# Wicca for Life

# Wicca for Life

~

## The Way of the Craft—
## From Birth to Summerland

~

# RAYMOND BUCKLAND

CITADEL PRESS
Kensington Publishing Corp.
www.kensingtonbooks.com

CITADEL PRESS books are published by

Kensington Publishing Corp.
850 Third Avenue
New York, NY 10022

All Kensington titles, imprints, and distributed lines are available at special quantity discounts for bulk purchases for sales promotions, premiums, fund-raising, educational, or institutional use. Special book excerpts or customized printings can also be created to fit specific needs. For details, write or phone the office of the Kensington special sales manager: Kensington Publishing Corp., 850 Third Avenue, New York, NY 10022, attn: Special Sales Department, phone 1-800-221-2647.

Citadel Press and the Citadel logo are trademarks of Kensington Publishing Corp.

First Citadel printing September 2001

10 9 8 7 6 5 4 3 2 1

Printed in the United States of America

ISBN 0-8065-2275-5

Library of Congress Control Number: 2001091779

# Contents

**20. The Tools of Witchcraft** 258

*Athame; Bracelets; Crowns; Besom; Wand; Priapic Wand; Cords; Scourge; Corn Dolly; Consecration of Tools; Ritual.*

**21. Personal Development of a Witch** 273

*Psychic Development; Affirmations; Meditation; Divination; Healing.*

**Appendix**

# Introduction

For many hundreds of years, the word *Witchcraft* has conjured up pictures of ugly old hags flying through the air on broomsticks, stirring bubbling cauldrons, worshiping Satan, and doing evil. For several centuries, during the Middle Ages, the church (believing what have since proven to be misconceptions of Witchcraft) persecuted millions: torturing and putting to death innocent people. In recent years, the truth has emerged that Witchcraft is simply a non-Christian (not *anti*-Christian) religion dating from ancient times and that its followers—known as Witches or Wiccans—are lovers of all living things, with desire to harm none. This book looks at these positive, nature-loving people and examines (chapter 1) how and why the misconceptions arose.

The change of attitude toward Witches is especially evident today in the media—in books, in movies, and on television. The Wicked Witch of the West of *The Wizard of Oz* has given way to the modern Wiccans of the Craft, who use their Wiccan powers to solve the everyday problems of modern life.

With an understanding of what Witches really are, this book then studies the makeup of a Wiccan's life, from birth to death, showing it as a model on which to build your own life. It shows how positive energies are used to promote health and happiness, in the Witches themselves and in others. Today, more and more people are turning to Wicca as their religion of choice. Here are the details of this belief system and how to live the Witch's life. This book even includes such simple yet important things as building a backyard refuge for wildlife.

As a religion and way of life, Wicca can be practiced by a group—known as a coven—or by the individual. The centuries-old teachings and techniques have been kept alive by family groups known as hereditary Witches. Now is an appropriate time to establish new hereditaries, new families of Witches, and to spread the word of Wiccan life.

By basing the whole of your life on the tenets of Wicca, you can develop lasting relationships that are filled with love. You can make use of ages-old magic to meet your goals and to create your own reality. This does not necessarily involve working complicated rituals, as in the ancient mysteries of Greece and Rome, for Wiccan rituals are simple and straightforward. The Witches of old were ordinary, common people. The tools they used and the rites they performed were of the simplest means, yet they were extremely effective. In this book, you will be shown how to make these tools and how to perform these rites. There is nothing here that the average person cannot do. It is a magic that has endured because it is so basic—and works so well.

We all have natural powers within us that can be brought out and used to bring about all that we desire. In some people, these powers come out naturally, but in others they need to be drawn out. Presented here are the lessons and exercises that will help you to do just that—draw out your natural powers and bring about all that you desire. Although this book is focused primarily on family Witchcraft, it should be equally useful for any other nonhereditary covens and also for solitaries. Here, in this book, is presented all that is needed to pass through the whole of your life in the Wiccan way. Here is *Wicca for Life*.

R.B.

# ~ 1 ~

# What Is Witchcraft?

The word *Witchcraft* comes from the Old Anglo-Saxon word *wicce-craeft*, meaning "the craft of the wise." For many people today, the word carries a wide variety of connotations, but originally it was quite specific.

For thousands of years before Christianity, there were many variations of Pagan worship. In the big cities of Greek and Roman times, the forms of religion were well organized, with dedicated temples and an established priesthood. But out in the country areas, the common people did not have this luxury. They worshiped the same deities, but their temples were the woods, the mountains, and the open fields. They were close to nature and, by virtue of this closeness, felt close to their gods. Every man and woman was his or her own priest, able to commune with divinity on the same level as the official priesthood in the towns and the cities. Although the principal deities worshiped were the same in most areas, the names that were used frequently varied in different areas of Europe and Asia, with local titles and appellations prevailing.

## The Beginnings of Religio-magic

By looking at the development of religio-magic from earliest times, we can fully understand the development of this relationship of men and women to the gods. Twenty-five thousand years ago, in upper Paleolithic times, humankind lived in awe of nature. Life was ruled largely by such factors as weather and successful hunting. Before the development of agriculture, it was necessary to kill and eat animals in order to survive. The australopithecines of East and South Africa, the first upright primates, evolved from primate vegetarians to become predatory meat-eating hunters. The cave art of the period shows magical images designed to bring about successful hunting.

As E. Adamson Hoebel points out in *Anthropology: the Study of Man*, "Upper Paleolithic art had the gross purposes of filling men's stomachs and of maintaining the population by serving as a magical aid in hunting and procreation." This early art is an important clue to those times. As Hoebel says, most of it was almost certainly for magical purposes. This is evident from the fact that the artworks were invariably painted in nearly inaccessible places, in niches in caverns deep in the bowels of the earth—places where they were obviously not just decoration but part of some ancient mysteries.

In that early time, humankind had a great fear of and reverence for nature: the thunder and lightning of a storm, the howling winds, the roaring waters of a raging river. Gods were seen dwelling within all of these things.

Humans, unlike other anthropoids, are omnivorous by nature. Early humans believed that the gods ruled the hunt and its success or failure. Therefore, to ensure its success, magical rituals were performed. These were addressed to the God of the Hunt in the form of theater—acting out the hunt with a successful conclusion. Many times one of the tribe would play two parts—that of the god and that of director of the actor-hunters. The "hunters" would suggest to the god what they would like him to do for them.

The God of the Hunt was believed to be horned or antlered (as were most of the beasts hunted). Therefore, the person officiating—in effect, the first priest—would dress in the skin of the animal to be hunted and wear a mask and its horns or antlers. There are cave paintings of such figures, the most famous of which is known as *The Sorcerer* and found in the Caverne des Trois Frères, in Ariége, France. There is another at Fourneau du Diable, Dordogne, France. In relatively recent times, Mandari hunters of eastern Sudan, Australian aboriginal hunters, and Native American hunters such as the Mandans have adopted the same techniques that were used in those ancient times.

Along with the God of the Hunt was a female deity who was especially important. This was the Goddess of Fertility. Primitive art includes paintings and carvings of animals copulating (at Le Tuc d'Audoubert, for example), together with figurines—dubbed Venus figurines—of pregnant human females. The copulating animals are obviously magical figures designed to promote growth and expansion of the herds to be hunted. Figures of human females were intended to magically ensure the tribes' increase in times of high mortality. The Fertility Goddess was later to become especially important, as fertility of the fields, along with its native wildlife, remained a constant concern.

Domestication of both animals and plants was a gradual process, eventually leading to the storage of food for winter use. This, in turn, led to a virtual elimination of dependence on successful hunting. The God of the Hunt dropped into the background, becoming more generalized as a god of nature, while the Goddess remained vital as a deity of fertility.

> *The proper study of mankind is man.* —Alexander Pope

As humankind spread across Africa, Europe, and Asia, these concepts of the deities also spread. The many gods and goddesses of wind, water, fire, and so forth, were always led by the two major figures—those of fertility and of hunting/nature.

Great civilizations, such as Greece and Rome, developed sophisticated hierarchies of gods and goddesses, but the country folk always had far simpler versions of the complicated rituals developed by the powerful priesthood in the cities and towns. In Western Europe, after the passing of the Roman Empire, the Celts held sway. Much of what we know as Witchcraft today comes from that Celtic way of life. As the editors of *The Celts* put it (The Emergence of Man series), "On the Continent, Celtic culture—with its rigidly structured social organization, its religion administered by the Druids, its eloquent tradition of heroic legends passed down orally from generation to generation and its fantastic art—merged with Roman customs and traditions, sometimes losing its Celtic identity altogether. In

England, Celtic culture gave way to various aggressors: Romans, Anglos, Saxons, Vikings, Normans." Indeed, these invasions brought great variety to British religious thought and practice. But the basic Celtic teachings remained. In the outlying villages and farms, religious beliefs were slow to change. The farmer and his wife and family still worshiped the Goddess of Fertility alongside the gods of nature and death, and what came after.

> The idea of dividing the Power Beyond into two, one good and one evil, belongs to an advanced and sophisticated religion. In the more primitive cults the deity is in himself the author of all, whether good or bad.
> —Dr. Margaret A. Murray, *The God of the Witches*

# Survival of the Old Religion

Many of the old rites lived on, both in practice and in legend. In early spring, it was accepted magical practice for a farmer and his wife to lie in the first furrow of a field and have intercourse to ensure that field's fertility and productivity. When the crops first began to appear, it was common for all to take up pitchforks, poles, and broomsticks and to dance around the fields, riding the poles like hobbyhorses. As they danced around the fields, the people would leap high in the air to show the crops how high to grow. It was simple imitative, or sympathetic, magic. At harvesttime, of course, it was time to thank the gods for all that had been produced. Many Pagan rituals and customs such as these are still found across Europe and elsewhere.

In the villages were invariably found one or two "wise ones," those who had the wisdom of herbs and of magic. As the local doctors, they tended the sick with herbal concoctions, decoctions, infusions, and macerations. They also knew the spells and charms passed on from generation to generation. These "doctors" were known by the old Anglo-Saxon name of *wicce* (feminine) or *wicca* (masculine). (In fact, the Saxon kings of England always had a Council of Wise Ones known as the Witan.)

When it came to the worship of the old gods and the forms of the rituals, the wise ones conducted the rites. They became the priests and priestesses of the countryside, leading groups from the villages or from neighboring farms in the major celebrations of the seasons. Later on, any followers of this Old Religion became known as Wiccans, or Witches.

These wise ones, then, were the original Witches. Although the late Dr. Margaret Murray, in her books *The Witch-Cult in Western Europe* and *God of the*

*Witches*, suggested that there was an unbroken line of Witchcraft from the early cave-dwelling days through to the Middle Ages, this is not so. There was a progressive line of *religio-magic*, yes, but this does not indicate that the actual form of the Witchcraft rites and customs of more recent times were the same as those performed by peoples of the upper Paleolithic age.

## The Rivalry of the New Religion

The rise of a new religion—Christianity—came to threaten and almost destroy the belief in, and worship of, the gods of nature. Unlike the "Old Religion" (as we might term Witchcraft), the "New Religion" was human-made and full of contradictions. Yet it became established and, for many hundreds of years, existed alongside witchcraft. Initially Christianity was content to gain converts gradually, but, as we shall see, in time it became more impatient.

In Great Britain, when a king of a particular region was converted to the New Religion, it was declared by the church that *all* his subjects were also similarly affected, even though the majority of them were still worshiping the old gods.

Between 597 and 604 C.E. (Common Era), during Augustine's mission to Britain, London remained Pagan but King Aethelbert of Kent was converted. After his death, Kent reverted to Paganism. In 604 C.E., similar events occurred with the king of the East Saxons—the king was converted, but upon his death his successor reverted to Paganism. The years 627 and 628 C.E. saw the conversions of the kings of Northumbria and East Anglia, respectively. The king of Wessex was converted in 635 C.E., and in 653 C.E. the king of Mercia. But by 654 C.E., it was necessary to reconvert the king of the East Saxons. So there was not a regular, smooth transition from the Old Religion to the New. Far from it; what had been part of everyone's lifestyle for generations would not easily be swept aside.

In an effort to appeal to more pagans, the New Religion adopted many of the ancient conventions. The Christian Trinity is a good example. This was based on the ancient Egyptian triad of Osiris, Isis, and Horus. The immaculate conception and the resurrection were copies of old Pagan beliefs found in many parts of the ancient world. Even the name *Jesus* was taken from the Celts' Esus, a nature god. The Pagan festival of Yule was adopted as Christmas (even to the inclusion of the phallic tree). Easter was based on the goddess Eostre's springtime festival. The festival of contact with the spirits of the dead, known as Samhain, became the Christian's All Souls' Day. And for many centuries there were priests who served both the Pagan and the Christian populations.

> *No opponents fight more bitterly and to the death than warring religions. True, the winner will sometimes wear its opponent's creeds like scalps—but not round the waist: Every effort is made to obliterate the memory of whence the creed came and the scalp is worn like a toupee and passed off as real hair. The Christian religion had done this in the very beginning . . . when in England the missionary monks acted on the advice of Pope Gregory the Great and incorporated local heathen customs into the conduct of the Christian year.*
> —Brian Branston, *The Lost Gods of England*

One giant step forward for the New Religion came when Pope Gregory (590–604 C.E.) issued instructions to his bishops in Britain that they were to take all pagan temples and consecrate them to the New Religion, installing new altars and rededicating the temple On the open sites of regular pagan gatherings, new churches were to be built.

"In this way," the pope said, "I hope the people (seeing their temples are not destroyed) will leave their idolatry and yet continue to frequent the places as formerly." He desperately hoped to fool, or even coerce, the people into attending Christian churches.

For a long time, Gregory's plans seemed to bear fruit, and more and more of the population became (at least nominally) Christian. But finally, the saturation point appeared to have been reached. By this time, the church fathers had enjoyed their taste of power and were determined that Christianity should be the *only* religion; all others were to be destroyed. This brought about the start of the persecutions, when anything non-Christian was automatically labeled *anti*-Christian and therefore undesirable.

> *In the north of Europe, the Old Religion persisted in spite of the coming of Christianity. Courts and courtiers might be Christian, but the forests were true to the phallic cycle and the old magicians. . . . [The] permanence of the central figure of the Old Religion emphasizes how strong it must have been in the first ten centuries of this era. King Edgar, AD 900, was regretting that it was even at that date more common in England than worship of the Christian God.*
> —Pennethorne Hughes, *Witchcraft*

# The Old Religion Slandered

The Old Religion was lumped together with Satanism (which itself was an offshoot of Christianity, for the older religions had no concept of an all-evil entity such as the Christian devil). This was where the word *Witchcraft* began to take on a strongly negative meaning when used by people other than the Wiccans themselves.

The wise ones, for example, had a knowledge of poisons, among other things. This was essential in order for them to administer to those who accidentally poisoned themselves by eating the wrong plants. Persecutors turned this knowledge against them, saying that they used the knowledge to poison others! In fact, King James I's later translation of the Bible took this line of reasoning. The original words of the Bible said, "Thou shalt not suffer a poisoner to live." James' translators—whether by ignorance or design—confused the Latin words *veneficor* and *maleficor* and chose to say, "Thou shalt not suffer a Witch to live," by virtue of her knowledge of poisons.

It didn't take long for the trickle of venom generated by the Christian Church to swell into a raging torrent. In 1235, Pope Gregory IX instructed the archbishop of Sens: "Thou shouldst be instant and zealous in this matter of establishing an Inquisition . . . to fight boldly the battles of the Lord." Thirteen years later, Alexander IV issued a papal bull against Witchcraft, with a second one two years later. By the time Pope Innocent VIII issued his bull, in 1484, printing had been invented; with it came wide distribution of such utterances in writing. The Inquisition came into its own with the reappearance of this bull two years later, as a foreword to a diabolical book written by two German monks, Heinrich Kramer and Jakob Sprenger. These men were designated by the pope "Inquisitors of these heretical depravities."

The "heretical depravities" to which the pope referred were the generations-old Pagan practices of promoting fertility of human, beast, and crop, and of worshiping the old gods. Kramer and Sprenger's book was titled *Malleus Maleficarum*—the "hammer of the Witches." Perhaps typical for two such monks, their writings and attacks focused on fertility and other sexual aspects of the Old Religion. Everything positive that Wiccans did was reversed and shown as negative. Rather than promoting fertility, Wiccans were accused of impeding it. They were said to "hinder men from generating and women from conceiving," to bring about sterility in all things, and to have sexual intercourse with demons. This nefarious volume would be used by trial judges for the next two hundred years, bringing about the torture and destruction of millions of men, women, and children on charges of "Witchcraft." Not until the very end of the nineteenth century was it discovered that the two German monks had forged a letter of support from the theological faculty of the University of Cologne, the official censor of books at that time. This, apparently, was done in order to give themselves more prestige.

The persecutions turned out to be a powerful tool for the unscrupulous. By making a charge of Witchcraft—or even suggesting someone might be a Witch—it was possible to get rid of an enemy, acquire land that was otherwise unavailable, or generate personal power. Persecution became very much a political tool. When someone was accused of Witchcraft, his or her land and goods became forfeit to the state or church. This was a great temptation for many, including Christian dignitaries.

In Scotland and throughout most of Continental Europe, being burned alive at the stake was the penalty for those found guilty of Witchcraft—and most people accused were so pronounced. In England and in New England, the penalty was hanging. The case of the so-called Witches of Salem village, in New England in 1692, was typical of what happened throughout much of Europe. Most of the accused were previously devout Christians, indicted simply by hysterical children, confused neighbors, or overzealous church officials.

Once accused, the victim had no defense. If the accused had a perfect alibi, then "spectral evidence" was admitted, which said that it was possible for a Witch to be in two places at the same time. Eventually, twenty people were put to death in this little New England village. Still, this was a very small number compared to Europe, where two or three hundred people might be executed on a single occasion, simply at the nod of a bishop. In France, for example, the bishop of Treves had a whole village put to death because of an especially harsh winter, which he determined had been caused by Witches. Not knowing who the Witches were, he executed everyone. In Germany, on February 16, 1629, Prince-Bishop Philipp Adolf von Ehrenberg executed 157 people.

> I never told my religion, nor scrutinized that of another. I never attempted to make a convert, nor wished to change another's creed. I have judged of others' religion by their lives, for it is from our lives, and not from our words, that our religions must be read.
> —Thomas Jefferson

# Apparent Death of the Old Religion

With persecution continuing so harshly for so long—literally hundreds of years—the many followers of the Old Religion obviously could not continue their practices, at least not openly. Outwardly it looked as though the New Religion, revering the Prince of Love and Peace, had effectively slaughtered all its rivals. Witchcraft, it seemed, no longer existed. In fact, from the early eighteenth century on, it became illegal even to believe in the existence of Witches.

But a religion that had been followed for thousands of years, generation after generation, was not to be simply stamped out, even by the severity of the Inquisition. Many true Witches went into hiding. No longer were there large groups of Pagans gathering together to worship, led by the local wise ones. Instead, families kept the religion among themselves. What became known as hereditary Witchcraft survived. The religious rites, together with knowledge of the old cures, charms, spells, and magic, were jealously guarded and handed down within a family.

But the negative connotations of the term *Witchcraft* had become entrenched. Early Christian missionaries would encounter native practices they did not understand in traditional societies, and invariably labeled such practices Witchcraft, since they could not fit them into biblical categories. For them, and many others, the word has become a synonym for *magic* or *sorcery*, and is found in books on African Witchcraft, Native American Witchcraft, Australian aboriginal Witchcraft, and others.

This was the state of the Old Religion until the middle of the twentieth century, and to an extent even today. In England, the last law against Witchcraft was finally repealed in 1951. This repeal meant that if there were any Witches still surviving, they could finally come out into the open once more, free of the fear of persecution. But those families that *had* survived had learned their lesson and were content to continue in secret, away from prying eyes. However, one man changed all this: Dr. Gerald Brousseau Gardner.

Gerald Gardner had spent his whole life fascinated by, and investigating, religio-magic. He lived for many years in the Far East, and had there become acquainted with the Dyaks, the headhunters of Borneo, and many local native tribes, learning their practices. Upon his retirement and return to his homeland of England, to his great surprise Gardner encountered a surviving coven of Witches. Because of Gardner's background, plus the fact that an ancestress of his had been burned as a Witch in Scotland in 1640, he was invited to join the group and was subsequently initiated. Finding that Witchcraft was actually the continuation of an ancient pre-Christian religion, and not at all the dark, evil practice he had always been led to believe it was, Gardner was delighted. He wanted to run out and tell the world how wrong it was. The members quickly told him, "No." They explained that the group had managed to remain alive only by keeping quiet about its existence. But some years later, upon the death of the group's leader and with the last law against Witchcraft repealed, Gardner published *Witchcraft Today*, the first book actually written by a Witch, giving the Witches' side of the story. This was to be the beginning of the reemergence of Witchcraft as a religion and the eventual establishment of Wicca as an accepted everyday practice around the world.

In this present book, as in my other books on Witchcraft, I hope to be able to help reestablish the Old Religion. There are today many covens in existence (I formed the first American one myself, in New York in 1963), as well as many solitary Witches. But with second- and even third-generation Wiccans now emerging, I feel the time is right to also encourage the establishing of new hereditary lines, or family traditions, as some call them. They are, in effect, covens that consist purely of family members. This book presents the material that will help individuals, groups, or covens, learn the Craft. Here are the religious rites, together with the charms, spells, and other magical practices, that will make you a Witch.

# ~ 2 ~

# How to Become a Witch

No one is born a Witch. You don't have to be the seventh child of a seventh child, have a star in the palm of your hand, be born on Hallowe'en, or be born with a veil over your head to be a Witch! Just as no one is born (for example) a Roman Catholic or Baptist, no one is born a Witch. You might be born into a Roman Catholic family or a Baptist family, but you don't become a member of that faith until you go through certain rites admitting you and then confirming you in it. So it is with most religions, including Witchcraft.

One of the advantages of Witchcraft, however, is that although the majority of Wiccans are initiated into a group, or coven, it is also possible for an individual to become a Witch by going through the necessary ritual without the aid of a priest or priestess. In the old days before the persecutions, many people lived alone, or far from the nearest village, and had no recourse to a religious leader of any sort. Yet they still believed in the gods and wished to worship them. Thus they appropriately dedicated themselves. I'll talk about such a Self-Dedication later in this chapter, and how it can be done today, but first let's look at the usual Initiation.

> *The term initiation, in the most general sense, denotes a body of rites and oral teachings whose purpose is to produce a decisive alteration in the religious and social status of the person being initiated. In philosophical terms, initiation is equivalent to a basic change in existential condition; the novice emerges from his ordeal endowed with a totally different being from that which he possessed before his initiation; he has become ANOTHER.* —Mircea Eliade, *Birth and Rebirth*

# The Mysteries and Initiation

Witchcraft is a "mystery religion," similar to the old Greek and Roman mystery religions. This means that it is a religion of initiation, with the initiate taking an oath of secrecy. (The word *mystery* comes from the Greek *meuin*, meaning "to keep mum" or "to keep secret.") A clear picture of the ancient mysteries is seen in Pompeii, Italy, where virtually all inhabitants—even the slaves—were admitted to the Dionysian mysteries. The Villa of Mysteries, site of the initiations, was situated on the Street of Tombs, set a little apart from the rest of the town, outside the Stabian Gate. The villa was owned by a woman who was also the High Priestess of the Dionysian mysteries.

The initiations took place in a room decorated with frescoes, made up of a number of scenes depicting a neophyte going through the ceremony. From this we have gleaned a good general idea of what took place, though we have no details since every person there took an oath of secrecy. This oath was honored to the point that, as I have said, all we know of the rites is what we can gather from the murals.

> All the mysteries operated after the same manner. They consisted in a sacred drama and a series of ritual acts, which reproduced the gestures and actions attributed to the Divinity. This is the principle of the Eucharist. . . . It was not an objective but a subjective drama, its essence being the repetition of that which according to tradition had been wrought by God. It was led up to by preliminary instruction, heightened in effect by visions and ecstatic suggestions conducting the initiated, himself an actor in them, to communion with God.
>
> —Professor Vittorio Macchioro, *The Villa of Mysteries*

The central theme of the Dionysian mysteries, and indeed of all mysteries, puberty rites, and the like, was what is termed a *palingenesis*; a rebirth. The neophyte is ending life as known up to that point and being reborn, starting life anew. In many religions, even today, such a fresh start is characterized by the taking of a new name, usually one of your own choosing. Again, this holds true in Witchcraft.

An Initiation may be broken down into parts. It starts with a catharsis; a spiritual cleansing. This may be a period of meditation, but invariably also includes a ritual bath. It is a bath in water to which salt has been added (salt is recognized universally as a symbol of life) and may also include various herbs, such as basil, cumin, yarrow, peppermint, lemongrass, and vervain. The old ceremonial magic *grimoire*, the *Key of Solomon*, gives a recipe for a ritual purification bath that includes basil, fennel, hyssop, lavender, mint, rosemary, thyme, valerian, and vervain.

> *Adding herbs or scented oils to the bath is one of the most relaxing, soothing, easy and effective forms of magic. In essence, a tub of water containing a bath sachet is nothing more than a huge pot of "herb tea," in which the bather brews.*
> —Scott Cunningham, *The Magic of Incense, Oils and Brews*

# Death and Rebirth

The palingenesis is a rebirth, but before the rebirth there must be a death, albeit symbolic. This is enacted in various ways in different societies. As shown on the walls of the Villa of Mysteries in Pompeii, it is symbolized by a ritual scourging. So it is in Wicca.

The initiate is blindfolded and bound (symbolizing the darkness and restriction of the womb) before being scourged by the priest or priestess. But this is not a whipping or lashing, to hurt and harm; it is purely symbolic. In Wicca, the thongs of the scourge are made of silk or a similar material. Once the "death" has taken place, the blindfold is removed for the rebirth. Various secrets are imparted to the initiate, the oath is administered, and he or she is then presented to the gods as a newly initiated priest and Witch.

*Note:* This is the initiation ritual in general terms. I'll give the full details of the Wiccan rites, step by step, for both coven Initiation and Self-Dedication, at the end of this chapter.

> *Being initiated into the witch cult does not give a witch supernatural powers as I reckon them, but instructions are given, in rather veiled terms, in processes which develop various clairvoyant and other powers, in those who naturally possess them slightly.*
> —Gerald Brousseau Gardner, *Witchcraft Today*

As I discussed in chapter 1, Witchcraft was able to stay alive during the persecutions by virtue of being practiced within close family groups, known as hereditary Witches. Mothers and fathers initiated sons and daughters. Occasionally there were gaps, for Wicca is not a religion that is forced on anyone, even within families. Sometimes an individual, or even a whole generation, opted not to become a part of it. At times this meant the end of the line for a particular family tradition. Over the centuries, of course, the remaining groups got fewer and fewer. If Gerald Gardner had not sown the seeds that sparked the revival of interest in Witchcraft, it is almost certain that the Old Religion really would have eventually died out. But even today, with the tremendous influx of new blood into Wicca—it has been described as "the fastest growing religious movement in America"[1]—there are very few family units as opposed to covens and solitaries. There is, perhaps, a need for new generations of hereditary Witches. It is hoped that, with this book, new family groups *will* be encouraged to begin.

# Wiccan Theology

Before entering into Wicca, there are some basics you should know. Witchcraft is a religion, as I have said and as I will frequently reiterate. As such it involves belief in and worship of gods and goddesses.[2] Exactly who are these deities? Wicca, having developed gradually over many thousands of years from a variety of religio-magical beliefs, does not have a formalized theology. Just as two different groups, or traditions, of Wiccans may use different names for their deities, so too may they have different views on how these gods originated—indeed, on the whole scheme of humankind. But the majority of Witches do agree on the following belief system: There exists an all-powerful, omniscient "energy form" (for want of a better term). The entity Lazarus, channeled by Jach Pursel, refers to it as "God/Goddess/All-That-Is." I think this is an excellent term, if a trifle cumbersome. The point is that in order for humans to relate to this energy form, it is necessary to put it into some form to which we *can* relate. The obvious one is a human form. If you have a des-

---

1. See my book *Witchcraft From the Inside*. (Llewellyn, St. Paul, 1995)
2. For *gods*, please understand *gods and goddesses*. I try to use *deities* as much as possible, to be nonsexist, but it does become cumbersome (as does *god/goddess*). Please understand that no disrespect is meant when I use the word gods when speaking of deities in the general sense.

perate need to pray for help or guidance, it makes sense that you feel more comfortable having an image in your mind that you are addressing. Hence, throughout history, we have worshiped a god or goddess, or a group of gods in human form or human form with animal head—or even in nonhuman form. It would be difficult to confide in some great, nebulous energy form, so early humankind created a "god of thunder" or "goddess of water," or "god of hunting," or "goddess of fertility."

The Wiccans of today follow this pattern, seeing the God and Goddess of Witchcraft in human form and, generally, understanding that they are that same God and Goddess of early times. For this reason, the Wiccan deities are still thought of as a Goddess of Fertility and a God of Hunting/Nature, or Mother and Father Earth.

Everywhere in nature is both male and female, both in the animal kingdom and in the plant kingdom. It seems only natural, therefore, that the deities would be both male and female. The Christian concept of a lone all-male deity does not make sense. Many Wiccan traditions think in terms of a balance between the two energies, while others place more emphasis on one over the other. As we saw in chapter 1, there was definitely more emphasis on the Goddess during the summer months, when it was possible to grow food, and more on the God in the winter months, when hunting was important. This balance is still found today in most traditions.

But this emphasis is sometimes extended. For example, feminist groups frequently laud the Goddess over the God even to the point of virtually ignoring him. In my opinion, religion is a very personal thing and you must discover what is exactly right for you; you should not have to compromise. For this reason, no one can say that any one view of worshiping, or acknowledging the deities, is more correct than another. If it's right for you . . . it's right!

I have been speaking of various traditions of Witchcraft. The situation is much like those found in Christianity and other religions. In Christianity, you can find Baptists, Episcopalians, Roman Catholics, Methodists, and many others. They are all Christians, holding the basic concepts of this religion, but they vary in their approaches to worship, in their rituals, in their hierarchies, and so on. So it is in Wicca. There are many different denominations (usually referred to as traditions). None is any more correct or authentic than another; all are valid. But though they follow the same basic precepts, they do vary in their forms of ritual, hierarchy, and even in the names they use for the deities.

So to consider whether Wicca is right for you, you need to consider whether you are right for Wicca. Does it make sense to you to see the deities in the way I have described? Can you relate to a closeness to the earth, to all nature, such as we find in Wicca?

> *You don't slap on a pentacle, wiggle into a black dress or dark pants and shirt, paint your fingernails a disgusting color, wear wild makeup and call yourself a Witch. . . . To be a Witch isn't a fashion statement.*
> —Silver RavenWolf, *Teen Witch*

## The Responsibilities of Wicca

Let's go a step farther. In Wicca—as it should be in all religions—there are certain responsibilities. You have a responsibility to yourself, to the earth on which we live, and to the fellow inhabitants of that earth, be they human or otherwise. In Wicca, there is a tenet, or law, to guide you: "An it harm none, do what thou wilt." This is known as the Wiccan Rede; the Witchcraft Law. The word *an* is Old English for "if," so the tenet means that *if* (and only if) it harms no one, you can do what you like. This sounds like license to have a good time, but it's not. It means that you can do whatever you like but *only so long as what you do harms no one* . . . and this "no one" includes yourself, of course. So right away there is a prescription against illegal drugs, alcohol, or anything of that sort. There are plenty of examples of how you can hurt others in obvious ways, but in Wicca you also need to keep in mind all the unconscious ways in which you can do harm. This Wiccan Rede is especially important when you are considering doing magic. We'll look more closely at this in the next chapter.

There is one other thing that needs to be kept in mind regarding doing no harm. Witches believe in a threefold return *in this life*. (It's "instant karma," if you like.) In some other religions, there is a belief that you will get your rewards and punishments after you die, in the afterlife. Because of this, many people think they can get away with things, not having to face up to their responsibilities until after death. Not so in Witchcraft. We believe that we are responsible for our actions right here and now. Do good and you will get back three times this good. But do harm and that, too, will come back to you.

It can be seen, then, that there is (or should be) *no* inducement to do harm, such as the working of black magic (negative, harmful magic) or anything related to it.

Thus Witchcraft is a *positive* religion, with Witches doing only good. To speak of a "black Witch" is a contradiction in terms. Some people speak of "white Witches," but that is really redundant: All Witches are, in effect, "white," doing only good.

---

## Golden Rules

*Golden Rules from many traditions lead to the same center.*

"An it harm none, do what thou wilt."
WICCA

"Do naught unto others which would cause you pain if done to you."
BRAHMANISM

"Hurt not others in ways that you yourself would find hurtful."
BUDDHISM

"Wherefore all things whatsoever ye would that men should do to you, do ye even so to them."
CHRISTIANITY

"Do not unto others what you would not have them do unto you."
CONFUCIANISM

"No one of you is a believer until he desires for his brother that which he desires for himself."
ISLAM

"What is hateful to you, do not to your fellowman."
JUDAISM

"Regard your neighbor's gain as your own gain and your neighbor's loss as your own loss."
TAOISM

"That nature alone is good which refrains from doing unto another whatsoever is not good for itself."
ZOROASTRIANISM

# Wicca Is Not Satanism

An obvious question is, what about Satanists? Satanic followers (to the chagrin of Wiccans) often refer to themselves as Witches. The name is a misnomer; the correct term is simply *Satanist*. In the early days of Christianity, the rule of the church was very harsh. The common people—farmers, serfs, servants—had their lives very strictly governed by the church. There were very few things they were allowed to do; much was forbidden. Even the sexual life of a married couple was strictly regulated. This regulation of life reached such a stage that there was, in effect, a rebellion.

Some people, finding that they got nothing at all from praying to the supposedly good God, decided they would try the opposite and pray to Satan instead. It is doubtful that this bettered their lives, but at least they had some satisfaction in opposing the rulings of the church. So Satanism came into being as a reversal, a denial, of Christianity.

The whole concept of an all-evil deity, Satan, was actually unknown to pre-Christian peoples. In the older religions, the gods were much more human, with good moods and bad moods. Consequently, there was no need for an all-evil being. But the Christian idea of an all-good God necessitated such an entity; it is impossible to have "white" unless you also have "black" as a contrast. The idea actually originated in Persia in the seventh century B.C.E. and was later picked up by Christianity. There is, then, a closer connection between Christianity and Satanism than there is between Witchcraft and Satanism.

A question that frequently arises is whether or not you can be a Witch and continue to be a Christian. This is like asking if you can be a Christian Buddhist, or an Islamic Jew, or any combination of religions. It is certainly possible to combine practices and beliefs on a personal level (in fact, it seems that most religions follow pretty much the same paths anyway . . . the "many paths that lead to the same center"). But such labeling seems not to serve a useful purpose. Let's look at the concept of a Witch-Christian, for example. It would be difficult to reconcile a belief in many gods—or even just the God and Goddess—with a belief in a single male God with a male son, together with admonitions to "have no other god but me"—let alone "Thou shalt not suffer a Witch to live"! If you are going to become a Witch, then become a Witch. You will find, as I have said, that the teachings of other religions—certainly the positive ones—are actually found in Wicca anyway. Wicca is a religion; it is not a game or a hobby.

In 1994, at the World Parliament of Religions held in Chicago, Illinois, Wicca was finally acknowledged by the other religions of the world (including Protestants, Jews, Roman Catholics, Buddhists, and so on) as a legitimate religion.

# Life After Life

One of the basic tenets of Witchcraft is a belief in reincarnation. Without this belief, the death of a child, for example, makes little sense. Ill health or traumatic near-tragedy; a luxurious life for some as opposed to a life of struggle for others; the sudden arrival of fame and fortune . . . such experiences seem to make little sense without a belief in reincarnation. However, if any occurrence, state of being, mishap, or good fortune is considered as an experience within a whole range of such, spread over a number of lives, then it does begin to make sense.

Wiccans believe that they pass through a number of lives. Each one is like mastering the individual lessons of a full curriculum. In one life, we may need to learn the humility of poverty; in another, the joy of full happiness and many blessings; in another, the tragedy of a loved one's death. All these, and many more, are necessary lessons and experiences on the road to completion. There is a view of karma (which is what this learning experience is) that says one life is dependent upon the previous one; for example, if you murder in one life, you will yourself be murdered in the next. But generally in Wicca (views differ from tradition to tradition), it is felt that one life is *not* dependent upon the previous. We simply pass through a large number of lives, amassing total experience.

Some people have recollections of their previous lives; in fact, most people can access these memories through various means of regression. But it should be accepted that each life is new. Whether you were a king, a queen, or a slave in a previous life has no bearing on your present incarnation. You're here to gather a whole new set of experiences, so concentrate on this present life and don't dwell on the past. You might encounter someone who boldly states he was Abraham Lincoln in a past life. Your response should be (in effect), "That's interesting. What have you done with *this* life?"

What happens at the end of this series of lives? No one can say. Many Wiccans believe that we then become "at one with the gods." Others believe we move on to another series of lives on another planet or solar system. Who can say? All we can do is to work to achieve the very best within us in each lifetime. It is this lifetime we must concentrate on.

# ~ 3 ~

# Initiation—The Beginning

In the old days before the persecutions, the followers of the Old Religion would gather together in an open field, in a clearing in a woods, on a mountaintop—just about anywhere they could find a small area of ground to use for their rituals. Because Wicca is a religion of nature, it was always preferable to meet out in the open. Of course, there were often times of the year when bad weather would preclude this. At these times, Wiccans would meet in someone's cottage—often the home of the local "wise one" who was also, invariably, the leader of the group.

At certain times of year, there were big celebrations known as Sabbats (we'll be studying these in chapter 19). Because these might draw huge crowds, permanent temples were often built to accommodate everyone, though open areas were still preferred. Generally, however, the group was few in number—about a dozen or so—and any small area was sufficient. Sometimes the group would meet beside a special tree, or by a sacred well. During and after the persecutions, of course, surviving groups had to meet in secret, in places such as isolated cottages or secluded clearings in the woods; the big gatherings came to an end.

## The Magic Circle

What was, and still is, important for the meeting was not its location, but the consecration of the area used. The easiest area to mark is a circle. It can be difficult constructing a square or rectangle on the ground with any accuracy, but a circle can easily be marked. This is usually done by sticking something into the ground, extending a string or rope from it, and then swinging the end around the central point, marking a circle. This circle would be made large enough to allow all the participants to stand comfortably within its boundaries.

The Circle is often referred to as a Sacred Circle or Magic Circle. It is regarded as a space "between the worlds," neither in this world nor yet in the next. It is a place to commune with the deity and be at one with the gods. Where established temples and churches are permanently consecrated for use, the Witches' Circle was consecrated for just that one meeting, since they might meet in a different place every time they got together. Today, many Wiccan groups meet in a house or apartment, and the Circle is often set up permanently. But even so, it is traditional to consecrate the circular area before the start of every meeting.

The ideal place to hold meetings is a room that can be kept just for this purpose. Today, many Witches have a spare room in a basement or attic kept strictly for the coven gatherings. Others clear all of the furniture out of a living room, family room, or dining room, replacing everything afterward. Those in small apartments can barely squeeze everyone into the available floor area. For solitaries (single Witches), a space as small as a closet can, and has, been used quite successfully.

When there is a coven comprised of nonrelatives, as opposed to a single family group, the meetings are often rotated among the different homes of the members. But most such groups seem to prefer a single, regular meeting place. This is usually the home of the group's leader.

The Circle can be marked by laying down a length of clothesline or other cord. If the temple is in a permanent room, it can be marked by painting the floor, by trailing a line of salt or sand, or in any other way that shows the boundaries clearly and distinctly. You don't need anything strange or unusual, like sulfur, and you don't need to draw an elaborate pentagram or any other geometric design within the Circle. Some people will permanently mark the Circle on a separate piece of carpet that can be unrolled and laid down for the meeting, then rolled up and put away again afterward. In the days of the persecutions, when Witches had to meet in secret for fear of being discovered, they identified the area of the Circle simply by placing pots and pans around the floor. These could easily be kicked away should they be discovered.

If you are a solitary Witch, then of course you can mark a Circle smaller than one in which you are trying to fit a number of people. The marking is intended simply to show the extent of the consecrated area, so that no one will accidentally wander out of it during the rites. What is most important is the actual consecration of the area. This is done with salt, water, and incense in a very simple ritual. Once done, the area is special; the place is now "between the worlds." Before I deal with the consecration of the Circle, let us consider what is within it, in the way of tools.

## The Altar and Its Tools

It is important to create an altar. This can be any suitably sized object: a small table, trunk or footlocker, wooden box, or similar item. Try to stick to wood rather than metal if you can. I've found that one about fifteen to eighteen inches deep by twenty-one to twenty-four inches long is a good size. You can have a round altar if you prefer (I, personally, prefer this), of about a twenty-four-inch diameter. The best height is whatever is most comfortable for you. There may be times when you will kneel before the altar, but most of the time you will be standing in front of it, so make it a comfortable height for this. Try to avoid having to lean forward, or stooping over it.

Place the altar within the circle. When you stand before the altar, facing it, you should be facing east (though some traditions prefer to face north). East, of course, is the direction in which the sun rises.

I recommend putting the altar right in the center of the Circle. Different traditions have different placements. Some put it right up close to the drawn line in the north, others in the east, still others in the center. I feel that if it is in the center, everyone can stand around it and be a part of the rituals. Off to one side, only the presiding priest or priestess can stand before it—blocking the view of all the other Witches. (Of course, if you are a solitary, this isn't a factor.)

I think it is important that all those present feel they are active participants; all are a part of the family of Witches and should at least be able to see what is going on. Throughout this book I'll be suggesting what I feel is a good way (not necessarily "the best" way) to do things. Understand that there is *no one right way*, nor is there a wrong way. Do what suits *you* best. So . . . I place the altar in the center of the Circle, facing east.

You may cover the altar with an altar cloth if you wish, though it's not mandatory. I think it's a nice idea, since you can change the cloth with the seasons. You might use a plain color (perhaps green for spring, yellow for summer, orange for fall, white for winter) or make nicely decorated cloths with embroidery, appliqué, paint, or whatever. The choice is yours. On the altar, and cloth, will go the coven tools.

In chapter 20 I detail how to make all these tools. Since I'd like you to read through the whole book before leaping in and starting doing things, I think it's more convenient to leave those construction details until later and not get bogged down here.

You will need an incense burner, candle or candles, deity figures, a small dish holding water and another one holding some salt, a large wine goblet, a plate, and your athame. A libation dish is also a good idea, and I like to add a small hand bell. Like the incense, the sound of the bell adds to the vibrations of the ritual. See page 24 for the placement and details of all these tools.

The exact positioning of the tools is again your choice. Some say that they must follow the positioning of the elements. East is associated with air, south with fire, west with water, and north with earth. With the altar tools, the censer (incense holder) is associated with air (because of the rising smoke of the incense) and therefore is placed on the east side of the altar; a candle goes with fire and therefore is placed in the south; water is placed in the west; and salt, associated with earth, is placed in the north. The trouble with this arrangement is that if you have the candle on the south of the altar—and especially if your altar is facing north—you are going to have to be reaching over it all the time, which could present a hazard. So I do not place my altar tools to tie in with the elements; I place them in what seem to me the most suitable positions.

I have the candles at the back of the altar (in the east), with the deity figures alongside them, on the outsides of the candles. Between the candles, and slightly into the center, is the censer—a swinging type. Directly in front of it sits the bell. To the left (north) side of the altar is the water, with the salt beside it. To the right go the goblet and plate of cakes. The athame is laid across the altar in the center, or a little to the front (west). When oil is added, it goes with the salt and water. A libation dish can be placed beside the wine goblet. Trial and error is good here. Set up in a way you like and see how it works out. Don't be afraid to change the position of anything.

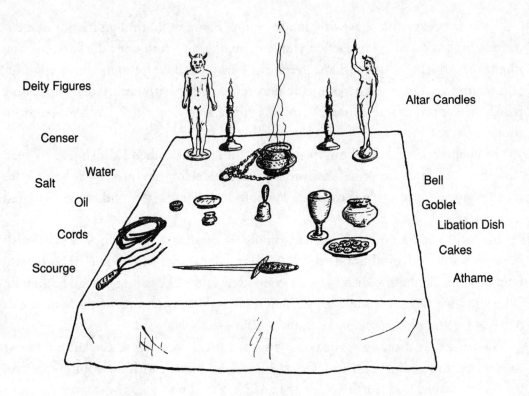

**Deity Figures**

**Censer**

**Water**

**Salt**

**Oil**

**Cords**

**Scourge**

**Altar Candles**

**Bell**

**Goblet**

**Libation Dish**

**Cakes**

**Athame**

*SUGGESTED ALTAR LAYOUT*

# The Witch's Personal Tool

The athame (pronounced *a-THAM-ay*) is the Witch's personal tool. It is a knife but not a weapon; it is designated for use only in rituals.[3] Every Witch should have one. The officiating priest or priestess may lay his or her athame on the altar while using other tools. In fact, anyone may lay theirs on the altar if they wish, but I recommend that those about the Circle hold the athame as much as possible so the altar doesn't get crowded. You can, of course, hang a sheath from your belt and place your athame in there when you need to.

Most Witches have figures representing the Lord and the Lady on their altar. Some simply use candles to represent them, some use symbols (such as a stag

3. This is not strictly true, since traditions differ so much. Some Witches believe that they should use their athames for *everything*, be it ritual use in the Circle or digging up herbs from the garden. There is certainly something to be said for this, since the more you use a tool, the more it absorbs your energies and becomes an extension of you.

horn for the God and a seashell for the Goddess), while others seek out appropriate statuettes. It is certainly a lot easier to find suitable figures today than it was forty years ago! Back then we had to comb antiques stores for bronzes or porcelain figures of appropriate look and size. These days there are several companies and individuals making a wide variety of deity figures, many of them specifically for Wiccans.

Traditionally, incense is burned during rituals. The old belief was that the smoke of the incense carried your prayers up to the gods, but—more important—the burning of incense creates and charges the atmosphere for religio-magical rituals. It doesn't matter whether you burn powdered incense sprinkled on burning charcoal, cones, or sticks of incense. My personal preference is for powdered incense, which is also the most economical. It can be purchased from New Age stores and also from church supply houses, as can the special charcoal you need. (*Warning:* Do not use barbecue charcoal!) You will need a good censer, or thurible, for powdered incense, but I feel that the swinging of the censer really adds to the ritual.

There should be fire on the altar in the form of a candle or candles. Some like just one altar candle; others prefer two, one on each side of the altar. As I've explained, exactly how you arrange the items on the altar is up to you, but don't let it become a catchall on which anything and everything is deposited. Remember that an altar is sacred and should be treated with respect. Even if, outside the Circle, it is just a humble coffee table, when in the sacred Circle, it is itself sacred.

For Initiations, you will have addititional items on the altar—things you won't need for regular Esbat meetings. These include a small bottle or dish of anointing oil, binding cords, and a scourge. For a Self-Dedication, just the oil is needed.

---

### Anointing Oil

Take a small bottle and fill it with mint of some sort. There are many different types of mint. My preference is for what's called catmint—*Nepeta cataria.* Pour in enough olive oil to cover the mint and fill the bottle. Again, there are many types of olive oil; choose a good-quality extra-virgin olive oil. Cap the bottle and let it stand in a cool, dry place for 24 hours, turning the jar upside down every 6 hours. At the end of the 24-hour period, carefully strain the liquid through a piece of cheesecloth into a bowl. Refill the bottle with fresh mint and pour in the oil from the bowl. Again cap it, store it, and turn it every 6 hours. Repeat this process over at least a 3-day period, using the same oil but refreshing the mint each time. At the end of the time, strain again, this time bottling the liquid. This is your anointing oil.

The bottle of wine and the wineglasses or goblets for all the coven members should be placed on the floor alongside, or under, the altar. (Incidentally, some Wiccans use the term *chalice* for their wine cup. To me this has Christian connotations, so I prefer *goblet*.) Cakes and wine are served at every meeting. They represent the necessities of life, the food and drink without which we could not exist. It is our opportunity to thank the gods for these gifts. (In the old days, the common people had ale rather than wine. I like to keep the old title of *Cakes and Ale* for this ritual, though many use *Cakes and Wine*. Either is acceptable.)

---

### Circle Cakes for Cakes and Ale

The cakes we use, we make from scratch, are oat cakes. We start by grinding oat groats to make into flour. This we do in a stone wheel hand grinder. For about half a dozen people, we use 4 ounces of flour. To this, add ½ teaspoon of baking powder, ⅓ teaspoon of salt, 1 egg, and about a teaspoon of butter or oil. Mix and add water until the texture is smooth, not too watery. If you want sweetened cakes, add sweetener to taste; you can also include small pieces of fruit such as diced apple, if you wish. Preheat a cast-iron pan—you can use cast-iron muffin tins if you like—lightly greased. Preheat the oven to 410 degrees. Pour the batter into the pan and bake for 30 minutes. It's good served hot or cold.

---

The cakes are usually made especially for the coven meetings. Some delight in forming them in the shape of crescent moons and stars, or such. They can be of any type you like, even store-bought cookies, if you do not bake. Wine or ale is traditional, but if you have a problem with alcohol, fruit juice or something similar is fine. The wine is poured into the large goblet on the altar, prior to the start of the ritual. The cakes are placed on the plate, also before the start.

Candles are placed around the Circle, standing on the marked line. There should be one at the north point (green, if you use colored ones, though white ones all around are fine), one at the east (yellow), one in the south (red), and one in the west (blue). Again, choice of color is up to you. I have listed what is traditional, but you may prefer another arrangement. One other possibility is to use all yellow candles around the circle in spring, green in summer, brown or orange in fall, and white in winter. Be creative. Enjoy yourself! These candles are lighted as part of the start of the ritual. If you wish light before you actually start, you can add other candles around the Circle, but place them farther out and not on the marked line. Some Witches add candles on stands outside the Circle, raising them up for better light. This can be especially helpful when you read from The Book of Shadows during the ritual.

I have said, in many places, that you can decide for yourself what you want to use and how you want to use it. I would emphasize, however, that you have a good reason for making any decision. Don't just decide on (for example) black candles around the Circle "because they look neat." There is a reason for everything used and done in Wicca (see my views on placement of the altar, page 22). There are also reasons why some things are *not* used. Not all reasons are right for everyone, however, which is why I make the point that you need to feel comfortable and do what is right for you—but with good reason.

## First Steps Into Wicca

Once you have your temple set up, you are ready to start along the path of Wicca. At each and every Circle, you will lay out the basic tools on the altar. For an Initiation or Self-Dedication, you will add the appropriate additional tools. Since I am focusing on how to start a new family tradition, or hereditary line, I will begin by giving you a Self-Dedication (which can also be used by a solitary). I'll follow this with a coven Initiation.

Many Witches say that you must be initiated by another, previously initiated, Witch. My question would be, who then initiated the very first Witch? Although in any established tradition you have to be initiated into a coven by a High Priest or High Priestess, it is not so in other situations. If you are starting a new tradition or hereditary line, or are going to be a solitary, then a Self-Dedication is just fine, and equally as valid as any other Witch's initiation.

No one should enter the sacred Circle without being properly prepared. This means taking a ritual bath at the very least. Better yet is to include a short period of meditation. If you don't want to meditate before every Circle, at least include it in your preparations for an initiation.

The ritual bath should always be taken, however. Such a bath simply involves warm water with a handful of salt stirred into it. Sea salt is preferable, though not essential. You can also add herbs if you wish, as I mentioned in chapter 2. Since it is a simple "dunking" in and out and not a lingering, soapy bath, coven members run a ritual bath, and each Witch jumps in and out, one after the other! You need only get fully wet by the salted water.

To meditate, sit comfortably in a chair. I recommend one with a straight back and with arms. Rest your arms on the arms of the chair. If you'd prefer to sit on the floor, that's all right, too. You can even lie flat on your back, though that may tend to send you to sleep! Wherever you sit, be sure your spine is straight; this is the key. Start by relaxing your body with deep breathing. Close your eyes and simply breathe deeply, breathing in to fill your lungs and breathing out to completely exhaust them.

Try to keep your mind blank. This is not easy. When odd thoughts from the day come creeping in, gently push them out again and concentrate on your breathing.

Relax your body in stages. First, concentrate on relaxing your feet, then your legs; your hands, then your arms; your lower body, then the upper; your neck, then your head. Feel all parts of the body gradually relaxing.

As you breathe in, imagine white light coming into your body and filling it. As you breathe out, see the grayness of negativity flowing out and away. Feel all the little aches and pains going away as the gentle relaxation of purity comes in. Keep this up for a few minutes. As the white light builds and fills your body—down through your legs to your feet and toes; down through your arms to your hands and fingers—see it expanding even beyond your body to form a ball or egg of white light all around you. This is your protective barrier to keep away all negativity. When you feel you have done this sufficiently, let your breathing return to normal and open your eyes. Remain sitting for just a moment longer before starting to move around. Whether you meditate before or after the bath is not important, though I recommend it before.

---

*What is meditation? Quite simply, it is a listening . . . listening to the Higher Self or, if you prefer, the Inner Self, the Creative Force, the Higher Consciousness; even the gods themselves. It can be all of these. Properly used, meditation opens the door to individual growth and personal advancement. Of all the techniques of advancement in the psychic and spiritual fields, meditation is by far the most effective. Coincidentally, it is also the most simple.*
—Raymond Buckland, *Buckland's Complete Book of Witchcraft*

# Wiccan Dress

What should you wear in the Circle? Many Wiccans solve the problem by wearing nothing at all; they do all their rituals in the nude. It is called skyclad, meaning "covered only by the sky." If you study many of the old paintings and woodcuts of Witches in the Middle Ages, you'll see that they are almost invariably naked. Occasionally they are dressed; once in a while, a combination is depicted, with some dressed and others nude. While a lot of Wiccans continue this skyclad tradition, other modern Witches prefer to wear ritual robes. Some even wear what amounts to everyday clothing. I say "what amounts to" because you should not just wear the same clothes you wear for the rest of the day.

Witchcraft is a religion, and within the Circle you are participating in a religious rite. You are between the worlds. Because it is something sacred, it is appropriate that you wear something "special." This can be nothing at all, it can be ritual robes, or it can be everyday-type clothing (even T-shirt and jeans) that is kept just for this purpose, and nothing else.

Let's look at robes. They can be any color. I recommend avoiding black. There is certainly nothing wrong with the color (though it is actually a lack of color), but it does contribute to the negative image that Witches are trying to avoid. White is very popular, as are the colors of nature: greens, yellows, browns. The color may not be important, but I feel that the material is. I suggest wearing natural materials like cottons and linens, even silk, and avoiding polyester and nylon. Apart from anything else, you'll be more comfortable.

In a coven, you don't all have to wear the same color but you should all be robed, or nude, or in everyday attire; don't mix them. One last comment—no one should be coerced into being naked if they do not wish to be. In fact, in Wicca no one should be coerced into anything.

---

*It's true that kids can be self-conscious about seeing pictures of a skyclad gathering and hearing grown-ups talk about sex. It is not true that their embarrassment or the pictures and discussions will do them any harm. Children have built-in defenses: they simply don't pay conscious attention to things they can't understand.* —Ashleen O'Gaea, *The Family Wicca Book*

# Names

In your devotions, you and those who follow you will be addressing the God and the Goddess. You may well want to decide upon names to use for them. If you want time to consider this, you can simply address them as "God and Goddess" or "Lord and Lady." I have used these simple terms in the rituals that follow in this book.

When you are ready, you may substitute names by which you best relate to those deities. In Saxon Witchcraft, the names used are Woden and Freya, the ancient Saxon God and Goddess. In Gardnerian, they are Cernunnos and Arada. Celtic Wiccan names include Herne and Cerridwen, and Dagda and Morrigan. There are many names from which to choose. Janet and Stewart Farrar's books *The Witches' Goddess* and *The Witches' God* are excellent sources.

Once again, find what is right for you. You may find yourself guided by your family roots. I urge you not to mix gods and goddesses of different origins, different cultures, however, such as a Greek god with a Celtic goddess. Although there is really nothing wrong with this for worship purposes, it can bring problems in dealing with your approaches to the theology of these gods.

Speaking of names, you may want to create a new name for yourself; this will be your Witch name. You are about to be reborn, and will be starting life anew. So why not start with a name of your own choosing, instead of one someone else gave you? Why not select a name that is right *magically*, using numerology to do it? Even if you are not good at math, it is not hard to do.

Start by finding your birth number. On a piece of paper, write down the month, day, and year of your birth. For example: 7.24.1982. (Be sure to include all four digits in the year you write down.) Now add these digits together: $7 + 2 + 4 + 1 + 9 + 8 + 2 = 33$. Add again to reach a single digit: $3 + 3 = 6$. The number 6 is your birth number.

Now to find a name that matches that birth number and is thereby the right name for you magically, having the same vibrations. Start by choosing a name that you like. For example, let's say you like the name Amanda. Write out the numbers 1 through 9 with the letters of the alphabet underneath them:

| 1 | 2 | 3 | 4 | 5 | 6 | 7 | 8 | 9 |
|---|---|---|---|---|---|---|---|---|
| A | B | C | D | E | F | G | H | I |
| J | K | L | M | N | O | P | Q | R |
| S | T | U | V | W | X | Y | Z | |

Now find the numbers that would equate to Amanda:

A = 1, M = 4, A = 1, N = 5, D = 4, A = 1

Adding those together, we get: 1 + 4 + 1 + 5 + 4 + 1 = 16; 1 + 6 = 7. This is not the same as your birth number, 6. To make it the same, you need to add a letter or number that would create a total equal to 6. If you add an 8, it would work: 7 + 8 = 15; 1 + 5 = 6. But the 8 letters are H, Q, and Z, which don't seem to fit very well . . . or do they? How about if you just put an H on the end of the name, making it Amandah? That gives you 1 + 4 + 1 + 5 + 4 + 1 + 8 = 24; 2 + 4 = 6, the same as your birth number. Amandah, then, could be a good Witch name for you. (You can put the H anywhere. How about Amandha, or Ahmanda?).

Try it with your own birth date and your own choice of name. You might have to add more than one letter, or even drop one. But usually, with just a little shuffling around, you can get the name you want. In fact, you usually—as in the above example—end up with an extra-special, unique name.

## Founding the Hereditary Line

For the founding of a hereditary line—a coven of Witches within your family—there has to be a first Witch, in the sense of the first one officially made a Wiccan. That first person can then go on to initiate others in the family, and so start the family tradition. (It works the same way when you start a coven—with a variety of people, of course.) I'll deal with these Initiations in a moment, but let me start with that first, all-important, Self-Initiation or Self-Dedication, as it's sometimes called.

This ritual should be done in private with no witnesses. For this I would strongly recommend that you be naked, going along with the thought of being reborn. Begin with Casting the Circle. "Casting the Circle," also sometimes known as "Erecting the Temple," refers to consecrating the ritual area.

In this and all following rituals, it is nice if you can memorize the words that are said—but if this is difficult, don't hesitate to read them. Ideally, you should have a good sense of what will be said so that you can say it and extemporize if necessary; the words should really be coming from your heart. If you must grope to remember the words, then you are losing your feeling for the ritual, which is not good.

Better, then, to read if you must. Later, you will make a Book of Shadows that will hold all your rites and rituals.

For now, you can place handwritten sheets of paper on a nice stand. An antique music stand next to the altar is ideal. Don't try to lay the paper on the altar and bend over to read it. That can get very awkward. When you need to walk around the Circle, speaking, don't hesitate to pick up the papers, or book, and take it with you. It's better to speak clearly and confidently than to grope for the words. Over the years, you will learn all that you ever use, but don't worry about it now.

## Casting the Circle

You are now in the ritual Circle you have drawn or marked, properly prepared, standing in front of the altar with all the tools on it. The Circle has been drawn on the floor as a physical demarcation. The candles beyond the Circle are alight for illumination, though not the four "point" candles (east, south, west, and north), nor the altar candles. The wine goblet is full. Now to consecrate the Circle.

Ring the bell three times. Then, using your dominant hand, take up your athame (if you do not yet have an athame, then you can just use your hand, pointing your forefinger), kiss the blade, and hold it high in salute. Say:

*Hail, Lord and Lady. Here I do build a temple of life in which to honor you. Assist me as I lay down the foundation stones on which I will build my cone of power.*

Lowering your athame, walk over to the east point in the Circle. Point the tip of the blade at the line drawn on the ground. Take your time, concentrating all your energies into directing a line of force flowing from your heart, down your arm, through your athame, and down into the ground on this line. Recapture that ball of white light you built in your pre-Circle meditation. As you breathe in, feel the energy building, and direct it down to the drawn line.

Slowly walk around the Circle, directing that energy as you go. Continue until you get back to the point where you started. In your mind, connect the ends of the line of power, then raise the athame in salute. Describe a pentagram in the air (see the illustration on page 33) to seal it, kiss the blade, and return to the altar.

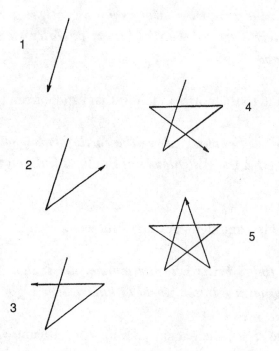

*DESCRIBING A PENTAGRAM*

Walk over to the east point in the Circle, taking with you matches or, better yet, a lighted taper. Light the east candle and say:

*Here is light at the east, where the life-giving sun rises each day. Here is erected the Watchtower[4] of Air, standing guard over this temple of the gods.*

Move on around to the south and light that candle from the taper, saying:

*Here is light at the south, where fires rise up to warm and illuminate the earth. Here is erected the Watchtower of Fire, standing guard over this temple of the gods.*

Move on around to the west and light that candle from the taper, saying:

---

4. The "watchtowers" are imaginary towers that you erect in your imagination to guard the Sacred Circle and help keep it free from any negative forces.

*Here is light at the west, where waters move gently to give the moisture of life to the earth. Here is erected the Watchtower of Water, standing guard over this temple of the gods.*

Move on around to the north and light that candle from the taper, saying:

*Here is a light at the north, where the earth forms a solid foundation for all life. Here is erected the Watchtower of Earth, standing guard over this temple of the gods.*

Return to the altar and light the altar candle(s), saying:

*Here is light that I bring into the temple. Let it light the way through the darkness of ignorance to the world of knowledge. Light to life, in all things.*

Extinguish the taper, then again take up your athame and dip the tip of the blade into the bowl of salt, saying:

*Salt is life. Let this salt be pure and let it purify my life, as I use it in this rite dedicated to the God and Goddess in whom I believe.*

Take three pinches of the salt and drop them into the water. Moving your athame blade across to the water dish, dip it in there, saying:

*Let the sacred salt drive out any impurities in this water, that together they may be used in the service of these deities, throughout these rites and at any time and in any way I may use them.*

Mix the water and salt with the athame blade, stirring in a clockwise direction three times around. Then lay down the athame and pick up the dish of salted water. Go to the east point of the Circle and raise the dish so it's level with your eyes. Say:

*I use this sacred liquid now in the building of this, my sacred temple. I dedicate it to the gods, in love and light.*

Lowering the dish, start once again to walk slowly *deosil* (clockwise) around the Circle, dipping your fingers into the water and sprinkling it along the line of the Circle as you go. Return to the east point where you started. Raise the dish briefly in salute then return to the altar. Put down the salt dish and take up the censer. Once again, go to the east point. Raise the censer and say:

> *The fire of this censer, with the fragrance of its smoke, serves to cement the foundation of this our temple, dedicated to the Lord and the Lady.*

Lower the censer and again pass along the line of the Circle, swinging the censer so that the fumes and smoke pass along it. When you return to your starting point, again raise the censer in salute and then return to the altar. Replace the censer and take up your athame. Raise your athame in salute and describe the pentagram over the altar. Say:

> *Lord and Lady, God and Goddess, I invite you to enter into this temple I have constructed to venerate you. Be with me here and witness these rites held in your honor. So mote it be.*

Kiss the blade and set down the athame.

*Note:* For a regular Esbat or Sabbat, you would continue the Casting of the Circle by consecrating all the Witches within it. This I will deal with on page 42. For now, let me continue with the Self-Dedication. For this rite, you should have a small dish or bottle of anointing oil on the altar.

Notice that there is no summoning of spirits of any sort. When erecting the four watchtowers, some traditions do call upon the "Guardians of the Four Quarters," often referring to them as sylphs, salamanders, undines, and dwarves. I consider this a very dangerous practice akin to ceremonial magic. Once you conjure something, you stand the risk of not being able to get rid of it.

For example, I have known of a coven that did not get rid of the salamanders of the south, the fire spirits. Just after the closing of the Circle, a fire actually broke out in the south of the room they were using. For guardians of the sacred Circle, who could do a better job than the gods themselves, the Lady and the Lord?

# Self-Dedication of a Witch

Ring the bell three times three, or nine times in all (with a brief pause between each set of three). Take up the anointing oil and dip your index finger into it. Draw a cross inside a circle on your forehead, in the position of the Third Eye (between the eyebrows). Then draw a pentagram, with the point upward, over your heart. Third, touch the oil to your genitals, right breast, left breast, and genitals, in this way describing a triangle. Replace the oil on the altar and pick up your athame. Hold it high in salute. Say:

> *God and Goddess; Lord and Lady. I am here a simple seeker of knowledge, a lover of life. I here dedicate myself to you and to your service. You are the ones I have chosen to serve. I do this of my own free will, with no pressure from any other. Guard me and guide me in all that I do, for all that I do is in love of you and of all life. Help me live my life with harm to none. Help me acknowledge the depth and beauty of all life, animal, vegetable, and mineral. The animals, birds, fish, reptiles, and all living things are my brothers and sisters. The trees of the forest, the plants, flowers, herbs, and all growing things are my brothers and sisters. The rocks, soil, sand, the rivers, lakes, seas, all waters of the earth and all that is of the earth are my brothers and sisters. Make me one with this family. Let me guard them and work for them as they all work for me.*
>
> *Lord and Lady, from this day forth I accept and will ever abide by the Wiccan Rede: "An it harm none, do what thou wilt." I pledge myself to you, the gods. I will always protect you as you do me. I will defend you against those who speak ill of you. You are my life and I am yours. So mote it be.*

Lower your athame and ring the bell three times. Take up the goblet of wine and raise it. Say:

> *To the gods!*

Pour a little into the libation dish (your offering to the gods) and say:

*As this wine drains from the cup, so let the blood drain from my body should I ever do anything to harm the gods, or those in kinship with their love. So mote it be!*

Drink to the gods. (You do not have to drain the cup! You can always pour more into the libation dish.) Replace the goblet and raise both hands high in salute. Say:

*As a sign of my being born again into the life of Wiccacraft, I here take upon myself a new name, by which I shall always be known within the Sacred Circle, which is the place between the worlds. Henceforth I shall be known as . . . [Witch name]. So mote it be!*

Lower your arms and ring the bell three times.

The above may be used by a solitary Wiccan, by the first to start a coven, or by the founder of a hereditary family group. In the case of the hereditary founding, the following should also be added.

Take up your athame and hold it in both hands over the position of your heart. Say:

*I further dedicate myself as the founder of a family line of Witches. I take upon myself the awesome responsibility of initiating others of my family, to build a new coven, the coven of . . . [name; for example, "the coven of Williamson" or "the coven of Johnson"] . . . in honor of the gods. Lord and Lady, help me in this undertaking. Let the coven prosper and endure. So mote it be!*

Now hold the athame over the altar and say:

*Now I consecrate this, the true tool of a Witch. It has all the powers of a magic wand and may be used in forming other instruments of the Craft. I here consecrate it, so that it may be properly used within this Circle and in the service of the gods.*

Sprinkle some of the water on the athame, then hold it in the smoke of the incense, saying:

*I cleanse and consecrate this, my magical athame, that it may serve as I serve the Lord and the Lady. May it be my strength and my love and may it never be used in anger nor to harm anyone or anything. So mote it be!*

Draw a pentagram in the air with it, kiss the blade, and lower it. You may now sit and meditate on what the Craft means to you and your family. It may be that, at this time, you will receive some indications from the gods that you are indeed in touch with them—some sight, sound, or inner feeling. Whether you do or not, relax and enjoy the knowledge of having finally come home to the Craft; of having finally become one of the members of the Old Religion.

If you feel like singing or dancing, or celebrating in any other appropriate way, do it! Now should follow the ritual of Cakes and Ale, or Cakes and Wine, but I will leave the details of this until I go through a coven Initiation (see page 41). The final step is always the Closing of the Circle, but we'll also look at that a little later on.

Note that nowhere in the Self-Dedication, or in the following coven Initiation, do initiates repudiate their previous religion. There are no words against any other faith. Should new Witches, at any future date, decide that Wicca is not the right religion for them after all, they are free to leave and either return to their previous faith or continue seeking elsewhere. Note also that an oath of secrecy is no longer taken.

# Oath of Secrecy

In times of persecution, it is obvious that an oath of secrecy would serve a useful purpose. It also served a purpose in the very early days of Paganism, long before the arrival of Christianity. At that time the purpose was a magical one. It was believed that to know a person's name was to have a power over him or her. This was especially true when working with spirits and entities.

In ceremonial magic (a practice and not a religion; it is not connected to Witchcraft), the aim of the rituals is to conjure certain entities, such as minor demons or devils, and to make them obey your commands. To do this, it was necessary to show your ability to have power over them. Part of this involved simply knowing their true names. By knowing these names and by using various words, tools, and symbols of power, it was believed possible to force these entities to do your bidding. In the same way, to know the name of your enemy's deities—and then conjure these deities—was to give you power over those gods and goddesses, and thereby over your enemy.

So in those days, it was important to keep the names of your gods secret. Regular, everyday names were used to refer to the gods—almost like nicknames—but the names used in rituals were secret, and guarded by the priesthood. When these names were revealed to a new initiate, he or she had to take an oath never to reveal them to anyone who was not also an initiate. Most of these ancient religions had their own ways of doing magic, so these methods were also kept secret.

This oath of secrecy is still a part of some modern Wiccan Initiations (in Gardnerian Wicca, for example). Although it may no longer be necessary, it remains part of that tradition's heritage. I do not include such an oath in the material in this book. If you feel strongly that there should be one, by all means add one.

# Libations

In almost every ritual, wine is poured into a dish and, frequently, a piece of cake is also put into the dish (see "Cakes and Ale," page 65). These are tokens of sharing with the gods and with others. In thanking the gods for the food and drink we need in order to live, we also think of the fact that while we have these things, there are others who have nothing. Symbolically, we indicate our wish to share with those less fortunate than ourselves.

What happens to these libations? At the end of the Circle, they are taken out and poured on the ground, to be absorbed by the earth. Some Wiccans with backyards and gardens will dedicate a small area especially for this purpose. Sometimes statutes of the deities will be placed about it. It may also include such things as bird feeders and baths. The food left there is frequently taken by animals, thus becoming a very real sharing from the Circle. If you live in an apartment and have no access to such an outdoor area, you can pour the wine into a potted plant and place the food on the windowsill, for the birds. Or you might have a window box you can use. Some Wiccans will make a trip to a nearby park just to leave their libations. As a last resort, you can pour them down the sink or disposal, knowing that they will eventually find their way to the earth.

# Starting a Coven

When the "first Witch" has completed the Self-Dedication, he or she is now ready to bring others into the Craft who wish to be a part of it. In a hereditary coven, these will be members of the family. The immediate family, as a whole, should decide just how far outside their group the coven should extend: Should they include cousins and second cousins, for example, or restrict membership to direct lineage only, such as sons and daughters, grandsons and granddaughters? What about those outsiders who marry into the family? These are important considerations, for too soon a family coven can grow large and unwieldy. The obvious answer, in this case, is to split up into two, or even more, family covens.

If you're starting a coven that's not a family line, of course you don't have these concerns. But you still have to consider just who to bring in. The scene has changed dramatically over the last forty years or so, and today many people wish to find a Wiccan coven. Whoever starts the coven should think seriously about what the criteria will be for admission.

First and foremost should be, how sincere is the person in wanting to join Wicca *as a religion*? With a wealth of television shows and movies dramatizing and romanticizing Wicca, many are drawn for the wrong reasons. They think it's "cool" to be a Witch, or they think they'll gain great powers, or believe it's all about working magic and casting spells, or doing drugs and having sex. In fact, there are many covens that never work magic and never cast spells. And no true Witches do drugs. There are many who are Wiccans simply because it is their religion and they wish to worship the gods.

And yes, there are also many covens that do work magic. However, their magic is only done when there is a very real need for it, and much of it is for the purposes of healing. I'll be talking about magic and healing in later chapters.

If you are starting a coven, draw up a list of "dos" and "don'ts." Do consider those who are sincere, those who have some true knowledge of what Wicca really is, those you feel would be a worthwhile addition to the group. Don't consider those who obviously have all the wrong ideas, who think it's the same thing as Satanism, who just want to dress up in black and frighten people, who are looking for power over others. I've purposely used the word *consider* above. Don't make any instant decisions on admitting members, but do get to know each person in order to find why he or she is attracted to your group. Ask questions and expect prospective members to ask questions of you. Find out what they have read; what they believe Witchcraft to be; what their views are on religion, life, environmental issues, and so on.

Traditionally, after first contacting a coven, there was a year-and-a-day waiting period before anyone could get initiated. This was plenty of time to check out would-be Witches, and to give some initial training to see how they responded. Few groups today make an applicant wait this long, however. Still, I cannot emphasize too strongly that you should not be in any hurry to bring in people who want to join your group. A coven is like a small family. All grow to be very close. Don't risk spoiling the group by admitting someone who may disrupt it.

Suppose you now have a person or a number of people whom you know are just right. Or you are ready to start your family Wiccan coven. How do you proceed? The person who has done the Self-Dedication is now referred to as the High Priestess (or High Priest, but I will use a female as an example). All Witches are priests or priestesses; they can perform the rituals by themselves if they wish. Once the Witch becomes a leader of a group, these priests and priestesses are termed High Priests or Priestesses.

## Coven Initiation

The coven Initiation differs from the Self-Initiation in that there can be more activity, since there is more than one participant! When you have a large coven, you can start to delegate parts of the rituals to different Witches so that as many as possible are actually participating. This is the ideal. Witchcraft is a religion of participation. Unlike most organized religions, you do not just sit in a large hall and watch what is going on; you are right in there as part of it. I consider this a very important part of religious experience.

I will next describe a coven Initiation with just the High Priestess and the initiate—as it would be for the first few Initiations. When you have a full coven, don't hesitate to rewrite this ritual so that all may have parts. Let the officiating priest play the lead, but let others join in. (In the appendix, I have included an example of an Initiation performed with a whole coven participating.) Opening the Circle with a whole coven, Cakes and Ale, and other rituals will be dealt with in chapter 4.

# Coven Initiation Ceremony

The High Priestess, properly prepared, stands in the ritual Circle in front of the altar. In addition to the regular tools are a container of anointing oil, a blindfold, a nine-foot length of red silken cord, and a scourge (see chapter 20). The initiate's own athame also lies on the altar, to one side. The candles beyond the Circle are alight but not the four quarter candles around the Circle itself nor the altar candles. The wine goblet is full.

Outside the Circle, to the east, stands the initiate. He[5] stands quietly until called for. (*Note:* The Sacred Circle is always entered and departed from the east.)

The High Priestess (HPS) rings the bell three times then takes up her athame, kisses the blade, and holds it high in salute, saying:

*Hail, Lord and Lady. Here I do build a temple of life in which to honor you. Assist me as I lay down the foundation stones on which I will build my cone of power.*

HPS lowers the blade and walks over to the east point in the Circle. She points the tip of the blade at the line drawn on the ground and slowly walks around the Circle, directing energy as she goes. She continues until she returns to the point where she started. There she raises the athame in salute and describes a pentagram in the air. She kisses the blade and returns to the altar.

HPS now walks over to the east point in the Circle, taking with her a lighted taper. She lights the east candle, saying:

*Here is light at the east, where the life-giving sun rises each day. Here is erected the Watchtower of Air, standing guard over this temple of the gods.*

She moves on around to the south and lights that candle from the taper, saying:

---

5. It is usual, but not mandatory, for a woman to initiate a man and a man to initiate a woman. In some traditions, the coven tries to maintain an even balance of male and female members—but not all traditions subscribe to this. There are, in fact, all-female covens and all-male covens. Many Witches do feel, however, that having both sexes present acts something like the two opposing poles of a battery and, magically, can be beneficial.

*Here is light at the south, where fires rise up to warm and illuminate the earth. Here is erected the Watchtower of Fire, standing guard over this temple of the gods.*

She moves on around to the west and lights that candle from the taper, saying:

*Here is light at the west, where waters move gently to give the moisture of life to the earth. Here is erected the Watchtower of Water, standing guard over this temple of the gods.*

She moves on around to the north and lights that candle from the taper, saying:

*Here is light at the north, where the earth forms a solid foundation for all life. Here is erected the Watchtower of Earth, standing guard over this temple of the gods.*

HPS returns to the altar and puts down the taper. Standing before the altar, she lights the altar candle(s), saying:

*Here is light that I bring into the temple. Let it light the way through the darkness of ignorance to the world of knowledge. Light to life, in all things.*

She again takes up her athame and dips the tip of the blade into the bowl of salt, saying:

*Salt is life. Let this salt be pure and let it purify my life, as I use it in this rite dedicated to the God and Goddess in whom I believe.*

She takes three pinches of salt and drops them into the water. Moving her athame blade across to the water dish, she dips it in there, saying:

*Let the sacred salt drive out any impurities in this water, that together they may be used in the service of these deities, throughout these rites and at any time and in any way I may use them.*

She mixes the water and salt with the athame blade, stirring in a *deosil* direction three times around, then lays down the athame and picks up the dish of salted water. She goes to the east point of the Circle and raises the dish, saying:

> *I use this sacred liquid now in the building of this, my sacred temple. I dedicate it to the gods, in love and light.*

Lowering the dish, HPS starts once again to walk slowly *deosil* around the Circle, dipping her fingers into the water and sprinkling it along the line of the Circle. She returns to the east point and raises the dish briefly in salute, then returns to the altar. She puts down the salt dish and takes up the censer. Again HPS goes to the east point, where she raises the censer, saying:

> *The fire of this censer, with the fragrance of its smoke, serves to cement the foundation of this our temple, dedicated to the Lord and the Lady.*

HPS lowers the censer and again passes along the line of the Circle, swinging the censer so that the fumes and smoke pass along it. When she returns to the starting point, she again raises the censer in salute and then returns to the altar. HPS replaces the censer and takes up her athame. She raises it in salute and describes the pentagram over the altar, saying:

> *Lord and Lady, God and Goddess, I invite you to enter into this temple I have constructed to venerate you. Be with me here and witness these rites held in your honor. So mote it be.*

She kisses the blade and sets down the athame. She dips her forefinger into the water and marks a cross within a circle on her forehead and a pentagram over her heart, saying:

> *Here I do consecrate myself in the names of the Lord and the Lady. I am here in peace and love, with honor to all life.*

HPS rings the bell three times three, or nine times in all. Then, taking up her athame, she faces the east, where the initiate waits outside the Circle. She points the tip of the athame at the initiate.

| HPS: | Who are you who stands outside this temple of the ancient gods? |
|---|---|
| INITIATE: | I am a seeker who has traveled far. I look for peace, joy, and the light of knowledge. |
| HPS: | Are you here of your own free will? |
| INITIATE: | I am. |
| HPS: | What steps brought you here? |
| INITIATE: | First curiosity, then learning, and finally love. Curiosity about the Old Religion; learning about the ancient ways; love for the gods, for life, and for my brothers and sisters of the Craft. |
| HPS: | What two words will bring you into this Circle, this temple of the gods? |
| INITIATE: | Love and trust. |

HPS lowers her athame, takes up the blindfold and cord, and goes to the east to face the Initiate. She "cuts out of the Circle." [6]

6. Cutting out of the Circle and returning into it are ritual actions. They involve cutting across the "lines" drawn by the person who constructed the Circle, in order to pass through, then rejoining them and sealing the join with a pentagram.

| | |
|---|---|
| **HPS:** | **All who bring such words are welcome.** |

She salutes him (kisses him; see "Salutes" in chapter 14) then blindfolds him and binds him as follows: With the initiate's hands behind his back, the nine-foot cord is placed over his left wrist, at the cord's center point. A knot is tied. The initiate's right hand is then laid across and the cord is tied 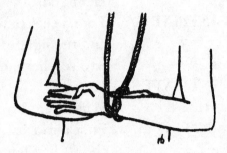 around the right wrist, tying the two together. The two ends of the cord are then taken up, one on either side of the initiate's head, and loosely looped around the neck to be tied in a bow on the right shoulder.

HPS guides the initiate over the lines of the Circle into the temple. She turns, closes and seals the Circle, then guides the initiate to stand before the altar. Then, HPS rings the bell three times. She takes up the salted water and marks a cross within a circle on the initiate's forehead, a pentagram over his heart, then touches it to his genitals: right breast, left breast, genitals.

| | |
|---|---|
| **HPS:** | **With this holy water I anoint and cleanse you, that you may be clean and pure within this Circle, the temple of the gods.** |

The initiate now kneels in front of the altar.

| | |
|---|---|
| **HPS:** | **I ask, why are you here in this temple of the gods?** |
| **INITIATE:** | **I am here to be made one with those gods. I wish to become one of the children of the Lord and Lady. I wish to be part of the family of Wicca.** |
| **HPS:** | **To do what you wish you must end life as you have known it. Are you ready to do that?** |
| **INITIATE:** | **I am.** |
| **HPS:** | **You will be setting your feet on the path that leads to purity, truth, and love. The first step is to leave your life of old; to face death and joyously pass beyond it. Are you ready to do so?** |

| | |
|---|---|
| **INITIATE:** | **I am.** |
| **HPS:** | **So mote it be.** |

HPS takes up the scourge and (lightly, so as *not* to hurt) strikes the initiate across the buttocks nine times.[7] She then lays down the scourge and rings the bell seven times.

HPS helps the initiate to his feet and removes the cord and the blindfold. She embraces him and gives him the threefold salute.

| | |
|---|---|
| **HPS:** | **Now you enter into the world newborn. To start life anew you will need a new name. What is that name by which you wish to be known, within this sacred Circle?** |
| **INITIATE:** | **I take the name . . . [Witch name].** |

HPS again consecrates him—forehead, heart, and sacred triangle—this time with the anointing oil.

| | |
|---|---|
| **HPS:** | **I consecrate you now in the names of the Lord and the Lady. Henceforth you will be known, in this sacred Circle and to all your brothers and sisters of the Craft, by your new name . . . [Witch name]. With this sacred oil I anoint and cleanse you, giving new life to one of the children of the gods. So mote it be!** |

HPS replaces the oil on the altar, salutes the initiate, then rings the bell nine times.

| | |
|---|---|
| **HPS:** | **Now I present to you the working tool of a Witch.** |

She takes the initiate's athame from the altar and presents it to him. They both hold it as she speaks:

---

7. This is the symbolic death found in mystery religions universally. An example may be seen in the seventh scene of the frescoes at the Villa of Mysteries in Pompeii.

| HPS: | This is the true tool of a Witch. It has all the powers of a magic wand and may be used in forming other instruments of the Craft. It must be properly used within the sacred Circle. |

HPS lets go of the athame, and the initiate holds it over the altar.

| HPS: | Now you must consecrate it, so that it may be properly used within this Circle and in the service of the gods. |

The initiate sprinkles some of the water on the athame, then holds it in the smoke of the incense.

| INITIATE: | I cleanse and consecrate this, my magical athame, that it may serve me as I serve the Lord and the Lady. May it be my strength and my love and may it never be used in anger nor to harm anyone or anything. So mote it be! |

He then draws a pentagram in the air with it, kisses the blade, and lowers it.

| HPS: | Now you are truly one of us. As such you will share our knowledge of the gods, of the arts of healing, divination, and magic. You will learn all the mystic arts. All these things you will learn as you progress down the path of the Old Religion. But first, I must caution you to always remember the Wiccan Rede: An it harm none, do what thou wilt. |
| INITIATE: | An it harm none, do what thou wilt. |
| HPS: | So mote it be. |
| INITIATE: | So mote it be. |

HPS gives the initiate the eightfold salute (see chapter 14). Then she and the initiate embrace and kiss. HPS takes his hand and leads him around the Circle, starting at the east point, where she raises her athame in salute.

| HPS: | Hail Lord and Lady. Here do I present, for the first time, the Witch . . . [Witch name] . . . , a brother of the Craft. A true member of the Old Religion. |

She leads him on to the south point, where she repeats the announcement, then to the west and to the north, repeating at each. Back at the east, HPS raises her athame again in salute and kisses the blade. She then leads the initiate back to the altar. There she raises the goblet, pours a libation, and drinks from it. She passes it to the initiate, who also drinks.

| HPS: | To the gods! |
| INITIATE: | To the gods! |

Now should follow the ritual of Cakes and Ale, or Cakes and Wine (see chapter 4), followed by singing or dancing or celebrating in any other appropriate way. The final step is always the Closing of the Circle. We'll look at this in the next chapter.

# The Book of Shadows

Witches keep their rituals, spells, herbal lore, and any and all other things pertinent to them in a book called The Book of Shadows. How it got this name is not known for certain, but it has been suggested that it comes from the time of the persecutions. Up until then, the Craft was a purely oral tradition, with everything passed on by word of mouth. But with the persecutions, groups of Witches became isolated, losing touch with others of the Old Religion. So that the rituals would not be lost, they were written down in a book, carefully kept and guarded by the coven leader. Since they were having to meet "in the shadows" at that time, the book became known as The Book of Shadows.

Many traditions use a book with a black cover, probably considered easier to hide. But some have earth-colored covers such as green or brown. It really doesn't matter what color the cover is these days. Personally I prefer green, a color I associate with nature.

The book is always handwritten. *It should not be typewritten or computer generated.* This is a book of magic. By the very act of writing, you are putting your energies into the book. As you write, you are concentrating on what is being put down on the pages and, in so doing, empowering the book with your energies. I will go into this in more depth in later chapters when I talk about making magical talismans.

The first page of the book is usually decorated with the words THE BOOK OF SHADOWS OF THE WITCH [NAME], IN HER [OR HIS] HAND OF WRITE. In other words, in her own handwriting.

Originally, as I have mentioned, there was just one book for the coven, kept in safekeeping by the High Priestess or High Priest. It was a large, weighty tome, including not only the rituals but also all the magical lore, herbal lore, and divinitory systems used by the members.

These days, individual Witches keep their own particular interests in their own personal books. A Witch who is interested in astrology, for example, will have all her astrology notes in the book, while another Witch may prefer herbal lore in his volume.

They will probably all contain the regular rituals—Esbats and Sabbats—but will then be personalized with the Witch's interests, together with the ways that this particular Witch has found magic to work best.

For a hereditary group, I suggest having a large, complete Book of Shadows that all family members can contribute to, kept by the head of the household. Individual family members will also have their own books with their own special interests included, if they wish.

Some Books of Shadows are quite creative with elaborate lettering, illuminated like ancient manuscripts. I think this is wonderful and can really make the book a work of art. If you do this, however, you will find it best to stick to plainer text for the words of any rituals. When doing a ritual in the Circle, you will probably be reading the words from the book (which can be placed on a stand beside or behind the altar). It is not easy to read fancy script in flickering candlelight, so make the ritual words as bold and plain as you can.

While some buy bound blank books to use, many Witches make their books from scratch. It makes a great project and, once again, means that you end up with a powerful, very personal book, due to all the energies you have put into it. You can make the cover out of hand-tooled leather, for example, or out of pieces of wood decorated with wood-burning tools. You can use parchment, or simulated parchment, sheets for the pages. Some Wiccans even make their own paper, which is not as difficult as might be thought.

One nice idea I came across was homemade paper scented with herbs and embedded with pressed herbs and flowers. (The lavender was especially good!) A dab of essential oil was added to the paper pulp mix, or an actual pressed flower or herb was added. It made a wonderful Book of Shadows.

> *If you would keep a book let it be in your own Hand of Write. Let Brothers and Sisters copy what they will, but never let the book out of your hands and never keep the writings of another. . . . Let each guard his own writings and destroy them whenever danger threatens. Learn as much as you may by heart and when danger is past rewrite your book.*
> —Gardnerian Book of Shadows

## Wiccan Jewelry

Now might be an appropriate time to discuss Wiccan jewelry. Once you are a Witch, you will probably feel like shouting the fact to the world. You could do this effectively by wearing appropriate jewelry, much as a Christian might wear a crucifix or a Jew wear a Star of David. The symbol most often associated with Wicca is the pentagram—the open, five-pointed star with a single point upward.

The pentagram symbolizes the life force. In many of the old books of magic, you will find illustrations of a man or a woman standing with legs apart and arms extended. Superimposed on the body is a pentagram.

Some people seem to consider the pentagram a symbol of evil. They especially think this of the inverted pentagram with the single point downward and the two points upward. In fact, no symbol is evil—or good—in itself. It is only so in context.

For example, the swastika is a symbol found in many places, used by many cultures. It has been a religious symbol since at least 10,000 B.C.E., appearing in India, China, Asia Minor, Japan, Persia, Scandinavia, ancient Greece, and Rome. It is also used by Native Americans. But when it was used by Nazi Germany, it became a symbol of evil. As used by, say, Hopi or Navajo tribes, however, it is not evil. So the symbol itself is neither good nor bad; it is simply a symbol. It is how it is used and by whom that matters.

In the same way, the pentagram is neither good nor bad; it is simply a symbol (whether right way up or inverted). As used by Witches, it is a positive symbol. As used by Satanists, it is a negative symbol.

Another popular Wiccan symbol is a crescent moon. This is used by itself, or in conjunction with a full moon, and in many other ways. For example, a popular Goddess symbol is a full moon with a crescent moon on either side of it. An equal-arm cross—an old representation of the sun—is also used. The *labrys*, or double-headed ax of ancient Crete, has been adopted by many feminist Wiccans, among others. The Thor's hammer is used also, as is the Egyptian ankh, or *crux ansata* (cross of life).

These symbols are used in pendants and rings, on bracelets and talismans. Some people almost cover themselves with them, with rings on every finger, dozens of bracelets, and lots of pendants. Others may only wear one small, discreet pentagram. With my English upbringing, I lean more toward understatement, but what you wear is up to you. Of course, you will find many non-Witches, or "wannabe" Witches, who smother themselves with pentagrams and the like just to look different. (These are usually the ones who also paint their fingernails black and wear grotesque makeup.)

Traditionally, all Witches wear a necklace while in the ritual Circle, as a symbol of the circle of rebirth (see "Life After Life" in chapter 2). The High Priestess generally also wears a silver bracelet as a sign that she is the coven leader. This is engraved with certain signs and symbols, depending upon the tradition to which she belongs.

In traditions that have degrees of advancement (see chapter 4), there is provision for a "Witch Queen" or "Queen of the Sabbat" and, as such, she will wear a crown. This is usually a simple band of silver with a silver crescent moon on the front. Some traditions have adopted this for any High Priestess, and some allow any female Witch to wear a crown. However, if everyone does it, then it is no longer special.

# ~ 4 ~

# Witchcraft in the Family

To belong to a family of Witches is something very special. Any coven is itself like a family, but to have it the other way around—your actual family is the coven—can be extraordinary. In the old days before the burning times, this was pretty much the norm. But with the persecutions and the eradication of so many followers of the Old Religion, it became the exception to find a family of Wiccans. Yet we have hereditary Witchcraft to thank for Wicca's survival. If it hadn't been for those few families that kept the beliefs going, that continued the ancient rites and magic, we would not have it today. In fact, we would probably all believe the Christian propaganda that has been so heavily laid on.

For hundreds of years, everything written about Witches and Witchcraft was written by those very people who had tried so hard to destroy the Old Religion. But thankfully, the hereditaries kept the true faith going.

Having Wicca as the family religion creates a very special bond among family members. This is also true—or should be—among members of any coven. The family is the coven and the coven is the family. You can share so much with brothers and sisters, with your parents and your children.

Yet no one should be forced into becoming a Wiccan just because the rest of the family has decided that it is the path for them. If there are family members who do not wish to participate, that is fine. If there are those who find another religion more attractive, that, too, is fine. The most important thing is that all should feel happy and comfortable in the religious rites they perform. If these should differ from your own, that does not make them wrong. It has been often said that there are many paths, yet they all lead to the same center. All should be encouraged to look at other faiths.

If a Wiccan child, brought up in Circles and with reverence for all life, hears of Satanism and hears others refer to Witches as "servants of the devil," he or she needs to know why many people think that way, and where the Christian devil fits into the scheme of things. It is important that everyone—and this holds true especially for children—be given the opportunity to compare personal experience with various presentations of religious belief, and not just Wiccan.

The only argument I have is with those who would try to force their beliefs on others. There is nothing more annoying (and many seem to share this feeling with me) than having people from another religion banging on your door and thrusting their literature in your face! There are some hateful little tracts that well-meaning but misguided people like to give to everyone, often in the form of little "comic" books. The Aquarian Tabernacle Church (a Wiccan church) of Washington has come up with a wonderful response. Pathfinder Press publishes similar tracts, but from a Pagan perspective! I keep a supply of their little "comic" booklet titled *The Other People . . .* readily available for handing out in response to those who force their literature on me. It works extremely well.

## Coven Leadership

Who leads a coven? Traditionally the oldest member of the family leads the group, though this does not have to be so. Let's look at a new family group. If the mother and father are the first to start the coven, then they will become its High Priest and High Priestess. And incidentally, it is not necessary to have both positions. You can have a High Priestess leading the rites, or a High Priest. It may well be, in fact, that the parents are not the best suited for the jobs. Oftentimes there are family members who are much better at leading rituals, or who have much greater knowledge from having studied the subject more. But let's examine what is probably the most common arrangement.

We will assume that the parents were the ones who started the family Witchcraft group. The mother was the first to perform the Self-Dedication, and then she initiated the father. From there, all family members were brought in. In time, others may show themselves to be better suited to the leadership roles. Or the parents (or one of them) may no longer wish to lead the group. Then this parent or parents will become what are known as Elders of the coven, there to help and advise on matters. For example, an older daughter may be the High Priestess (perhaps with no High Priest position), and the parents may be members of the coven, but as its Elders.

In the Saxon tradition of Witchcraft, the coven leaders are voted in by the coven. They then hold the position for a year. At the end of this time, there is a new vote. If they've done a good job, they will probably be voted back into the positions. But if they have not, or if someone else would like the post, they may relinquish it. In this way, it is possible for everyone to have the experience of leading the rites and having the responsibilities that go with running a coven. I think this system has much to recommend it.

## Degree Systems

Another system that might be considered is the degree system. Many Wiccan traditions have such a policy. In this, Witches are initiated to the First Degree. They stay there for at least a year, learning and experiencing. At the end of this time, if the High Priestess and High Priest think they are ready, they will be raised to the Second Degree. There, they have more things to learn and will start helping with conducting the rituals and Casting the Circle for the coven rituals.

After a further year, they are eligible for the Third Degree. A Third Degree Witch may become a High Priest or High Priestess. In a coven outside the family traditions, they would then be encouraged to break away and form a new coven. They would certainly be eligible to perform Initiations. If they did not wish to break away, they would be considered Elders of the coven.

So both a family coven and any other new coven can consider these approaches. They can have the people who start the group as their leaders, and keep them in those positions, or they can vote in the best-qualified people as leaders. Or—in both situations—they can incorporate a degree system (it doesn't have to be three degrees, though this is most common) of advancement for the individual Witches.

Leadership of a coven entails more than just playing the leading role in the rituals. The coven leader(s) will arrange the rituals, deciding (with the help of the Elders, if there are any) on the dates they will be held and exactly what rituals will take place, perhaps even writing new rituals. They will see that plenty of supplies are always on hand: candles, incense, charcoal, wine, cakes. They will delegate duties, if necessary. They will decide on the best ways to work magic (see chapter 7) and what follow-up there needs to be. They will arrange the training of the members of the coven.

The coven as a whole should decide on how they wish to dress for rituals. They should also be consulted on as many aspects of the rituals, and practice of the Craft, as possible.

## The Wiccan Esbat Ritual

The regular meetings of a coven, other than the Sabbats (which we will look at in chapter 19), are known as Esbats. These might be just for worship—to thank the gods for their blessings and to ask them for what is needed—or they might be used to perform coven magic.[8] Esbats are held at least once a month, at the full moon, though they can be held more often if desired. In fact, many covens meet at least once a week.

The general pattern of an Esbat is: (a) consecrating the meeting place (Casting the Circle), (b) inviting the gods to attend, (c) prayers, (d) giving thanks (Cakes and Ale), (e) doing magic, *if needed*, and (f) parting (Closing the Circle). If the Esbat is at, or near, the full moon, then the Drawing Down the Moon ritual is included prior to the Cakes and Ale.

I will give this, and all other rituals, as for a whole coven or family to perform. If there is only a solitary, or just two or three Witches, they you can adapt the words and actions for the number present. Don't hesitate to rewrite any of the rituals given in this book, for your own use, to suit what you like.

---

8. Magic can be done by individuals or by groups such as covens. Covens working magic can put a lot more power into it than individuals, since they can draw energy from all the members.

## ESBAT RITUAL

Let us name the participants: High Priestess (HPS), High Priest (HP), maiden, squire, witches 1, 2, 3, and 4.

All are properly prepared. The High Priestess and the High Priest stand in front of the altar, which has all the tools on it. The other Witches stand in the Circle around the altar. So far as it might be possible, the Witches should stand alternating male and female. The candles are alight beyond the circle, but not the four quarter candles around the Circle or the altar candles. The wine goblet is full.

The High Priestess rings the bell three times, then takes up her athame, kisses the blade, and holds it high in salute. All others in the Circle likewise raise their athames in salute, kissing the blade.

**HPS:** **Hail, Lord and Lady. Here I do build a temple of life in which to honor you. Assist us as we lay down the foundation stones on which to build our cone of power.**

HPS and others lower their blades. HPS walks over to the east point in the Circle. She points the tip of the athame blade at the line drawn on the ground and slowly walks around the Circle, directing energy as she goes. She continues until she returns to the point where she started. There she raises the athame in salute and describes a pentagram in the air. She kisses the blade and returns to the altar.

Witch 1 now walks over to the east point in the Circle, taking with him a lighted taper. He lights the east candle.

**Witch 1:** **Here is light at the east, where the life-giving sun rises each day. Here is erected the Watchtower of Air, standing guard over this temple of the gods.**

He returns to the circle and passes the taper to Witch 2. She takes it and moves around to the south, where she lights that candle from the taper.

**Witch 2:** **Here is light at the south, where fires rise up to warm and illuminate the earth. Here is erected the Watchtower of Fire, standing guard over this temple of the gods.**

She returns to the Circle and passes the taper to Witch 3, who moves around to the west and lights that candle from the taper.

**Witch 3:**    **Here is light at the west, where waters move gently to give the moisture of life to the earth. Here is erected the Watchtower of Water, standing guard over this temple of the gods.**

He returns to the Circle and passes the taper to Witch 4. She moves around to the north and lights that candle from the taper.

**Witch 4:**    **Here is light at the north, where the earth forms a solid foundation for all life. Here is erected the Watchtower of Earth, standing guard over this temple of the gods.**

Witch 4 goes to the altar and puts down the taper, then returns to her place in the Circle. Standing before the altar, the High Priest lights the altar candle(s).

**HP:**    **"Here is light that I bring into the temple. Let it light the way through the darkness of ignorance to the world of knowledge. Light to life, in all things."**

HPS dips the tip of her athame blade into the bowl of salt.

**HPS:**    **Salt is life. Let this salt be pure and let it purify our lives, as we use it in this rite dedicated to the God and Goddess in whom we believe.**

She takes three pinches of the salt and drops them into the water. Moving her athame blade across to the water dish, she dips it in there.

**HPS:**    **Let the sacred salt drive out any impurities in this water, that together they may be used in the service of these deities, throughout these rites and at any time and in any way we may use them.**

She mixes the water and salt with the athame blade, stirring in a clockwise direction three times around, then lays down the athame and picks up the dish of salted water. She hands it to the maiden, who goes to the east point of the circle and raises the dish.

> **MAIDEN:** **I use this sacred liquid now in the building of this, our sacred temple. I dedicate it to the gods, in love and light.**

Lowering the dish, she starts to walk slowly *deosil* around the Circle, dipping her fingers into the water and sprinkling it along the line of the Circle. She returns to the east point and raises the dish briefly in salute, then returns to the altar. She puts down the salt dish.

The High Priest takes up the censer and passes it to the squire, who goes to the east point, where he raises the censer.

> **SQUIRE:** **The fire of this censer, with the fragrance of its smoke, serves to cement the foundation of this our temple, dedicated to the Lord and the Lady.**

He lowers the censer and again passes along the line of the Circle, swinging the censer so that the fumes and smoke pass along it. When he returns to the starting point, he again raises the censer in salute and then returns to the altar. HP replaces the censer and takes up his athame. All raise their athames in salute and describe a pentagram in the air.

> **HPS:** **Lord and Lady, God and Goddess, I invite you to enter into this temple we have constructed to venerate you.**
> **HP:** **Be with us here and witness these rites we hold in your honor.**
> **ALL:** **So mote it be!**

All kiss their blades.

HPS dips her forefinger into the water and marks a cross within a circle on the forehead of the High Priest, followed by a pentagram over his heart, saying:

**HPS:** Here I do consecrate you in the names of the Lord and the Lady. Let us be here in peace and love, with honor to all life.

They salute. HPS gives the dish of holy water to the High Priest, who then does the same to her. He dips his forefinger into the water and marks a cross within a circle on the forehead of the High Priestess, followed by a pentagram over her heart, saying:

**HP:** Here I do consecrate you in the names of the Lord and the Lady. Let us be here in peace and love, with honor to all life.

They salute. All of the Witches in turn move around and stand before the High Priestess or High Priest. HPS consecrates the male Witches and HP consecrates the female Witches. Each returns to his or her place after being consecrated and saluted.

**HP:** All hail the four quarters and all hail the gods!
**ALL:** All hail!
**HPS:** We bid the Lord and Lady welcome and invite them to join with us, witnessing these rites we hold in their honor.
**HP:** Now the temple is erected and all within it duly consecrated. Let none leave this sacred space without good reason.[9] So mote it be.

The maiden rings the bell three times three, or nine times in all.

**HPS:** Blessings be upon all of us. What we have, we have through the love of the Lord and the Lady. Let us give thanks to them for these blessings.
**HP:** If any among us have anything to request of the gods, then let them ask now. Know that what we need may not come easily.

9. It is best not to break the Circle once it has been cast unless absolutely necessary. This is especially true when working magic, since any breaking and resealing the Circle weakens it.

**The gods help those who help themselves. But the first step to gaining your desires is to put those desires into words.**

HPS: **Yet always remember the Wiccan Rede: An it harm none, do what thou wilt. Whatever you do, whatever you may ask for, make sure it harms no one, not even yourself.**

There follows three or four minutes as all silently, in their own way and in their own words, thank the gods for what they have and ask for what they need.

The maiden rings the bell three times.

If it is a full moon—or close to one—then the Drawing Down the Moon ritual should follow (see below). If not, the coven goes straight into the Cakes and Ale rite (see page 65).

# Drawing Down the Moon

This ritual is performed at every full moon. The coven should meet at least once a month, preferably at the full of the moon. In Charles Godfrey Leland's book *Aradia, Gospel of the Witches*, Aradia, the daughter of Diana, says to her followers: "Once in the month, and when the moon is full, ye shall assemble in some desert place, or in a forest all together join to adore the potent spirit of your queen, my mother, great Diana." Witches have always followed this admonition and always meet at the full moon to worship the Goddess. Traditionally, at this meeting the High Priest will ask the Goddess to descend into the body of the High Priestess and, through her, speak to the gathered Witches.

*Lovely Goddess of the bow!*
*Lovely Goddess of the arrows!*
*Of all hounds and all hunting*
*Thou who wakest in starry heaven*
*When the sun is sunk in slumber.*
*Thou with moon upon thy forehead.*
*Who the chase by night preferrest*
*Unto hunting in the daylight,*
*With the nymphs unto the music*

*Of the horn—thyself the huntress,*
*And most powerful: I pray thee*
*Think, although but for an instant,*
*Upon us who pray unto thee!*

"To Diana," in Charles Godfrey Leland's
*Aradia, Gospel of the Witches*

## THE FULL MOON—DRAWING DOWN THE MOON CEREMONY

This ritual is preceded by the regular Esbat ceremony (see page 56).

The maiden rings the bell seven times. HPS stands in front of the altar, facing away from it, toward the assembled coven. They all sit or kneel in a circle around the altar. HPS stands in the "God position" (see the illustration below). HP kneels before her and raises his athame.

God
Position

Goddess
Position

**HP:**      **Our Lady, Great Mother, who was of old known by many and various names: Aphrodite, Bride, Cerridwen, Diana, Gana, Isis, and many others. Mother of us all, bringer of life and love, bearer of all fruitfulness, I invoke you and call upon you to de-**

scend into the body of this your High Priestess. Touch with her hands, kiss with her lips, speak with her voice to these, your loving and faithful followers.

HP gives HPS the eightfold salute, then draws a pentagram with his athame, lowers it, and sits back. HPS moves into the Goddess position.

HPS: I am the one who watches over you, whether you be awake or asleep. I am mother to you all and to all life. That you should pay me homage at this full of the moon is pleasure for me and brings great joy. Let my worship be in your hearts. Behold, all acts of love and pleasure are my rituals, therefore let there be beauty and strength, power and compassion, honor and humility, mirth and reverence within you.

And if you seek me, know that your seeking and yearning avail you not unless you know the mystery—that if you don't find what you seek within you, you will never find it without. For behold—I have been with you from the beginning, and I am that which is attained at the end of desire.

Know that, together with my Lord, I weave the web of life for each and every one of you. I am at the beginning and at the end of life and of time. I am Maiden; Mother; Crone. Wherever you may be, if you need me then call upon me and I will be there. For I live deep within each and every one of you. I am life and I am love. Be true to me and I will always be true to you. Harm none and love all. So mote it be.

*Note:* These are the words spoken by the High Priestess in this ritual. But it sometimes happens that the Goddess herself actually does come down into the body of the High Priestess. When this happens, you will find that the Lady speaks her own words . . . words just seem to come into the head of HPS and she relays them to the coveners; she acts as a "channel" for the Goddess. When this happens, of course, there is no need for the above.

HPS lowers her arms back to the God position and closes her eyes. There follows a few moments of silence. Then the maiden rings the bell three times, and the coven proceeds into the Cakes and Ale rite (see page 65).

# Alternatives

In Gardnerian and some other traditions, the "Charge of the Goddess" is spoken by the High Priestess at the Drawing Down the Moon. Some may prefer this to the shorter address I give above. The charge is lengthy and loosely based on material in Leland's book *Aradia*, together with material by Gerald Gardner, Doreen Valiente, and a couple of bits from Aleister Crowley:

*Listen to the words of the Great Mother who was, of old, also called among men Artemis, Astarte, Dione, Melusine, Aphrodite, Cerridwen, Diana, Arranrhod, Bride, and by many other names. At mine altar, the youths of Lacedemon in Sparta made due sacrifice. Whenever ye have need of anything, once in the month, and better it be when the Moon is full, then shall ye assemble in some secret place and adore the spirit of Me, who am Queen of all the Witcheries. There ye shall assemble, ye who are feign to learn all sorcery, who have not as yet won its deepest secrets. To these will I teach that which is yet unknown. And ye shall be free from slavery and as a sign that ye shall be really free, ye shall be naked in your rites. And ye shall dance, sing, feast, make music and love, all in my presence. For mine is the ecstasy of the spirit and mine is also joy on earth. For my law is Love unto all beings. Keep pure your highest ideals, strive ever towards it. Let none stop you or turn you aside. For mine is the secret that opens up the door of youth and mine is the cup of the Wine of Life and the Cauldron of Cerridwen, which is the Holy Grail of Immortality. I am the Gracious Goddess who gives the gift of Joy unto the heart of men. Upon earth I give knowledge of the Spirit Eternal, and beyond death I give Peace and Freedom and Reunion with those who have gone before. Nor do I demand ought in sacrifice, for behold I am the Mother of All Things, and my love is poured out upon the earth.*

*Hear ye the words of the Star Goddess. She is the dust of whose feet are the Hosts of Heaven. Whose body encircleth the universe.*

*I am the beauty of the Green Earth, and the White Moon amongst the stars and the mystery of the Waters, and the desire of the heart of man. I call unto thy soul "Arise and come unto me," for I am the Soul of Nature who giveth life to the universe. From me all things proceed and unto me all things must return. Beloved of the gods and man, thine inmost divine self shall be enfolded in the raptures of the Infinite. Let my worship be in the heart that rejoiceth; for behold, all acts of love and pleasure are mine rituals, and therefore, let there be beauty and strength; power and compassion; honor and humility, mirth and reverence within you.*

*And thou who thinkest to seek me, know that thy seeking and yearning avail ye not unless you know the mystery, that if what thou seekest thou findest not within thee, thou wilt never find it without thee. For behold—I have been with thee from the beginning, and I am that which is attained at the end of desire.*

# Cakes and Ale

This is the ritual in which Witches can thank the gods for the necessities of life: the food and drink that we need in order to live. It also serves as something of a midritual break after the preceding religious rites. When everyone has some wine and a cake, they can relax and may bring up any subject to discuss. This includes any magic or healing that they feel needs to be done. The coven can then discuss whether or not to do it, and whether it needs to be done immediately or can be planned for the future. If it is to be done during that ritual, then members need to discuss exactly how it should be done most effectively. (We will look at the working of magic in chapter 7.)

If no magic or healing is to be done, then the Esbat Circle may finish with entertainment: singing, dancing (be careful not to break the Circle!), storytelling, acting out traditional ritual plays, or the like. If there is no entertainment, then the coven goes directly to Closing the Circle (see page 67).

## CAKES AND ALE[10]
(Cakes and Wine)

Let one of the Witches be given the job of pouring the wine and seeing to it that everyone's wine goblet is kept filled. At the start of the rite, he or she should

---

10. This ritual has been known by both names: Cakes and Ale and Cakes and Wine. It is probable that the country folk—the true Pagans—in the old days could only afford ale. (In fact, they may even have preferred ale!) I have stuck with that name, but you can call it what you will and can use whichever drink you prefer. And as I've mentioned before, if you don't want alcohol, fruit juice is fine.

ensure that there is plenty of wine in the large goblet on the altar (which becomes the High Priestess' goblet).

The maiden rings the bell three times.

| | |
|---|---|
| **SQUIRE:** | **Now is the time for us to give thanks to the gods for that which sustains us.** |
| **HP:** | **Let us never forget what we owe to the gods.** |
| **ALL:** | **So mote it be!** |

HPS lifts the full wine goblet from the altar and holds it close to her body, between her breasts. HP takes his athame and holds it between the palms of both hands, slowly lowering the blade into the wine as he speaks:

| | |
|---|---|
| **HP:** | **As the athame is to the male, so is the cup to the female. In like fashion may the one join to the other and bring fruitfulness.** |

HP removes his athame from the goblet. HPS pours some libations (and says "To the gods" as she does so) and takes a drink from the goblet. She then holds it for HP to drink from it. He does, then takes the goblet from her and turns to hold it for the nearest Witch to drink from it.

This process continues, passing the goblet around the Circle, with each Witch holding it for the next Witch to take a drink. When it has gone all the way around, the goblet is returned to HPS. HP now takes up the plate of cakes and holds them to his chest. HPS dips her athame blade into the wine and then touches it to each of the cakes. (Make sure there are enough cakes for everyone!)

| | |
|---|---|
| **HPS:** | **May the gods bless this food as they bless our daily lives. Let us remember that without the gods we would have naught. Enjoy these symbols of all that we delight in. I urge you all, however, to remember to share what you have with those who have nothing.** |

HPS takes a cake, breaks off a small piece (with the words "To the gods!") and puts it in the libation dish, then holds the plate so that HP can take one. He holds the plate for the first Witch and so on around the Circle. When all have cakes, they sit down. All individual wine goblets are then filled and passed around and all sit and enjoy their cake and the wine. General talk and relaxation is enjoyed.

If there are any matters that need to be discussed in Circle, now is the time to do so. Then if there is work[11] to be done, it is executed. If not, then the coven closes the Circle (see below).

## Closing the Circle

All stand and raise their athames in salute.

**HP:** Thank you, Lord and Lady, for this time we have spent in your presence. We came together in love and friendship; so let us go our separate ways.

**HPS:** Our thanks for watching over us, for guarding us, and for guiding us. Help us spread the love of the Craft throughout all lives we may touch.

HPS and HP salute. All coven members walk around the Circle to pass the HP and HPS, saluting them as they pass. When all are back in their places, the ritual continues:

**MAIDEN:** Merry did we meet, so merry may we part.
**SQUIRE:** And merry may we meet again.
**ALL:** So mote it be!

HPS goes to the east and, with her athame, cuts across the lines of the Circle.

**HPS:** This Circle is now open.

All may now leave the Circle if they wish. It is no longer closed and consecrated.

11. Magic.

# Wiccan Life Within the Family

Wiccan love and brotherhood or sisterhood are not confined to within the ritual Circle. They exist throughout life. After a Circle, most brothers and sisters excitedly discuss what they have just been through. Sometimes there are special experiences to share; for instance, someone might have had a psychic message or vision during the prayer meditation or during the Drawing Down the Moon. Or someone may have gotten an idea for a ritual or entertainment for a future Circle and wants to share it or discuss it.

One of the joys of a Wicca family, for both the parents and the children, is that there can always be communication. Both know that it is safe and comfortable to share thoughts, feelings, problems, questions, doubts, fears, apprehensions, joys, and all the many vicissitudes of life. No one will criticize, blame, or scoff. All are willing to accept life's responsibilities and all are aware that life is seldom "fair." There is always someone to listen, to sympathize, empathize, cry with, or laugh with. There are always hugs available and kisses if needed. This is certainly how it should be. Many, if not most, of the troubles within families in this age are due to a lack of communication.

An example of how communication can help with raising children is in the fact of death. Death, it is said, is all part of life! And so it is. The death of a relative, or even of a pet, is an excellent opportunity to discuss the ramifications of death and rebirth, of reincarnation, with your children. Once death is seen as the end of a learning time, as a graduation of sorts, then it loses much of its mystique and possible threat. Death is something to be looked forward to (though not sought out), not something to be afraid of. This sort of knowledge frequently puts the Wiccan child far ahead of the non-Wiccan child in terms of acceptance of life and what it includes.

# Extended Family

How large should the family Wicca circle be? There are no hard and fast rules. I have known small family groups, consisting of two parents and one or two children only, and I have known of large family groups, with uncles, aunts, nephews, and nieces included. With the larger groups, there were, in effect, two covens.

Parents and children of two (related) families would meet at their own homes for the Esbats but would join together, like some big family reunion, at one of the homes for the Sabbat celebrations.

More frequent is the situation of a family coven that just one cousin (for instance) hears of and wants to join. Perhaps his or her immediate family is not of the same inclination. I think the family coven should be willing to accept the cousin in such a situation, but on one condition. They should do so only with the knowledge and permission of the cousin's parents until the child is of age.

Being together in a coven certainly develops and maintains understanding among all members, and especially between parents and children. It puts everyone on the same level; children don't feel they are being "talked down to" or merely tolerated. Yet the parents, as Elders or High Priest and High Priestess, are still the authority figures. Over the years there remain strong ties so that, even when the children have grown and married, they still belong to the family coven.

Raising a Wiccan family can have its problems, but most come from outside. Depending upon the age of the Wiccan children, they may or may not understand the wisdom of keeping their religious beliefs to themselves when at school. Older children *are* aware of when it is appropriate to refer to religious matters, but younger ones can unthinkingly let slip references that might raise the eyebrows of other children, especially those from a strict Christian background. Many are the Wiccan parents who have had to repeatedly march up to their offspring's school to have a judicious word with the teacher or principal! Yet this does not become a problem if the children are given the right training. We are all proud of the Old Religion; many of us do want to shout out about how fine it is. But we have to be realistic and choose our time for shouting and our time for quiet complacency.

---

*There was a rumor that my great grandmother had left a book of spells and herbal cures, written in her own hand, but nobody seemed to know what had happened to it. Years later an aunt of mine discovered it among lots of old papers when she was cleaning out a shed at the bottom of her garden. It was all damp and mildewed and most of the writing had faded away. I did manage to make a copy of the parts that were still legible. . . . The last pages dealt with spells, and there were several mystical figures which could have had something to do with ancient rites.*
—Patricia Crowther, *Witch Blood! The Diary of a Witch High Priestess*

The rites in Witchcraft are in no way negative. All is life affirming, with respect for nature and for all life. Yet we do not share the details of our rites with non-Wiccans (known as *cowans*). We do not let others read from our Books of Shadows. The reason is, simply, that non-Wiccans do not have the training, are not aware of the whole picture, and so would not appreciate the symbology of much that we do.

It is a sad fact of life that there is not truly a sense of freedom of religion in the United States. We have made tremendous strides in this direction in the last decade or so, but still we are far from being generally accepted without question. There are Witches who would lose their jobs—and even their lives—if it were known what they were, simply because of the misconceptions that still abound. And there are many children whose lives are plagued by ignorant fellow students who learn they are Wiccan and taunt them unmercifully. All we can do, at the moment, is to keep fighting the battle of ignorance and keep trying to straighten out the misconceptions. Slowly (very slowly) but surely we are making headway.

# Wiccan Teachings on Life

There are many issues about which Wiccans—like other people—do not agree: abortion, vegetarianism, racism, homosexuality, the death penalty. All of these should be discussed by the family group, with feelings shared openly and honestly. It is all right to disagree, so long as there is good reason. Everyone should have a reason for their opinion.

---

*We watch a lot of Public Broadcasting (PBS). We find that the shows we see on this network affirm Wiccan perspectives more often than not. . . . These shows emphasize life's interconnectedness, and noticing the connections is a chance to point out (to our children) that this is exactly what Wicca teaches us. Even the bits about hard science—programs about the basics of quantum physics, the development of the human body within the womb, or unified field theory, for instance— are lessons in Wicca. The scientific method has taught us nothing which cannot be expressed in the Craft's traditional terms.*

*—Ashleen O'Gaea, The Family Wiccan Book*

There are some issues where it would seem there is no room for disagreement. The environment is one. With pollution increasing at a frightening rate worldwide, Wiccans everywhere should be greatly concerned. Most are, and do what they can to help. Wiccan families can certainly make this a top priority. What *can* be done? Here are some projects that families can work on together.[12]

- It takes one 15-year-old tree to make enough paper for just seven hundred grocery bags, so save that tree and take your own cloth bags to the store with you. Do not use plastic grocery bags since they are not biodegradable (even those that claim they are!).
- Permanent press clothes and non-iron bed linens are treated with formaldehyde resin. Avoid them and use natural fabrics whenever possible.
- Use water-based markers and pens, since permanent ones contain harmful solvents such as ethanol, toluene and xylene.
- Use paper plates and cups, not styrofoam ones. Styrofoam is actually polystyrene foam made from a carcinogen. It is completely non-biodegradable.
- Add brewer's yeast and garlic to your pet's food. Fleas hate it and this way you can avoid your pet absorbing the nerve-damaging chemicals in commercial flea collars.
- Don't throw out old newspapers with the garbage—recycle them. Recycle everything you can: cans, cardboard, bottles, plastic. If you don't get recycling pick-up, take the items to the closest recycling center.
- Keep hazardous materials in their original containers and make sure they are labeled. Keep them out of the reach of small children. Dispose properly of old motor oil, paint, car batteries, oven cleaners, paint thinner, drain cleaners, mothballs, furniture polish, pesticides, and so forth.

There are many things such as the above which you can do to help the environment. Check them out and work as a family, and a coven, to do them.

Most Wiccans also do all they can to help save the animals. One worthwhile, and enjoyable thing you can do is to build a backyard wildlife refuge. It can be as

12. Taken from *50 Simple Things You Can Do to Save the Earth*, published by The Earth Works Group, Earth Works Press, Berkeley, 1989.

simple or as complex as you like. The extra benefit is for you—you get to see a lot of wildlife up close and enjoy the antics of birds and animals you might never normally see.

Hummingbirds are attracted by brightly colored plants, especially red-colored ones such as morning glories. Bird feeders can be set up with sunflower seeds, corn, and thistle seeds. Heated birdbaths are appreciated in winter. Food scraps of all sorts are enjoyed by crows. Blue jays like peanuts (crack them, if possible, to help the birds get into them). Check with your local office of the Audubon Society and with the National Federation of Wildlife to see what you can best do for the animals native to your area.

Where I live, we get a tremendous variety of birds, plus rabbits, chipmunks, wild turkeys, deer, foxes, skunks, opossums, and others. We have a small farm and have created hedgerows and planted trees to help the wildlife. But even in a city environment, you can put bird feeders on balconies and make a heated birdbath.

Another way many Wiccans help is to adopt a section of local highway and to periodically pick up any and all garbage, such as empty bottles and cans, fast-food containers, and the like. Keeping the earth beautiful is also keeping it safe and healthy. Do what you and your coven family can.

---

*In 1980 there were 4.4 billion people on Earth. In 1990, there will be 5.2 billion. Every day some of these human beings move into places on the planet where only plants and animals used to live. Forests are cut down. Wetlands, oceans, ice caps, and prairies are invaded.* —Russell Train, *World Wildlife Fund*

---

In the year 2000 there are an estimated 6.1 billion people; by 2020 there will be 7.5 billion; by 2050, 9.1 billion! We are losing as many as three species per day, and this will soon be three species per hour. The Nature Conservancy, in 1989, estimated that by the year 2000 as much as 20 percent of all earth's species would be lost forever.

# Aspects of the Goddess and the God

In Wicca, we think of different aspects of both the Goddess and the God. In order to relate to them, it is easier to see them according to our needs. A young man in love might want to relate to a young aspect of the Goddess, or of the God, while a married woman expecting a child might feel more comfortable with a more mature aspect of the Goddess. Elderly people are more comfortable with older aspects of the deities. So we speak of the Maiden-Mother-Crone Goddess—the young, mature, the older aspects of her.

The Maiden is pure, virginal (unmarried, not necessarily nonsexual), and very much her own woman. The Mother is Creatrix: sensuous and full-bodied, whole and ripe. The Crone is wisdom and knowledge. She is still sexual, but purely for pleasure, not procreation.

In ancient mythology (and even in some traditions of Wicca), these different aspects were sometimes given different names. Antevorta, the Roman Maiden Goddess, was known in her Mother aspect as Carmenta and in her Crone aspect as Postvorta. The Irish Goddess Morrigan is Anu, Banbha, and Macha as a triad. The God, too, had his three aspects: as a young, middle-aged, and old man (developed by the Christians as Father, Son, and Holy Ghost). So the Lord and the Lady can be all things to all people.

> *How can a goddess be three persons and one at the same time?*
> —St. Augustine

# ~ 5 ~

# Witchcraft and Birth

There are many ancient creation myths. Gerald Gardner gives a Wiccan one in his book *Witchcraft Today*. It is as follows:

> Now G[13] had never loved, but she would solve all mysteries, even the mystery of death, and so she journeyed to the nether lands. The guardians of the portals challenged her. "Strip off thy garments, lay aside thy jewels, for naught may ye bring with you into this our land." So she laid down her garments and her jewels and was bound as are all who enter the realms of Death, the mighty one.
>
> Such was her beauty that Death himself knelt and kissed her feet, saying: "Blessed be thy feet that have brought thee in these ways. Abide with me, but let me place my cold hand on thy heart." And she replied: "I love thee not. Why doest thou cause all things that I love and take delight in to fade and die?" "Lady," replied Death, "'tis age and fate, against which I am helpless. Age causes all things to wither; but when men die at the end of time, I give them rest and peace and strength so that they may return. But you, you are lovely. Return not; abide with me." But she answered: "I love thee not." Then, said Death: "As you receive not my hand on your heart, you must receive Death's scourge." "It is fate, better so," she said, and knelt. Death scourged her and she cried: "I know the pangs of love." And Death said: "Blessed be," and gave her the fivefold kiss, saying: "Thus only may you attain to joy and knowledge."

13. The Goddess.

And he taught her all the mysteries, and they loved and were one; and he taught her all the magics. For there are three great events in the life of man—love, death and resurrection in the new body—and magic controls them all. To fulfill love you must return again at the same time and place as the loved ones, and you must remember and love her or him again. But to be reborn you must die and be ready for a new body; to die you must be born; without love you may not be born, and this is all the magic.

This is obviously a variation on Ishtar's descent into the underworld, and many other such stories. But in this myth can be found many parts of a Wiccan Initiation. Most Witchcraft traditions stipulate that the initiate must be "naked and un-adorned"—in other words, skyclad and not wearing any jewelry of any sort. This ties in with the Goddess being told to lay aside her clothes and her jewelry in order to be able to enter into the "nether lands"—the world of the dead. In the myth, the Lady is scourged, as a symbolic death, and afterward new knowledge is revealed to her. Again, this is as it is in an Initiation. In some traditions (such as Gardnerian), this myth is acted out at various times, as a ritual drama.

The descent of the Goddess into the underworld—whether it be in search of a lost loved one, as with Ishtar and Tammuz, or in search of an object, as with Freya's descent and search for her sacred necklace Brosingamene—symbolizes the vegetation dying off for the winter months. The return of the Goddess is the return of life in spring, the rebirth of the world. The Wiccan year is seen as a wheel, ever turning. Marking this turning are festivals that tie in with the agricultural year.

These festivals are a good indication of the Craft's ancient lineage, together with its connection with the life-earth link. If we go back far enough, the year was divided into just two halves: summer and winter. In summer, it was possible to

---

### Season's Eatings

It is traditional to eat apples and nuts at Samhain, in England. They can also be used for divination. At Imbolc, pancakes are eaten in England, while rabbit is the custom in Ireland. For Beltane in Scotland, oak cakes are made with nine prominent knobs on them. These are broken off one at a time and offered to nine deities of domestic animals. Strong ale is drunk in England at this time. Oat cakes are served again at Lughnasadh in Scotland; in England, bread made from the new grain; in Ireland, it is traditional to give your sweetheart a basket of blueberries.

grow food for sustenance, but throughout the winter it was necessary to rely on success in the hunt. We saw, in chapter 1, how the Goddess of Fertility came to predominate at the one time, and the God of Hunting at the other. The change from summer to winter took place around the end of October (what is now celebrated as Samhain, or Hallowe'en), and the return around the end of April (Beltane or May Day). These times were marked with great rejoicing; with festivals and celebrations.

Later, the midpoints of these two halves were similarly observed. Halfway through the winter, at February Eve (Imbolc), it was felt necessary to generate energy to help the God on through to spring. Halfway through summer, at August Eve (Lughnasadh), a similar celebration encouraged the Goddess in her period of reign. These became the four major Sabbats, or celebrations, of the Old Religion.

At some point, the cross quarter days were added—the summer and winter solstices and the spring and autumn equinoxes. So we have a wheel of the year with four major Sabbats and four minor ones. I'll look at all of these Sabbats in more detail in chapter 19, and give the rituals that are enacted to celebrate them.

Although one diety may be more prominent than the other over a certain period of the year, it does not mean that the other one is "dead." During the summer months the God is still very much around, but he is more active in his feminine aspects, just as the Goddess' masculine aspects are more in evidence during the winter months.

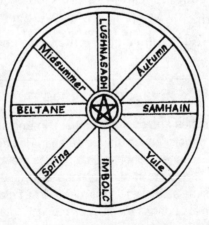

THE WHEEL OF THE YEAR

# "A-Conjurin' Summer In"

The Old Religion was very much a celebration of life, with fertility a major aspect of it. At the big Sabbat celebrations, therefore, it was not unusual for the celebrants to pair off after the religious rites and do further celebrating alone together. A poem by Rudyard Kipling has been adopted by many Witches as their May Eve chant. It really says it all:

> *Oh, do not tell the priests of our rites*
> *For they would call it sin;*
> *But we will be in the woods all night*
> *A-conjuring' Summer in!*

To be born at the time of one of the Sabbats was to be recognized as a "child of the Sabbat" in that you were almost certainly conceived at the celebrations nine months before. Such a Sabbat child was considered a blessing.

Wiccans welcome and celebrate all new life. The birth of a child is a very special occasion. Let us look for a moment at the other end of the spectrum—at death. There are many stories, most of them well documented, about mothers "knowing" when their child has died, even if it occurred thousands of miles away. This was especially evident during the major wars. A man would be killed, and his mother back home would know it at that same instant. Frequently, the mother (or someone else very close) would awake in the night, knowing that a death had occurred. The reason is that there is a very strong psychic bond between the two people.

To return to birth, an amazingly strong psychic bond is established right from the beginning, from birth. It is an invisible (though to some psychics, actually visible) umbilical cord that remains in place for all time. Before we all became so "sophisticated," these psychic bonds were much more prevalent and accepted. Today, outside the Craft, there are few who acknowledge them, unless forced to do so through such a death as I've described.

Witches believe that, ideally, when our spirit is reborn in a new body, it will be reborn among spirits known and loved in past lives. This was a hope and comfort during the burning times, when Witches hoped that they would return to be with coven members in the future. It could well be, therefore, that your newborn child was your brother, mother, closest friend, or coven High Priestess in a previous life.

Whether or not this is actually so would be difficult to prove, though enough evidence has been forthcoming through hypnotic regression to confirm the theory to any intelligent mind. With such a belief, it is no wonder that a Wiccan birth is hailed and celebrated. However, each new life is just that—new. There should be no dwelling on past lives, however fascinating it might seem to regress and discover the previous relationship. Get on with the present life and the present relationship. There are plenty of new lessons to learn and new experiences to be had.

In recent years, it has become common for parents-to-be to sing, talk, even play music to an unborn child. Indeed, there are books on prenatal care that recommend such stimulation. It has been found that a fetus will actually change position to better hear what is being projected! Witches seem to have been aware of this for generations, whispering the names of the gods, singing songs of the Old Religion, or simply muttering words of love and promise to the mother's swollen body.

Many Witches elect to have home births or use a midwife. Natural childbirth is an option again chosen by a large number of Wiccans. Those who have their child in a hospital will take any magical item felt needed to ensure a smooth delivery. This could include talismans, amulets (a key and a cowrie shell are both very potent, the shell being sacred to Aphrodite), even an athame tucked under the pillow! Even in the hospital, a mother can call upon the Goddess, if only mentally, as she gives birth and immediately following.

> *In ages past, when all babies were born at home with the aid of a midwife, many of these women were as skilled at reading signs and omens as they were at delivering babies. Any strange occurrences that coincide with the time of birth should be noted and may possibly be an omen that predicts something about the future of the child.* —Pauline Campanelli, *Pagan Rites of Passage*

As for the mother's preparation, this should include working with the chakras (pronounced *SHÂRK-rers*), a Sanskrit word meaning "wheel" or "disk." The seven chakras correspond to seven glands in the body, making a connection between the physical and spiritual bodies as follows:

- First chakra: Lumbar or base—renal.
- Second chakra: Spine—gonads (ovaries and testes).
- Third chakra: Solar plexus—adrenal.
- Fourth chakra: Heart—thymus, cardiopulmonary plexus.
- Fifth chakra: Throat—thyroid, parathyroids.
- Sixth chakra: Third Eye—pituitary.
- Seventh chakra: Crown—pineal.

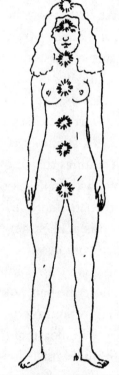

Psychic energy known as "kundalini," or serpent power, can be developed and sent up the line of chakras. Hindu occultists visualize a coiled serpent at the base of the spine, between the anal and genital areas, near the coccyx, waiting to be aroused and rear up, through the chakras, to the crown.

To raise the fiery serpent on a regular basis is good at any time, but it is especially beneficial for an expectant mother. Not only does it empower her, but it also contributes to the welfare of the expected child. As the vital force flows through the nervous system, a state of well-being and peace is achieved. The unconscious mind clears of all negativity and is filled, instead, with positive energy. The kundalini operates in a very natural, calm, relaxed, and contemplative atmosphere. As the chakras are opened in succession, greater awareness and perception of life are received. Perhaps most important, a channel is opened to the Higher Self. This, perhaps, is what establishes the connection between mother and child.

POSITIONS OF THE CHAKRAS

# Awakening the Chakras

There is a simple exercise for awakening the chakras. Be sure to choose a spot where you will not be disturbed, so that you can relax and be at ease. Sit as comfortably as possible, with your back straight. If necessary, make sure your back is supported. Close your eyes and breathe deeply.

As you breathe in, visualize white light flowing into your body, gradually filling it—down your arms and into your fingers; down your legs and into your feet and toes. As you breathe out, visualize all the dark negativity leaving your body. See the aches and pains, worries and depressions flowing out of you.

Once you have filled your body with white light, concentrate on the area of your first chakra—at the genital area.[14] The color associated with this center is red. Visualize a red disc or wheel spinning at this spot. See it spinning clockwise. Let it spin faster and faster. Keep it spinning for a while, then gently slow it down. As it slows, gradually move it upward, introducing yellow light into it so that it turns from red to orange. Move up to the position of the second chakra, whose color is orange. Start the orange disc spinning rapidly, clockwise, at your spine. Continue in this way, spinning discs at each of your chakra points, having them gradually change color as they move up.

The base chakra is red and the spine, orange; the solar plexus, yellow; heart, green; throat, blue; Third Eye, indigo; crown, violet. When you have mentally spun the chakras at all seven points, slowly return to white throughout the body, relax, and open your eyes.

This chakra awakening can be introduced to your child, once he or she is born. As you hold the baby, focus your mind on the chakra points on the child's body and go through spinning his or her chakras. If you do this as a regular regimen, it will contribute immeasurably to the baby's health and well-being.

Working with color can be very beneficial in many areas, but is particularly useful for a very young child's health. Every time you lay down the child for a nap, visualize white light enclosing him or her as protection. Keep this up for a while, then gradually change the white to green, the color of healing. Spend some time visualizing this green light around the child. This is an old Witch practice to ensure good health at all times.

14. There is some disagreement on the actual positions of the chakras. Some books state that the first is between the anal and genital areas, with the second at the genitals themselves. Then comes the stomach, followed by the heart, throat, Third Eye, and crown. But other books state—as I also prefer—that the base chakra is at the genitals, the second at the spine, the third at the solar plexus, and so on. Also, some state that the crown is the sixth chakra and the Third Eye is the seventh, while others reverse these two. Decide which you prefer and stick with it.

# Wiccaning

As soon as possible after the birth, Witches dedicate the child to the gods. This ritual is known as Wiccaning. In it, the parents of the child announce to the Lord and the Lady that they will raise their child to honor the old gods. It is *not* making the child a Witch. Whether or not the child does become a Witch is up to that child at a later date, when able to make such a decision. At that time, the child will go through the Initiation or Self-Dedication. For now, though, there is the Wiccaning.

## WICCANING RITE

The Wiccaning ritual may be done at any Esbat rite. It may only be done at a Sabbat with the full consent of everyone present, since it should not detract from the main celebration of the season and tribute to the gods. It may be done as a rite in itself, in which case the Circle is cast and the Wiccaning is performed followed by Cakes and Ale and Closing of the Circle. If the Wiccaning is done as part of an Esbat or Sabbat, it is performed just prior to the Cakes and Ale.

The Circle is cast, with all within it properly prepared. The parents stand to the east, immediately behind the altar, holding the child. (If it is a single parent, that parent will speak both parts.) If there are God and Goddess parents, they stand to the west. If there are not, the words attributed to them are spoken by the parents.

HP and HPS kiss. The Maiden rings the bell three times.

**SQUIRE:**    **There is a newcomer to this, our family of Witches. Let us make her [him] welcome.**

All turn to face the parents and child and raise their athames in salute.

**All:**    **All hail!**
**HP:**    **What is the name of this child?**

The parents give the name by which the child will be known when in the sacred Circle, until such time as she chooses her own name.

HPS:  We welcome you . . . [name].

HP:  We greet you with much love.

HPS:  Do you wish your child to join with us in worship of the Lord and the Lady?

PARENTS:  We do, for without knowledge of the gods of old no life is complete.

HP:  Well said. May you be doubly welcome.

HPS:  Now present your child to the four quarters.

The parents turn outward, at the east, and raise the baby in their arms to the gods.

PARENTS:  Here we do present . . . [name] . . . as a child of the Old Religion, to be accepted by the Lord and the Lady. So mote it be.

They move around to the south and repeat the presentation, going on to the west, and then the north. They return to the east and turn back in, to face the altar and the other coven members.

HP:  Now bring the child before the altar.

The parents move around to stand between HP and HPS, facing the altar. The maiden rings the bell seven times. HPS dips her fingers in the salted water and draws a cross within a circle on the baby's forehead and a pentagram on her chest, over the heart.

HPS:  Lord and Lady, we ask that you bless this child.

HP:  Watch over her, guarding and guiding her throughout life.

HPS:  When the time is right, bring her to this sacred Circle once again, to dedicate herself anew to the gods, on her own behalf.

FATHER:  May the Lady and the Lord smile down upon . . . [name] . . . always.

| | |
|---|---|
| **MOTHER:** | May they guard her and guide her along the path of life. |
| **FATHER:** | May they help her see that which is right and discard that which is wrong. |
| **MOTHER:** | And may they bring her at last, of her own desire, to this our Old Religion family. |
| **ALL:** | So mote it be! |
| **HP:** | Who speaks as God and Goddess parents for this child? |
| **GODPARENTS:** | We do. |
| **HP:** | Come forward. |

The godparents move forward and take the child from the mother. The parents fall back into line with the other coven members.

| | |
|---|---|
| **HPS:** | We charge you both, in the name of the Lord and of the Lady, to take this child by the hand and to lead her along the winding road of life. Teach her the ways of the Craft, but tell her also of other religions and their beliefs, that when the time comes she may make a reasoned decision. |
| **HP:** | Tell her the tales of the Craft of old, of the burning times and the times in hiding. Tell her of our many lives, both here and hereafter. |
| **HPS:** | Teach her to love all life. To live in harmony with all nature and all things. |
| **HP:** | Teach her of the Lord and the Lady, of love and happiness. Teach her the Wiccan Rede. |
| **GODPARENTS:** | All this we swear to do, for the child, for her parents, and for the family of the Craft. |

The parents come forward again, and the godparents return the child to them. All take their places in the circle of Wiccans.

| | |
|---|---|
| **HP and HPS:** | We bid welcome to . . . [name]. |
| **ALL:** | Welcome! |

Then shall follow the ceremony of the Cakes and Ale.

A coven Wiccaning is the same as a hereditary Wiccaning. Either one may be adapted for the number of participants. If the High Priest and High Priestess happen to be the father and mother, then the HP and HPS parts may be spoken by the maiden and the squire. If the Wiccaning has to be done by a solitary, it follows the same pattern, with the words suitably reworked to fit the single ritualist.

Godparents are not necessary, but are traditional and should be chosen with care. Look for those who really do care about the child and have her best interests at heart. Look, also, for those who are most likely to be close by as the child grows up, especially in the early years. These days many people relocate. It is not always possible to see what lies ahead, but a godparent close by will have more influence than one many miles away. If you can find people with a good knowledge of the Craft, that is certainly a bonus. At the very least, choose those who are sincerely dedicated to the Old Religion. The statements made in the Wiccaning ritual should not be taken lightly.

For a hereditary coven, it's fine to bring in Witches from other covens or other families to become the godparents, if necessary. They need not be permanent members of the family coven to act in this capacity; just Wiccans.

The child will be brought up to honor and respect the Old Religion and the Lord and Lady. But from here there are two stages that may take place. At about the age of six, seven, or eight (much depends upon the individual child), he may be brought into the coven in an actual Initiation ritual. At this time, he will take a new name that he has chosen himself. Then, probably around puberty, there will be a repeat of the Initiation as a confirmation that he is fully old enough to decide for himself.

If at this time he has decided that the Craft is not for him after all, however, then he may leave the coven. This, in fact, applies to everyone. No one should be there under duress. All who change their minds and decide to leave the Craft are free to do so at any time. And by the same token, they will be welcomed back if, later still, they want to return.

When children belong to a coven, they will attend the rites. If there is magic to be done, they should leave the Circle after the Cakes and Ale and before the actual magical work.

*There was in Florence in the oldest time a noble family, but grown so poor that their feast days were few and far between. However, they dwelt in their old palace. . . . Round this palace was a large garden, in which stood an ancient marble statue of Diana, like a beautiful woman who seemed to be running with a dog by her side. She held in her hand a bow, and on her forehead was a small moon. . . . One day [the children] came home with many flowers which had been given to them, and the little girl said to her brother: "The beautiful lady with the bow ought to have some of these." Saying this, they laid flowers before the statue and made a wreath which the boy placed on her head. . . . What was their amazement when they found early the next morning before the statue a deer freshly killed, which gave them good dinners for many a day; nor did they want thereafter at any time game of all kinds.*
—Charles Godfrey Leland, *Aradia, Gospel of the Witches*

# Protective Space

Back to our newborn child. Bringing a new life into the home calls for a special cleansing of that home. It's a good idea to do this just before the child is born—as close as possible to the delivery day.

For this cleansing you will need water, salt, incense, and a bell. This rite can be done by anyone, but the homeowner is probably the best choice.

Do the rite of consecrating the water and salt. You do not have to be in a consecrated Circle. You may, if you wish, just stand the salt, water, and incense on a table to start with. Take up your athame and dip the tip of the blade into the bowl of salt. Say:

*Salt is life. Let this salt be pure and let it purify my life, as I use it in this rite dedicated to the God and Goddess in whom I believe.*

Take three pinches of the salt and drop them into the water. Moving your athame blade across to the water dish, dip it in there. Say:

*Let the sacred salt drive out any impurities in this water, that together they may be used in the service of the Lord and the Lady, throughout these rites and at any time and in any way I may use them.*

Stir the water three times, clockwise, with the tip of the athame. Then take the salted water, incense, and bell to the front door of the house. If you have assistants who can help carry things and pass them as needed, that would be good. If not, you can put them on a small tray and take it around with you. You will be going first to the front, main entrance to the house, then to the back (or side) entrance, then to any other entrances. You will then be going to each room in the house, one by one, in any order.

At the entranceways, strike the bell three times. Dip your fingers in the salted water and sprinkle it on the door itself and all around the door frame. Then hold the incense so that the smoke censes the door and frame. Say:

*Lord and Lady, guard this entranceway, cleansing all who pass through it. Keep out any and all impurities, that those within this house may be protected by your light and love.*

Ring the bell seven times. Proceed to the next door and do the same thing. When you have completed the doors, proceed to the rooms. There you will ring the bell three times, then sprinkle the cense every corner of the room, and every corner of every closet that may be in the room. Then stand in the center of the room and say:

*Lord and Lady, guard this room, cleansing all who come within it. Keep out any and all impurities, that those within this house may be protected by your light and love.*

Ring the bell seven times. Proceed to the next room and on through the house, doing the same cleansing in each and every room. Don't forget any cellar, basement, or attic.

This is a good house cleansing and may be done at any time you feel it is needed. Some conclude by walking all around the outside of the house, sprinkling and censing. That is certainly an option.

# A Birth Tree

A tradition found worldwide is to plant a tree for a child's birth. It was thought that the child's life and that of the tree were then connected; as one grew and developed, so did the other. Apple trees were common, as were oaks. In England, the ash and the yew were each described as the "tree of life."

One old custom among followers of the Old Religion was to deposit the child's umbilical cord under the tree at the time of its planting. This made the magical connection.

If you are able to plant a tree, choose one carefully and plant it with a small ritual, dedicating it to the gods and to the well-being of the child.

# The Fairy Godmother

Many of the old fairy stories feature a godmother who is either good or bad, presenting blessings or (usually delayed) curses on the newborn child. The curse of the wicked godmother was mainly poetic license on the part of storytellers, since the negative gift frequently turned out to have its uses, anyway!

In the early days of the Craft, it was not unusual for a Goddess mother to give the child a gift of, for example, second sight (being able to see into the future), or of healing, or something similar. These may or may not have been true gifts, but they came from an awareness on the part of the giver of the child's potential. Through meditation, or even using such tools as tarot cards or astrology, it was often possible for a psychic to get a feeling for what a child would later excel at. To then "give that gift" was, in effect, to let the parents know in which direction the child should be headed. It might all be psychological, but more often than not the recipient of this "gift" would indeed do well in the indicated field.

Today, this feeling for what the child might develop can often be underscored by a physical gift such as a deck of tarot cards, or a book on herbs or astrology. Gifts appropriate for the Craft are always welcome. Many—if not most—of these gifts probably will not be used for some years, until the child grows. But in the case of tarot cards, for example, some parents will let the infant child handle them and gaze at the pictures, feeling that a connection will be established. Certainly the very fact of their having been given contributes to the vibrations around the child.

> As our children grow, their energy bodies develop along with their physical bodies. With the maturing connections between the physical and energy bodies, we naturally develop the potential to utilize these magical abilities. Whether this potential lies dormant or is actualized depends largely on the environment within which the child is raised. —Kristin Madden, *Pagan Parenting*

# ~ 6 ~

# Witchcraft With Siblings

I have said that Witchcraft generally (and not just with hereditaries) is what I would term a "family religion." Coven members invariably grow closer to one another than they are to their regular family members. Within Wiccan rituals, there is frequent mention of the "brothers and sisters of the Craft." All of this is then doubly true for hereditary covens, in which blood brothers and sisters are also Wiccan brothers and sisters.

Most non-Witch children would give their eyeteeth to have similar-thinking brothers and sisters, so hereditaries are most certainly blessed. It is no wonder that there is far less arguing and sibling rivalry in Wiccan families than in *cowan* ones. No matter what other differences exist, what contrary directions Witch siblings may go when it comes to hobbies and interests, there is always the one major common ground of the Craft.

Wiccan children as a whole seem far more mature than other children. Because of their connection to nature, they have a greater grasp on life—on its responsibilities and its rewards. They have a greater understanding of the place of birth and death in the life pattern. And they have the grounding of the Wiccan Rede, with its enjoinder to harm none.

For many modern Witches, the sensation of coming home that is found in Wicca is partly due to a personal acceptance of the intuitive process that brought the older heritage back into prominence. For a successful transition, the baseless fears induced by mainstream faiths for the purpose of controlling their members must be discarded, and the individual must be opened up to the power of the Goddess and the God. The deities of Wicca are not the punishing deities of conventional religions. When the Witch talks of a loving God and Goddess, there are no lists of laws, dietary demands, dogmas, worship formats, or even "witness"-type acknowledgements required. There is but one major rule to remember: "what is sent comes back."
—Ann Moura (Aoumiel), *Green Witchcraft—Folk Magic, Fairy Lore and Herb Craft*

## Peace Signs and Talking Sticks

This is not to say that Witch children never fight or argue! They are only human in this respect. But they have an understanding of the need for harmony and for nonselfish attitudes. There is more occasion to talk out differences than in other families. When one child has a major problem, he or she knows that it can be brought up before the whole family; there will be many concerned minds ready and willing to help find a solution.

A scene repeated in most homes with children, probably more times than could be counted, is of a girl or boy storming into a brother's or sister's room and accusing the other of having done something that hurt, brought about embarrassment, or in some way worked negatively on the accuser: borrowing a sweater without permission and then staining it, for example. Giving away a secret, "stealing" a friend, antagonizing someone admired—these are more typical examples.

A good technique used by some Witches is to allow the accuser to rant and rave for a few moments, to get it out of the system, and then to draw a pentagram in the air with the forefinger. This is a sign that the other must stop; the point has been made. The accused may then speak for a period to explain his or her actions. It's amazing how often this simple exchange will calm the situation to the level where it can be rationally discussed. However, if there can be no immediate resolution, the matter will be taken to the family coven.

When anything of importance is being discussed in the Circle, it can help restore a calm, nonemotional atmosphere by using what the Native Americans call a "talking stick." In the Craft we use a wand, someone's athame, or a similar talking

TALKING STICK

stick made especially for this purpose.[15] The High Priest or High Priestess passes it to whomever wishes to talk; this person then decides to whom it goes next, so that all may give their point of view. No one may speak unless he or she has the stick in hand. In this way, it is possible to get all views without having several people talking at once, which frequently leads to shouting and unnecessary emotion.

# For Harmony

A frequent cause of friction among siblings is sharing a room. Many of the problems—never all of them!—can be allayed through following the ancient Chinese art of feng shui (pronounced *fung shway*), observed by many practicing Wiccans. Much of the art is being aware of unconscious associations. For example, the sharp edge of a desk or table may unconsciously be thought of as a threat. It can be softened by placing a trailing plant there, covering the hard edge and seemingly eliminating the threat. The art can be applied to a bedroom (or even a whole house) to make it much more comfortable and enjoyable, eliminating unconscious problems.

The start of the makeover is what's known as a *bagua* (pronounced *"bag-WA"*) map: a breakdown of the room, or house, into sections with indications of what is governed by each section (see the illustration on page 91).

15. Making one can be a coven project. It can be a short length of broomstick handle or a piece of wood cut from a fallen tree. Decorate it with Wiccan and coven signs and symbols.

*BAGUA*

| WIND | FIRE | EARTH |
|---|---|---|
| Wealth; Power | Reputation | Partnership; Marriage |
| THUNDER | *The Belly* | LAKE |
| Family; | *of the* | Creativity; Future; |
| Health; Strength | *Dragon* | Pleasure; Children; Joy |
| MOUNTAIN | WATER | HEAVEN |
| Knowledge; | Career; | Support; Trance; |
| Spirituality | Finding Yourself | Helpful People |

Draw a rough sketch of the bedroom—the one being shared—and superimpose the *bagua* over it. Wherever the door to the room is, place that along the career side so that your door actually falls into the knowledge/spirituality section, the career section, or the helpful people/travel section.

Now consider where the two beds are placed. They should each be placed where, when lying in them, the person has a clear view of the door. If that's not possible, then hang a mirror for a clear view. (Incidentally, mirrors should be hung high enough that you don't chop off your head when you look into them.)

Looking from the door, the center of the left wall is your family/health/ strength section. Placing something green there—a color of healing and life—will help bring a truce in any argument. You might also put something green in the partnership corner (far right). In that corner, too, place a photograph of the two siblings together, in some happy moment. If no photo is available, try two candles (one each in their astral colors—see the appendix) or two flowers. If you use flowers, make sure to keep them watered and fresh!

Watch out for clutter, since it inhibits the life force that should flow freely through the room and the house. This clutter should especially be avoided in that partnership corner—no piles of baseball mitts, footballs, sneakers, or books. Don't keep the laundry hamper there. Keep this corner clean and fresh and the partnership will stay that way also.

Try to avoid having a bed underneath a beam or a sloping section of the ceiling. And if there is a television in the room, or a computer, it is best to keep it in a closed closet when not in use.

A final word on color. As far as possible, avoid primary colors in rooms shared by siblings. In fact, try to avoid them altogether. Softer colors, such as pastels, will be more soothing. The red end of the spectrum will stimulate, while the blue end will soothe.

# Creating Bonds

There are many coven projects that can be undertaken by coven and family members, especially brothers and sisters. These can include making a coven Book of Shadows, constructing a special altar or tools, decorating a temple room, writing rituals, making and consecrating talismans (see later chapters on doing this), and many more. But tasks about the home can also be given a Craft flavor to make them more acceptable. For example, the one who has the job of taking out the libations might also be the one who takes out the garbage (or vice versa).

Some hobbies can apply directly to the Craft, and can be shared by siblings, including candle making, incense blending, robe making, wine making or beer brewing, jewelry making, and gardening—perhaps with emphasis on herbs.

# Ritual Dramas

A special part of the major Sabbats can be the enacting of a ritual drama. (Actually, there is no reason why this can't be included in any ritual, Esbat or Sabbat.) If one of you has an idea for a new ritual, everyone will pitch in and contribute to it to help make it a success.

Look to the deity names your coven uses. What is the background? Is it Celtic, Greek, Roman, Teutonic? Whatever the origin, investigate the background, the myths, of the area. The Irish gods and goddesses are colorful—the Dagda, Lug, Balor, Brigit, Danu, Anu, Macha—and all have their stories. Other gods, other cultures, are equally colorful and full of wonderful material for drama.

There are stories of descents into the underworld, of returns, of deaths, births, resurrections. There are battles and conquests, discoveries and partnerships. All are ripe to be made into small plays that can be acted in or near the Circle as part of the coven's celebration.

The Farrar's book *Eight Sabbats for Witches* focuses on the dual personality of the God as Oak King and Holly King. Just this image alone gives material for a wide range of presentations.

Siblings can get together on such projects, dividing the labor and having fun with the myths. Costumes can be made and—always a fun and favorite pastime—masks can be made and worn.

Helping one another with rituals is also bonding. Older children can help their younger brothers and sisters when it comes to how to move in the Circle, carrying and handling the athame, entering and leaving the Circle. If yours is a tradition with degrees of advancement, then the older ones, who have already passed through the lower degrees, can help the younger ones prepare for the rites.

And just studying the history of the Craft together, or comparing notes with siblings, can be very beneficial and help create the special bond found in members of a Wiccan family, be it hereditary or simply coven.

---

*Children can be grounded in Wicca very gently. Notice how good the bath feels at the end of the day; make it feel better with herbs. Notice how good it feels to take a deep breath when you watch the sunrise. See how a candle or a crackling fire is hot and bright like the Sun. Aren't rocks strong like mountains, maybe the northern mountains? Isn't it cozy and safe under the bedclothes, dark like a cave deep in the Earth? Isn't it neat that sometimes when you're thinking about somebody, they call or you get a letter from them?*

*—Ashleen O'Gaea, The Family Wicca Book*

# ~ 7 ~

# What Is Magic?

Many people seem confused over Witchcraft and magic. Television shows and movies frequently contribute to the confusion, leading people to want to become Witches just so they can do magic, cast spells, and make charms. Yet it is not necessary to become a Witch to do this. So what is the difference between Witchcraft and magic? The short answer is that Witchcraft is a religion and magic is a practice.

## Religion Vis-à-Vis Practice

The essence of a religion is a belief in deity and the worship of that deity, or deities. Many religions use magic in their rituals (the transubstantiation of Roman Catholicism is an example), but not all. There are many religions—including branches, or traditions, of Wicca—that do nothing more than honor their gods. The worshipers ask for what they need and give thanks for what they receive. The rituals may well vary in their complexity. Some are very simple, while others incorporate great ceremony. But essentially, the worshipers gather solely for religious purposes.

Magic, on the other hand, does not have to be tied to religion at all. You do not have to be a Witch to do magic, nor do you have to be a Jew, Catholic, Protestant,

Buddhist, Taoist, or anything else. You can even be an atheist and do magic. Magic is a practice and, in itself, does not involve any connection with deity.

There are many types of magic: high magic, low magic, sympathetic magic, folk magic, ceremonial magic, healing magic, and more. As I've mentioned, some religions do incorporate some of these forms of magic into their rituals. Many Wiccans do so.

The point is, if all you want to do is cast spells and work magic, you do not need to become a Witch, since Wicca is first and foremost a religion. There are many books on working magic, of all types, that have nothing to do with Witchcraft.

## Magic and What It Is

I think the best definition of magic was made by Aleister Crowley,[16] who said, "Magic is the art or science of causing change to occur in conformity with will." In other words, it's making something happen that you want to happen. This can be done very simply or in a very complex and elaborate manner—whichever you feel most comfortable with.

> The subconscious mind is older, in terms of evolutionary development, than the conscious mind, and it retains one trait of its immemorial past in the fact that . . . it works by images, not words.... If, therefore, one consciously introduces carefully selected images into the subconscious mind one can evoke the corresponding emotion.          —W. E. Butler, *Magic: Its Ritual Power and Purpose*

An example of simplicity is to pray for something very hard and have it happen. This is magic. It can be passed of as "coincidence" by the skeptic, as can any magic, but if a thing is done time and again, with equally successful results, the idea of coincidence wears a little thin. (Personally I don't believe in coincidence.)

The fact that simply praying can cause change to occur indicates that the most powerful ingredient in working magic is the mind. It is necessary to have a very real desire for the change—usually a great *need* for it. In this way, the emotion of

16. Some pronounce Crowley's name to rhyme with *cow-ly*, but the man himself said, "It is Crowley . . . to rhyme with 'holy'!"

the need builds the burning desire and translates into the energy, or power, necessary to accomplish the act. And for this very reason, magic cannot be done "just to show that I can do it!"

Because of this desire or need for the end result, it can be seen that *the best person to do magic is the person who desires the end result.* No matter how inexperienced, the person can actually put far more power into the working of the magic by virtue of having a burning desire to see it succeed. To ask someone else to work magic for you—even someone acknowledged to be a "great magician"—is actually second best, since this person will not, and cannot, have that same deep-rooted inner desire.

> The first requisite of occult work is the ability to concentrate well. In later work it will be found that the astral imagery is so interesting that concentration is very easy to achieve, in fact one achieves it unconsciously. However, one must not be a "fair weather worker" and should be able to concentrate at will and also to make the screen of consciousness a blank, free from intruding images and thoughts.
> —Gareth Knight, *Occult Exercises and Practices*

## Types and Forms of Magic

Let's look in a little more detail at some of the different types and forms of magic.

*Sympathetic* is one type of magic. It can also be called *imitative magic,* since you are using an object to represent that which you wish to affect. There are many forms that sympathetic magic can take. For example, candle burning is a form of sympathetic magic. Here, candles are used to represent people and things. By certain manipulations, you can exert forces on those people and things the candle represents. There are probably more forms of sympathetic magic than any other type. *Image magic*—using dolls or poppets to represent a person or persons—is another form of this.

*Ceremonial magic* is quite different (and not really a part of Wicca, though some traditions do dabble in it). Here, there is a belief in spirits, entities, or whatever you wish to call them. Many of the old *grimoires*—the old books of ceremonial magic—actually term them "demons." I will stick with entities.

The belief is that each entity has its peculiar expertise. One will be able to locate buried treasure, for example, while another has the gift of tongues. One may be able to teach herbal lore, and another can cause the erection of magnificent buildings. Various ceremonial magicians of the past have reportedly conjured each and every one of these many entities and learned both their names and their areas of expertise. Each requires a particular, intricate rite of conjuration.

It is only by conjuring the entity, and causing it to appear to the magician, that the latter is able to show his or her power over the other and, thereby, demand the required knowledge. The entity is, apparently, very loath to be drawn into this world and therefore may want to harm the magician who brought it here. This practice entails working within a very detailed, protective, magic Circle with all sorts of talismans of protection worn, and with the working tools constructed to precise recipes. This is very definitely *high magic*.

*Folk magic*, in contrast, is extremely simple *low magic* using ordinary, easily found items. As in Wicca, nothing is conjured and forced to appear; consequently, there is no danger from doing this type of magic. This is the magic of the Romanies, or Gypsies, and of the "Hedge Witches." Sometimes deities are asked to bless the work, but most folk magic has no visible religious connection.

*Poppet magic* is a form of imitative or sympathetic magic. Figures are made to represent the people to be affected, and can be made of wax, clay, cloth, straw—just about any substance. It is not necessary that they look exactly like the person they have been made to represent. Sometimes an object belonging to the person is incorporated in the construction, but again, this is not essential. There is, however, a part of the ritual in which the poppet is named for the person. Astrological signs, or similar designs, may be drawn on the figure to help make the connection and exact identification. Frequently, poppets are made of cloth and stuffed with appropriate herbs, whether for healing, or love, or whatever. Poppet magic has been performed for thousands of years, with examples found in ancient Egyptian times and even as far back as Paleolithic times, twenty-five thousand years ago.

*Healing magic* is a type of magic that can be done in various forms, from hands-on to using poppets or plackets or similar items. The aim, of course, is to help heal someone who is sick, which can be done with the person present or at a distance. Although you might consider healing a positive, unselfish act, it is important to get the permission of the person to be healed before proceeding with it. Many are sick because it is part of their life's learning and experiencing process. To heal them without consultation could possibly interfere with this process. Do not, therefore, assume that all who are ill are desperate to be healed.

*Placket magic* is the use of small "plackets," or "pockets," to accomplish the healing, or other, process. (The word *placket* is an Old English word that means both "pocket" and "vagina"!) These are made of felt or a similar material, and in a color or colors appropriate to what is being sought. A photograph of the person, or something belonging to him or her, is placed inside the pocket and kept there for a period of time. The placket is made about three or four inches square, depending upon the size of the photographs that are to be inserted.

*Sex magic* is simply using the tremendous power generated in the sex act by directing it to achieve the end desired. I'll be looking at this in more detail in chapter 14. In fact, all of these forms of magic will be used and dealt with in detail as we progress through this book.

---

### Astral Colors

Here are the correspondences of various colors, used in such things as candle magic, color magic, placket magic, and poppet magic.

*BLACK*—Absence, anonymity, confusion, evil, discord, loss, stress, neutrality, indecision.

*BROWN*—Earthiness, hesitation, neutrality, stalemate, uncertainty.

*DARK BLUE*—Changeability, depression, honor, reverence, uncertainty.

*GOLD (Yellow)*—Attraction, charm, confidence, persuasion, positivity, protection.

*GREEN*—Fertility, finance, healing, luck, nature.

*GREENISH YELLOW*—Cowardice, discord, jealousy, sickness.

*LIGHT BLUE*—Health, healing energies, patience, tranquillity, understanding.

*ORANGE*—Adaptability, attraction, encouragement, stimulation.

*PINK*—Honor, love, morality.

*PURPLE*—Ambition, business progress, "old soul," power, nobility, religious depth, tension.

*RED*—Courage, good health, sexual love, strength, vigor.

*SILVER (Gray)*—Cancellation, neutrality, stalemate.

*VIOLET*—Healing, peace, spirituality.

*WHITE*—Purity, sincerity, truth.

# When and Where to Use Magic

Magic is not something to be used willy-nilly, or on a whim. It is a tool that must be used responsibly. I've mentioned that it should not be attempted just to prove that you can do it (it probably won't work in that case, anyway!), nor to impress someone. It should only be used when there is a very real need for it, and when the objective cannot be accomplished by more conventional methods.

This is especially true of healing. Always go to a properly trained medical person first. These days, there are hospitals and individual medical practitioners who are happy to cooperate with an alternative form of healer.

Having said all this, the first consideration now is exactly when to do your magic. You will find that the timing depends upon what it is you want to do. There are best times for doing love magic, best times for money, and so on. Of course, in an emergency you don't worry about this; just do the magic immediately. The added pressure and need, because of the urgency, will reinforce your power and overcome any possible negativity from not being able to perform the work at the most appropriate time.

There are two main considerations in deciding the best time: moon phase and planetary hours. The simpler of these is to go just by the phases of the moon. In fact, most Witches work according to the moon; very few bother with the niceties of planetary hours, though they do use the planetary rulers, as we shall see.

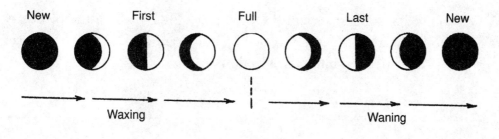

**PHASES OF THE MOON**

In simplest terms, constructive magic is done during the waxing (increasing) phase of the moon, and destructive magic done during the waning (decreasing) phase. When I say "destructive" magic, I am not speaking of *harmful* magic!

Harmful magic is never done in Wicca. Constructive magic would be something like increasing love, money, or situation. Destructive might involve getting rid of a bad habit, having your hair cut (so it will grow back more slowly), getting rid of negative forces, or the like.

When working on constructive projects, the power you project into the magic will grow as the moon grows in size. No magic is going to happen in a flash, like a fairy godmother waving her magic wand! It will take some time, depending upon the objective. Some magic can take several months to come to fruition. But most is resolved within one moon's phase—one month.

Some rituals need to be repeated a number of times, often three. If this is the case, then arrange it so that the final working of the spell is done as close to the full moon (or new moon, if you are doing something destructive) as possible. For this, you will need to consult a calendar that gives moon phases.

---

### The Rising of the Moon

The *new moon* always rises at sunrise.
The *first quarter* always rises at noon.
The *full moon* always rises at sunset.
The *last quarter* always rises at midnight.
For each day following the above, the moon will rise about fifty minutes later than the previous day.

---

Which would be the best day to do the magic? Here's where the planetary rulers come in. Each day of the week is ruled by a different planet—which, in turn, governs various activities and interests, as follows:

| Day | Planet | Activity |
| --- | --- | --- |
| SUNDAY | *Sun* | Agriculture, beauty, creativity, fortune, guardianship, hope, money, self-expression, victory |

| Day | Planet | Activity |
| --- | --- | --- |
| MONDAY | *Moon* | Ancestors, childbearing, dreams, healing, instinct, memory, merchandise, purity, theft, virginity |
| TUESDAY | *Mars* | Enemies, initiation, loyalty, matrimony, prison, protection, war, wealth |
| WEDNESDAY | *Mercury* | Business, communication, debt, fear, loss, travel |
| THURSDAY | *Jupiter* | Clothing, desires, harvests, honor, marriage, oaths, riches, treaties |
| FRIDAY | *Venus* | Beauty, family life, friendship, fruitfulness, growth, harmony, love, nature, pleasures, sexuality, strangers, waters |
| SATURDAY | *Saturn* | Building, doctrine, freedom, gifts, life, protection, real estate, sowing, tenacity |

If you are planning to do some magic regarding a marriage, then, you would do it on a Thursday. Tuesday is also good for matrimony. The same is true on several subjects: More than one day might be applicable. Think carefully as to which is the most appropriate. In this case, if it is the actual marriage Thursday is the day. But if it has to do with the state of matrimony, perhaps several years after the wedding it-self, Tuesday is the better day. An added indication in this case is that Thursday is also good for oaths, so in terms of the marriage vows, this would seem to back up the choice of Thursday.

Look, then, at the calendar and see which Thursday falls closest to the full moon on the waxing side (that is, before it actually becomes full rather than just after). This is the best day to perform the magical ritual. If you are going to do more than one ritual then this is the day to do the final one in the series. If you want to repeat the ritual three times, for example, and this means the first time will fall within the waning cycle, don't worry, since it will be the end of the waning. The other two will definitely be in the waxing phase, with the final ritual close to the full moon. What time of day, or night is best? This is where planetary hours come into it. Unless you are doing something like ceremonial magic, you don't need to fine-tune to such an extent.[17] But if you do want to have everything possible going for you, I have given a table of planetary hours in the appendix.

As to where to do your rituals, I have already spoken of your temple and the sacred circle (chapter 3). But if you haven't yet set up a temple, or are away from home, simply choose a spot where you will be undisturbed. You don't want to hear radios, television, the sounds of traffic or voices, or the telephone. You need to feel *secure*, so that you can put all your attention into the magic you are doing. You don't need a lot of space; in fact most magic can be done in little more than a five-foot-diameter circle, as you will see as we progress.

# The Cone of Power

When you work magic, you generate power that builds up from the line of the Circle you have drawn and consecrated and forms roughly into a cone shape, enclosing you. This is both a protective barrier—keeping out all negativity—and a wall against which to build the pressure of the power until releasing it.

The consecrating of the Circle is therefore the most important step in working magic. It's true that much folk magic does not include this step, but other precautions are taken there, and it is somewhat different from the magic done in a Wiccan Circle.

In a coven setting, just before starting to do the magic, the leader of the group should repeat the Circle consecration as an extra sealing, or reinforcing, of the area. This is especially necessary if anyone has broken the Circle by leaving and reentering it since its original casting. The Circle must be secure to contain the power that is raised.

In coven work and hereditary Wicca, the magic is done after the Cakes and Ale.

---

17. For full details of calculating planetary hours and using them, see my book *Advanced Candle Magick*. (Llewellyn, St. Paul: 1996)

In fact, during the relaxed "intermission" of eating the cake and drinking the ale or wine, the group will discuss what magic is to be done and consider the best way to do it. The dance, the chant, the focus, and the method of projecting the power will all be covered so everyone knows exactly what is expected of them.

The main theme, when all has been considered, is to raise the power and project it to the desired object. Power can be raised in a variety of ways, but basically it is a case of working yourself up to *ekstasis*—a state of ecstasy. Dance and rhythm are the two main ingredients for this. Dancing around the Circle, gradually building up the speed, accompanied by a steady, rhythmic beat, is the most common way. Some groups use traditional steps, but most extemporize. Records of the Witches of old dancing at their Sabbats speak of them leaping high in the air or interlocking arms, back to back, and whirling around, lifting one another off their feet. In fact, the waltz is said to have originated from a Witch dance known as "La Volta."

Many covens have a "designated drummer" who sits close up against the altar and provides the beat to which the others dance. The traditional drum used by the Witches of old was known as a tabor, and was similar in appearance to many of the flat native American drums or the Irish bodhran. But a drummer is not a necessity. The beat can be kept by clapping hands, beating the ground or floor, or slapping your thighs.

## Magical Chants

A worthwhile tool for building power is the chant. The exact wording should be decided upon when planning the work. It should be short and to the point, with a clear rhyme and solid beat. Some groups will insist upon old, frequently unintelligible chants that are supposed to be "mystical"—"*Eko tane mare syam! Abijl ala, nuno actenal nehn!*" What does this mean? It's actually from the Seventh Book of Moses, a book of ceremonial magic. It would, therefore, have no relevance to any Wiccan working, and especially not to any specific working.

Apart from anything else, you should never chant *anything* the meaning of which you do not know. Who knows what you might conjure up! Your chant should be short, simple, and focused on the object of the exercise. Suppose you are trying to help a coven member find a new apartment. Then, use something like, "Bring [name] peace; find her a home. Let her rest and cease to roam." Better yet would be just a couple of lines: "[Name] finds a home; no more to roam!" Stress the alternating syllables: "[Name] *finds* a *home*, no *more* to *roam!*" This way you can stamp or clap or whatever on that beat.

By choosing such a short, pertinent phrase you can dance and chant without really thinking about it. This is important because, in doing magic, you need to be focusing on the *end result*. In the above example, you do not think of the person— let's call her Jane—*looking* for an apartment; you think of her having *found* one and being happily settled in it. You see Jane with a big smile, enjoying her new home. This is your focus, and that's why you don't need to try remembering a lot of words as you dance and chant.

# Projection of the Power

As you dance, you will find that you get faster and faster, working up to a climax. What happens when you reach this climax? In some covens, the High Priestess will signal the moment and everyone will stop, perhaps collapsing on the ground, and direct all their pent-up energy into her, the High Priestess. She will then direct that massed energy to the chosen target. The only problem with this, to my mind, is that not everyone reaches the climax of their potential at the same time. I think it far more effective to let the individual coven members stop when they feel they can drive themselves no farther, drop to the ground, and themselves direct their energy to the target. Both methods give the same total blast of power from the entire group. The latter method offers that extra edge, when everyone is able to give full capacity without having been cut short.

# Cord Magic

There are times when you need to do magic, but—while it is the best time to do it, perhaps just before the full moon—it is not the best time to direct it. For example, if someone is to undergo an operation that will take place in the waxing cycle of the moon, you will want to send healing energies to that person, but you know that moon phase is not the best time to get the most power. So, what you can do is work the magic, building up as much energy as possible immediately before the full moon (the very best time), and then *store* that energy to be released during the waning phase, when the person is really in need of it. You can store the energy in your magical cord.

> The art of knots is a very ancient one. The twining and interlacing was a way of warding off the Evil Eye. The idea was to avert and mislead the eye of any malevolent person by the tracing of knots. The beautiful designs of Celtic art display this form of magic very expressively.—Patricia Crowther, *Lid Off the Cauldron*

In Olaus Magnus' *Historia de Gentibus Septentrionalibus* of 1555, a woodcut shows a Witch selling a knotted rope to some sailors. This was a cord into which magic had been worked to generate winds. If the sailor found himself becalmed, he could untie one of the knots; a wind would come up. The more knots he untied, the fiercer the wind would become. According to Magnus:

When they had their price they knit three magical knots . . . bound up with a thong, and they gave them unto the merchant sailors, observing that rule, that when they unloosed the first, they should have a good gale of wind; when the second, a stronger wind; but when they untied the third, they should have such cruel tempests that they should not be able to look out of the forecastle to avoid the rocks.

The best-known Wiccan cord magic spell can be done by an individual, by a couple, or by a whole coven. It involves tying nine knots in your cord while building up the power and directing it into this cord. This power buildup can be done by dancing, chanting, the sex act, or however you work best in building power. If it is being done by a coven, then the coven leader will do the actual tying of the knots as the coveners project their power into her or him. If it is done as a couple, then they will take turns tying a knot. As a solitary, of course, you would tie all the knots yourself.

Holding the cord and concentrating the energy, the first knot is tied in the middle ———X——— with the words "By knot of one, this spell's begun."

The next knot is tied at one end X———X——— with the words, "By knot of two, this spell comes true."

Sorcerer selling Mariners the Winds tied up in
Three Knots of a Rope
Olaus Magnus, *Historia de gentibus septentrionalibus.*

The next knot is at the other end X———X———X "By knot of three, so mote it be."

Then a knot between the middle and one of the end ones X——X——X——X "By knot of four, this power I store."

The same thing at the other end, between the end knot and the middle one X—X—X—X—X "By knot of five, the spell's alive."

Next, between the first two X-X-X——X——X——X with "By knot of six, this spell I fix."

Then, the same at the other end X-X-X——X——X-X-X with "By knot of seven, this spell I'll leaven."

The next knot should be next to the center X-X-X-X-X——X-X-X with "By knot of eight, I'll cast the fate."

And finally, the last knot X-X-X-X-X-X-X-X-X with "By knot of nine, what's done is fine."

All the energy is finally released into that last knot, seeing the finalizing of the work you want to do. If you are working sex magic, this is where the knot is tied at the climax. All the raised power is now stored in that nine-knotted cord.

The release of that stored power is done at another, later, ritual. It can be done all at once, if necessary, or by untying one knot each day for nine days, building up to the best time. The knots should be released *in the same order in which they were tied;* not the reverse order. This way it is the final knot, which absorbed the most energy, that is untied at the climax again.

There is a simple, yet effective cord magic spell that can be performed by a solitary witch using a short, disposable cord. This should be nine inches in length and, again, red in color. At the ritual, sprinkle it with the salted water at the altar, and hold it in the smoke of the incense. Then wrap it around your personal ritual cord. Carry the intertwined cords to the east and hold them up, saying:

> *I bind these cords together as I would bind my spell.*
> *I bind the cords; I bind the spell.*
> *I bind my power—work it well!*

Repeat to the south, west, and north, then return to the altar and unwrap the cords. You will now work with the short one. Sitting, standing, or kneeling, concentrate on the aim of the spell; the intent. Build up the power and energy within yourself as you feel best. Visualize the finished act. Then stand and, stamping out a rhythm, dance three times around the Circle *deosil.* Tie a knot in the cord each time you pass the east, making three knots in all, directing your power into the knots as you tie them. Tie the knot in the middle first, then one at each end. Return to the altar and lay the knotted cord on it. Touch your athame to it and say:

> *Here is my power, deep in this cord. It is tied within so that it may not escape.*

Take the knotted cord to the east and hold it up, saying:

> *The air will carry this magic.*

Go to the south and say:

*The fire will marry this magic.*

Go to the west and say:

*The Water will bear this magic.*

Go to the north and say:

*The earth will wear this magic.*

Return to the altar and again wrap the now-knotted cord around your personal ritual cord. Carry the intertwined cords to the east (then south, west, and north) and hold them up, saying:

*I bind these cords together as I would bind my spell.*
*I bind the cords; I bind the spell.*
*I bind my power—work it well!*

Return to the altar and, unwrapping the two, again lay the knotted cord on the altar, leaving it there till you have ended the Circle. Afterward, keep the cord on your person for seven days, sleeping with it under your pillow at night. Then bury it beneath an oak tree or a thorn bush for the most powerful magic.

# Safeguards for Magic

If you are not in a coven Circle or any consecrated Circle, when you want to work magic (and magic can be done just as effectively by a solitary as by a group), you *must* prepare yourself by cleansing yourself and the area in which you are working. I do, however, recommend casting a Circle if at all possible, using your athame. But even if you are doing candle magic, color magic, hands-on healing, or something similar, and are unable to cast a regular Circle, you must cleanse first. I have talked about this before, but it bears repeating.

Sit comfortably in a chair. I recommend one with a straight back and with arms. You can rest your arms on the arms of the chair. If you'd prefer to sit on the floor, then that's all right, too. Wherever you sit, be sure your spine is straight; this is the key. Start by relaxing your body with deep breathing. Close your eyes and simply breathe deeply—breathing in to fill your lungs and breathing out to completely exhaust them. Try to keep your mind blank. This is not easy. When odd thoughts from the day—from your job or your personal life, for example—come creeping in, gently push them out again and concentrate on your breathing. As you breathe in, imagine white light coming into your body. See it filling your body. As you breathe out, see the grayness of negativity being pushed out and away. Feel all the little aches and pains going away as the gentle relaxation of purity comes in.

Keep this up for a few minutes. As the white light builds and fills your body, see it expanding even beyond your body to form a ball or egg of white light all around you. This is a protective barrier for you, and will keep away all negativity. See it expanding to fill the area in which you are going to be working.

If you are doing a healing on someone who is present, then let it include that person, too. When you feel you have done this sufficiently—and the time will vary from individual to individual—let your breathing return to normal and open your eyes. Always do this before any magical or psychic work.

# Grounding

Some suggest that it is necessary to "ground" the power after doing magic. My feeling is that any power that has been raised is extremely positive energy, so the grounding is not necessary. If there *is* any power left, it can only benefit you, not harm you. However, some individuals feel happier grounding, and there is certainly no harm in doing so. All that it entails is connecting with the earth. You can do this by dropping to the ground and lying flat on it, with the palms of your hands flat on the ground. Or you may just crouch and place the palms of your hands on the ground. (Some feel they need to actually slap the ground to make the contact.)

Either way, you are allowing any surplus energy to be absorbed into Mother Earth and not leaving yourself still charged up. When I say "flat on the *ground*," don't worry if you are twelve floors up in a high-rise apartment! The energies will travel down through the structure to where it is embedded in the earth and so will complete the grounding operation.

## Law of Threefold Return

Remember the Law of Threefold Return: Everything you do will return to you, but at three times the strength. Do good and it will return threefold. But do harm and that, too, will come back on you three times as strongly. There should, therefore, be no inducement to do harm.

# ~ 8 ~

# Witchcraft in School

For most of us, the years spent in school are the most impressionable ones. These years can be the happiest of times, but for some they bring nothing but misery. Yet, for the Wiccan child, there is no reason why this should not be a truly wonderful period of life.

A Wiccan child does not automatically have all things going for him or her. In fact, quite the reverse . . . if there is any hint of interest in the metaphysical, they may well be immediately labeled "weird" by their peers. Television and movies are beginning to change this, however, making the previous object of ridicule and scorn now an object of envy and admiration. The times are changing slowly, however, so let's see how we can speed up the process.

---

*Ever remember, you are the "Hidden Children of the Goddess." If tempted to admit or boast of belonging to the Craft, you be endangering your brothers and sisters. For though now the fires of persecution have died down, who knows when they may be revived? Many priests have knowledge of our secrets and they full well know that much religious bigotry has died down or calmed down, that many people would wish to join our Craft if the truth were known of its joys and the churches would lose power. . . . So ever keep the secrets.*

—Book of Shadows

# In or Out of the Closet?

To what extent, if any, should a child show connection to the Craft? Legally, there should be no problem in this area. Just as some children are permitted to wear and display crucifixes or Stars of David, so should a Wiccan child be able to wear a pentagram or similar symbol. But what *should* be is not the same as what is! Much depends upon the part of the country in which you live, and the open- or closed-mindedness of your community. Wherever you are, it is possible to initiate a lawsuit to obtain your religious rights if you have to (and the ACLU has been wonderfully helpful on this score in numerous cases across the country involving Wicca), but ideally confrontation should be avoided. It is one thing to be granted your rights; it is another to have to live with your fellow students in an atmosphere of tension and antagonism, after having won them.

Start by not overstating your position. In other words, a small, discreet pentagram or pentagram ring is fine. But to overload yourself with rings, pendants, tattoos, bracelets, earrings, and necklaces that shriek "Witchcraft!" is foolish so far as the true Craft is concerned, and more so for your unobtrusiveness at school. It is the student who dresses all in black, with ghoulish makeup, black fingernail polish, and occult jewelry who is not the true Witch. Similarly, one who infers that he or she will curse you or cause dire things to happen is definitely not a Witch.

There is no connection between Witches and vampires, Witches and Satanists, Witches and warlocks. (*Warlock* is from the old Scottish word *warloga*, meaning "traitor" or "deceiver." It was a term applied during the burning times to one who turned in his fellow Witches to the authorities. It is never used among Witches themselves today.)

Remember, Witchcraft is a positive religion with love for all life.

---

*A nasty thing happens to teens when they talk to their friends about the Craft—they lose a lot of them. Here's where you separate the true friends from those who have no clue. This happens to adults too. Once you start moving to a higher level of consciousness, it is natural that those people who aren't on your wavelength will drift away. Some will go quietly and others will raise a big stink in the process. . . . You may cultivate a new set of friends rather quickly, or you may be a loner for a while. That's a chance you're going to have to take if you speak out.*

—Silver RavenWolf, *Teen Witch*

# Handling Verbal Attacks

The first thing to learn is not to fight back. When someone accuses you of being a Witch or dabbling in Witchcraft, simply ask, "What do you mean by Witch?" or "What do you mean by Witchcraft?" Make them explain themselves. Invariably, the answer will be one connecting Witchcraft to Satanism and black magic. Here is the opening to begin correcting the misconceptions. Quietly and level-headedly explain how these erroneous ideas came about. Stress the antiquity and the positivity of Witchcraft, the Craft of the wise. Take the "friends sharing information" approach to prevent an immediate rejection of your ideas. To do this well, you need a good understanding of the background of the Craft.[18] But then, as a Witch, you should have that.

Some will claim that you do not believe in or worship God. The response, of course, is that you *do* believe in and worship God. But more than that, you also honor a Goddess. It is obvious that everywhere in nature there is both male and female. Why, then, would this not be so with the deities? You can point out that in Christianity, Mary has, in many ways, taken over the role of the Goddess. So you most decidedly do worship a god, who is a good and loving god, just as they claim to do.

Try not to be drawn into arguments over passages in the Bible. You can counter by asking if the person is aware of what the Koran, or the Talmud, the Veda, or the Bhagavad-Gita has to say on things. Almost certainly they will admit they don't. Agree and say, "Of course we don't, because these holy books are not of our religion. In the same way, your Bible is not of my religion, so I'm not familiar with its contents." You can go on to explain that they must obviously follow the teachings in which they believe, but they cannot expect followers of all other religions to follow those same teachings. "Yet," you might add, "it's said that all roads lead to the same center. There are many similarities among all such holy books, including yours and mine." In this way, it's difficult for them to insist that something is "right" simply because it is written in the Christian Bible.

18. Check out my book *Witchcraft From the Inside* for a good overview.

## The Media and Witchcraft

Many young Wiccans these days find themselves looked upon as authorities where movies and television series concerning Witchcraft are concerned. However askance other students might have looked at you before, when there has been a recent large- or small-screen showing of "Witches" at work, they will not hesitate to ask how accurate it was, and other searching questions. This is always wonderfully fertile ground in which to sow the seeds of truth about the Craft.

There are many books available today about Witchcraft and its ways. Check out the bibliography in the appendix to this book, and don't hesitate to recommend books to any who show a real interest in the subject. As Witches, we do not proselytize; we do not go out seeking to convert others to the Craft. But we do believe in correcting misconceptions as much as we can. If we can get others to read worthwhile books on Wicca, even if they are not interested in becoming Witches themselves, they will indirectly help spread the word.

## Using the Power of Witchcraft at School

I have talked about magic and the fact that it can be used when there is a real need for it. This need can certainly arise for the young Witch at school. It can be there in the areas of popularity and friendship, academics, athletics, homework, dating, and others where peer pressure can build to an almost intolerable level. The need can also be there regarding the modern threats of drugs and physical harm.

Witches, of course, do not use drugs. There is no need. We can obtain that wonderful sense of well-being by our own powers. Building white light within and around you, sitting in a consecrated Circle, meditating—all these things can give you a far greater, and less destructive, "high" than can damaging drugs.

At times, the need can arise for the use of magic at school. Let's look at some of those specifically. As we saw in chapter 7, the best place to do magic is alone in an area where you will not be disturbed, such as a consecrated Circle. This can be constructed as we saw in chapter 3. If there are two or three of you who are working together, all should be properly prepared and work inside the Circle. (You can adjust the wording of the following rituals from "me" to "we," and similar, where necessary.) I have used a variety of magical methods in the following pages, including candle magic, poppets, and plackets. Don't be afraid to experiment once you've got a little experience. "Mix and match," as it were! Try using different methods to cast the same spell, and see which gives the best results.

Incidentally, if others ask you to do magic for them, say no. As I have mentioned previously, the most powerful and effective person to do magic is the one primarily affected by it. So anyone wanting magic done should be encouraged to study it and do it for themselves.

The following rituals should be read through several times, if necessary, before you attempt to do them. Become thoroughly familiar with them. Have everything ready ahead of time for doing them. And—most important—do them only if there is a *real need*. Magic should not be treated lightly; spells should not be done just for the sake of doing them. Magic done in this frame of mind almost certainly won't work.

# Rituals for Friendship and Popularity

## TO ATTRACT NEW FRIENDS

Cast and consecrate the Circle in the usual way, lighting all the candles, consecrating salt and water and yourself. The regular altar items should be moved to one side. In the middle of the altar, place a petitioner candle to represent yourself. This should be in your own astral color (see the appendix). The primary color is best, but the secondary will also work. If you cannot find one in the correct color and need to get on with the ritual, use a white one and scratch your name on it before consecrating it. (See the illustration on page 122 for how to consecrate a candle.) Close up against it place an orange candle—the color of attraction. In a circle around these two central candles, stand a number of white candles representing potential friends. (Do not name any of them, for you must not try to influence a particular person to do something he or she would not do naturally.) The outer circle of candles should be about six inches out from the central one. All these candles should be consecrated before use.

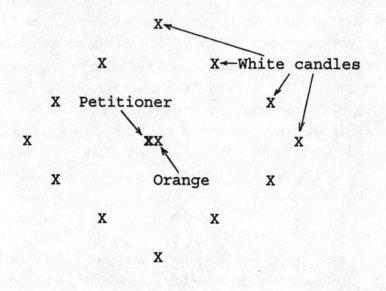

Make sure the incense is alight. Ring the bell three times. Light the central petitioner candle, which represents you, and say,

*Here I light the spirit of myself, [name], who desires to be encircled by good friends. Let my spirit shine out as this flame shines, attracting all I desire to me.*

Light the orange candle and say:

*Here is the light of attraction. May it be the energy that draws to me all that I desire.*

Light each of the surrounding candles, in a clockwise manner. As you light them, say:

*Here shine the lights of those I wish to join me in friendship. Their flames are symbols of the minds and hearts that will reach out to me and join with me. Together we will make a great light, a symbol of all that is good and right.*

Take up the incense and move it, clockwise, all around the outside of the circle of candles. Replace it. Ring the bell seven times.

Sit or kneel and meditate on the *types* of people you would like to become your friends; those interested in the same sports, hobbies, and so on, that you enjoy. In your mind, see them coming forward, smiling, and hugging you in friendship. See all of you taking hands and forming a large circle. Keep up this imagery for as long as you can. Then, relax and snuff out the candles between finger and thumb to lock in the energy. Do the circle ones first, then the orange, and finally the petitioner's candle.

You may now drink to the gods, first pouring libations. Say:

*To the gods!*

This ritual should be repeated for three nights in a row.

At the start of the second night, move the outer circle of candles inward, toward the center, so that they are closer to the central two (petitioner and orange). On the third night, move them in so that they are all touching the central ones. If you use candleholders, then it is sufficient for the holders to all be touching.

Stand and raise your athame in salute. Say:

*Thank you, Lord and Lady, for this time spent together. We came together in love and friendship; so let us go our separate ways. My thanks for watching over me, for guarding me, and for guiding me. Help me spread the love of the Craft throughout all lives I may touch.*

If several coven members are in the Circle, they walk around the Circle to pass you, embracing and kissing you as they pass. When all are back in their places, say:

*Merry did we meet, so merry may we part. And merry may we meet again. So mote it be.*

Everyone should repeat:

*So mote it be!*

Go to the east and, with your athame, cut across the lines of the Circle. Say:

**This Circle is now open.**

All may now leave the Circle if they wish. It is no longer closed and consecrated.

This ritual should be done during the week immediately preceding the full moon. It is best done on a Wednesday, Thursday, and Friday. You should see results from this almost immediately. By the end of a month, you will have at least three new friends who will be loyal and trustworthy.

## TO INCREASE YOUR POPULARITY

Cast and consecrate the Circle in the usual way, lighting all the candles, consecrating salt and water and yourself. On the altar, along with the regular altar items, place a bowl of flowers or of flower petals. Ring the bell three times and say:

**Lord and Lady, help me spread my love around me as I spread these beautiful flower petals about this sacred Circle.**

Taking up the flowers, or the bowl of petals, walk slowly around the Circle *deosil*, casting petals outward. As you do so, say:

**I cast these petals from me,**
**To meet the love around.**
**My life attunes to others,**
**With joy it will abound.**
**My friends and fellow students**
**All look to me anew.**
**I am a loyal companion**
**With friendship ever true.**

Repeat this twice more—three times in all—each time walking the Circle and sprinkling petals. Then return to the altar, replace the bowl, and meditate on the object of your desires. See, in your mind, yourself as a popular student, sought after by many. Relax, ring the bell seven times, and drink to the gods.

*To the gods!*

Stand and raise your athame in salute. Say:

*Thank you, Lord and Lady, for this time spent in your presence. We came together in love and friendship; so let us go our separate ways. My thanks for watching over me, for guarding me and for guiding me. Help me spread the love of the Craft throughout all lives I may touch.*

If several coven members are in the Circle, they walk around the Circle to pass the HP or HPS, kissing as they pass. When all are back in their places, say:

*Merry did we meet, so merry may we part. And merry may we meet again. So mote it be.*

Everyone should repeat:

*So mote it be!*

Go to the east and, with your athame, cut across the lines of the Circle. Say:

*This Circle is now open.*

All may now leave the Circle if they wish. It is no longer closed and consecrated.

This ritual should be done during the week immediately preceding the full moon. It should be done on a Friday (best), a Thursday, or a Sunday.

## TO DEVELOP UNDERSTANDING

Cast and consecrate the Circle in the usual way, lighting all the candles, consecrating salt and water and yourself. On the altar, along with the regular altar items, place a pile of small white stones (each about the size of a walnut), a pile of black stones, and a pile of gray stones that you have gathered over a period of time preparatory for this ritual. There should be at least seven stones in each pile.

Also on the altar are four small pouches or bags (it's good if you have made these yourself), which should be light blue in color. They can be of any material, but a natural fabric such as cotton, linen, silk, or even leather is preferable.

Ring the bell three times. Take up the four bags and walk *deosil* around the Circle. Place one bag in the east, one in the south, one in the west, and one in the north. Return to the altar.

Place all the stones in the center of the altar, or on the floor in front of the altar. With your right hand (or left, if you are left-handed), mix up the stones.

Ring the bell three times, and then pick out four white stones from the pile. Carry them around the Circle, *deosil*, stopping at each of the four quarters and laying a stone on top of the bag there. Return to the altar. Mix the stones again and then ring the bell seven times.

Pick out four black stones from the pile. Carry them around the Circle, *deosil*, stopping at each of the four quarters and laying a stone on top of the bag there. Return to the altar. Mix the stones again and then ring the bell nine times.

Pick out four gray stones from the pile. Carry them around the Circle, *deosil*, stopping at each of the four quarters and laying a stone on top of the bag there. Return to the altar.

Now, sit or kneel and meditate on what it is you desire—the developing of understanding in whatever field you feel you need it. When you feel you have done this sufficiently, ring the bell three times and walk once more around the Circle. At each of the four quarters, stop and fill the bag with the three stones that lie on top of it. Carry the bag with you as you move on to the next quarter. When you have all four filled bags, return to the altar. Hold up the bags together, between your hands, and say:

*Here have I developed understanding, as I wished. In all directions, the positives and negatives have mellowed with the neutral to become a perfect balance that is easily understood. I will guard this knowledge so that it may remain with me for as long as I desire. So mote it be!*

Pour libations and drink to the gods. Stand and raise your athame in salute. Say:

*Thank you, Lord and Lady, for this time spent in your presence. We came together in love and friendship; so let us go our separate ways. My thanks for watching over me, for guarding me, and for guiding me. Help me spread the love of the Craft throughout all lives I may touch.*

If several coven members are in the Circle, they walk around the Circle to pass the HP or HPS, kissing as they pass.

When all are back in their places, say:

*Merry did we meet, so merry may we part. And merry may we meet again. So mote it be.*

Everyone should repeat:

*So mote it be!*

Go to the east and, with your athame, cut across the lines of the Circle. Say:

*This Circle is now open.*

All may now leave the Circle if they wish. It is no longer closed and consecrated.

This ritual should be done during the week immediately preceding the full moon. It is best done on a Wednesday. The bags of stones should be kept in a safe place; many Witches bury them under an oak tree or thorn bush.

## TO BRING SELF-CONFIDENCE

Cast and consecrate the Circle in the usual way, lighting all the candles, consecrating salt and water and yourself. The regular altar items should be moved to one side.

In the middle of the altar, place a petitioner candle to represent yourself. This should be in your own astral color (see the appendix). The primary color is best, but the secondary will also work. If you cannot find one in the correct color and need to get on with the ritual, use a white one and scratch your name on it before consecrating it. (See the illustration on page 122 for how to consecrate a candle.)

Close up against it place an orange candle—the color of attraction. In a circle

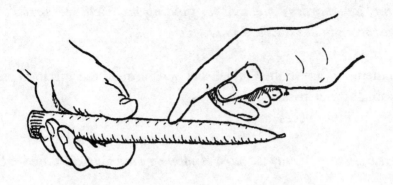

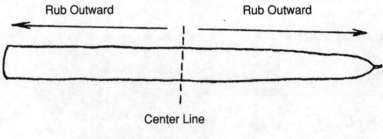

CONSECRATE A CANDLE

around these two central candles, stand a number of white candles. The outer circle of candles should be about six inches out from the central one. All these candles should be consecrated before use.

Make sure the incense is alight. Ring the bell three times. Light the central petitioner candle, which represents you, and say:

*Here I light the spirit of myself, [name], who desires to be filled with self-confidence. Let my hesitations and uncertainties fall by the wayside and let my spirit shine out as this flame shines, exuding faith and trust in myself and in all my thoughts and actions.*

Light the orange candle and say:

*Here is the light of attraction. May it be the energy that draws to me all that I desire.*

Light each of the surrounding white candles, in a clockwise manner. As you light them, say:

*Here is the confidence I will build in myself. As these candle flames burn strong and true, so will my confidence in myself develop and blaze up, filling me with the light and power of my own convictions. I draw this energy into myself, knowing it will do me only good.*

Take up the incense and move it, clockwise, all around the outside of the circle of candles. Replace it. Ring the bell seven times.

Sit or kneel and meditate on yourself. See yourself fully self-confident, able to handle any situation and deal with any person, no matter how important they may appear to be. See yourself growing in stature so that you actually look down (physically) on others around you. Yet know that with this new self-confidence you will still retain the spirit of love and humility that makes you who you are. Keep up this imagery for as long as you can.

Then, relax and snuff out the candles between finger and thumb, to lock in the energy. Do the circle ones first, then the orange, and finally the petitioner's candle.

You may now drink to the gods, first pouring libations. Say:

*To the gods!*

This ritual should be repeated for three nights in a row.

At the start of the second night, move the outer circle of candles inward, toward the center, so that they are closer to the central two (petitioner and orange). On the third night, move them in so that they are all touching the central ones. If you use candleholders, it is sufficient for all the holders to be touching.

Stand and raise your athame in salute. Say:

*Thank you, Lord and Lady, for this time spent in your presence. We came together in love and friendship; so let us go our separate ways. My thanks for watching over me, for guarding me, and for guiding me. Help me spread the love of the Craft throughout all lives I may touch.*

If several coven members are in the Circle, they walk around the Circle to pass the HP or HPS, kissing as they pass. When all are back in their places, say:

*Merry did we meet, so merry may we part. And merry may we meet again. So mote it be.*

Everyone should repeat:

*So mote it be!*

Go to the east and, with your athame, cut across the lines of the Circle. Say:

*This Circle is now open.*

All may now leave the Circle if they wish. It is no longer closed and consecrated.

This ritual should be done during the week immediately preceding the full moon. It is best done on a Friday, Saturday, and Sunday.

# Rituals for Academics

## TO INCREASE YOUR GRADES

*Note:* You cannot increase your grades by magic alone. It is said that the gods help those who help themselves. This means that you must still study and work hard. But you *will* then see the results of that work and study in the form of increased grades. In exams, it will seem that only those questions to which you know the answers will be asked.

Cast and consecrate the Circle in the usual way, lighting all the candles, consecrating salt and water and yourself. On the altar, along with the regular altar items, place a small square of paper (about three inches by three inches), a pen, and a bottle of red ink. (Please do not use a ballpoint or marker! Use an old-fashioned dip pen.) The paper should be a linen-based one. It can be pure white or simulated parchment. You will also need to have a copy of one of the magical alphabets (see the appendix) for reference. (You need not be too familiar with the alphabet you will be using, as detailed in chapter 15, where I talk about making talismans for protection.)

Ring the bell three times.

Sit or kneel and contemplate your position in the academic world. Do you know where you want to go; what you would like to do when you graduate? Do you have long-term goals? If not, this might be a good time to ask the gods to bring you enlightenment as to which direction you might go. There is no need to completely commit yourself to anything at this time, but it is helpful to have a general idea of your life's ambition(s).

Then focus your mind on your present situation and the state of your grades in general. You obviously *want* to improve them, or you wouldn't be doing this ritual, so think of them improving. See yourself excited as you receive higher and higher marks. Know the joy of being recognized as someone more than capable. Ring the bell seven times.

Now take the pen and paper. You are going to make a talisman to bring you that concentration and ability to score well. Draw four horizontal lines equidistant across the paper and four vertical ones crossing them, much like an overlarge tic-tac-toe layout. In the spaces between the lines, you are going to write certain words of power, but you will be writing them in one of the ancient magical scripts. You will be writing:

| A | L | L | U | P |
|---|---|---|---|---|
| L | E | I | R | U |
| L | I | G | I | L |
| U | R | I | E | L |
| P | U | L | L | A |

You will notice that some of these words or names of power are there forward, backward, up, and down. This *sigil* is from an old *grimoire*, or book of magic, from the fifteenth century.

Write each of those letters in a square, in the given order, but do not use the regular alphabet; use the magical alphabet equivalent of the letter. In this way you will have to concentrate on what you are doing and so put your energy, your power, into it. You can use any one of the magical alphabets: Theban, Angelic, Runic, or Malachim. Choose one you are not familiar with, so that you will really have to concentrate on what you are doing.

When you have completed the magic square, hold the piece of paper in the smoke of the incense and say:

*As I have worked my power and my energies into this talisman, so let it work for me, bringing me that which I desire in the way of improved grades for my schoolwork. So mote it be.*

Ring the bell nine times. Lay the paper on the altar for the ink to dry thoroughly.

Stand and raise your athame in salute. Say:

*Thank you, Lord and Lady, for this time spent in your presence. We came together in love and friendship; so let us go our separate ways. My thanks for watching over me, for guarding me, and for guiding me. Help me spread the love of the Craft throughout all lives I may touch.*

If several coven members are in the Circle, they walk around the Circle to pass the HP or HPS, kissing as they pass. When all are back in their places, say:

*Merry did we meet, so merry may we part. And merry may we meet again. So mote it be.*

Everyone should repeat:

*So mote it be!*

Go to the east and, with your athame, cut across the lines of the Circle. Say:

*This Circle is now open.*

All may now leave the Circle if they wish. It is no longer closed and consecrated.

This ritual should be done during the week immediately preceding the full moon. It is best done on a Wednesday, a Saturday, or a Sunday. After the ritual, when the ink is dry on the talisman, take it and place it under your pillow. Sleep with it there for three nights, then carry it with you at all times. You may, if you wish, place it in a small, white linen bag.

## TO DO WELL IN AN EXAMINATION

Do the same ritual as above ("To Increase Your Grades"), but use the following words to write on the talisman you create:

| M | I | L | O | N |
|---|---|---|---|---|
| I | R | A | G | O |
| L | A | M | A | L |
| O | G | A | R | I |
| N | O | L | I | M |

This ritual should be done during the week immediately preceding the full moon. It is best done on a Sunday but may be done on a Wednesday or a Saturday.

## TO CREATE HARMONY WITH YOUR TEACHER

Cast and consecrate the Circle in the usual way, lighting all the candles, consecrating salt and water and yourself. On the altar, along with the regular altar items, place two photographs: one of you and one of your teacher. If you do not have a photograph of your teacher, create a drawing of him or her. It doesn't matter if it isn't a good one—just concentrate on the teacher as you do it, telling yourself "This is a picture of [teacher's name]."

Also on the altar is a "placket," a pocket made by sewing together two squares of material, leaving one side open. The best material for this is felt, but it can be of any other natural material. One side should be yellow, and the other light blue. It should be large enough to allow you to slide the two photographs (or drawings) into it.

Ring the bell three times.

Take up the photograph of yourself and, holding it up, say:

*Here am I. I wish to relate well to my teacher; to get along well, to work harmoniously, and to have no misunderstandings or arguments.*

Hold the photograph in the smoke of the incense, then lay it down on the left side of the altar. Take up the photograph (or drawing) of your teacher and, holding it up, say:

*Here is [teacher's name], an understanding, patient teacher who is able to work well and harmoniously with me. He [she] has the patience to explain things well and to make sure I understand everything.*

Place the photograph on the right side of the altar. Take up the placket and hold it open over the incense, so that the smoke of the incense goes up into the placket. Then replace it in the center of the altar. Take your photograph in your left hand and your teacher's photograph in your right hand.

Place them together, face to face, and hold them in the smoke of the incense. Concentrate and see the two of you working well together, in perfect harmony. Slide the two photographs into the placket. Ring the bell seven times. Say:

*Thus do we come together in our thinking and in our working. Two in perfect harmony. So mote it be!*

Ring the bell nine times.
Stand and raise your athame in salute. Say:

*Thank you, Lord and Lady, for this time spent in your presence. We came together in love and friendship; so let us go our separate ways. My thanks for watching over me, for guarding me, and for guiding me. Help me spread the love of the Craft throughout all lives I may touch.*

If several coven members are in the Circle, they walk around the Circle to pass the HP or HPS, kissing as they pass. When all are back in their places, say:

*Merry did we meet, so merry may we part. And merry may we meet again. So mote it be.*

Everyone should repeat:

*So mote it be!*

Go to the east and, with your athame, cut across the lines of the Circle. Say:

*This Circle is now open.*

All may now leave the Circle if they wish. It is no longer closed and consecrated.

This ritual should be done during the week immediately preceding the full moon. It is best done on a Friday, though it may be done on a Wednesday.

Keep the placket safely on your person during all school hours.

# Rituals for Dating

## TO REJECT AN UNDESIRABLE

Cast and consecrate the Circle in the usual way, lighting all the candles, consecrating salt and water and yourself. On the altar, along with the regular altar items, place a piece of paper, pen, and ink (as in "To Increase Your Grades," on page 124; use a dip pen and ink, not a ballpoint or marker pen), reference for a magical alphabet (again, as in "To Increase Your Grades"), dish, and matches.

Ring the bell three times.

On the piece of paper, write the name of the admirer you wish to discourage. Write it in one of the magical alphabets, concentrating on the person all the time you are writing. *Do not wish him or her ill.* Simply see the person as having lost interest in you and wandering away from you. Hold the paper in the smoke of the incense and say:

*Here is [name]. She [he] is a nice person but not a person to whom I wish to be close. Let her be filled with new interests that will overcome her interest in me. Let there be new light and joy in her life, so that she moves easily and happily away from my sphere of influence.*

Hold the paper over the dish and set fire to it. Let it burn and allow the ash to drop into the dish. Say:

*As this symbol of [name] becomes nothing but dust, let her interest in me also become nothing but dust. Let it be something to look back upon but not to look forward to. Let this fire cleanse. And where there are endings there are also beginnings, so let her life be filled with all good things. So mote it be!*

Ring the bell nine times.
Stand and raise your athame in salute. Say:

*Thank you, Lord and Lady, for this time spent in your presence. We came together in love and friendship; so let us go our separate ways. My thanks for watching over me, for guarding me, and for guiding me. Help me spread the love of the Craft throughout all lives I may touch.*

If several coven members are in the Circle, they walk around the Circle to pass the HP or HPS, kissing as they pass. When all are back in their places, say:

*Merry did we meet, so merry may we part. And merry may we meet again. So mote it be.*

Everyone should repeat:

*So mote it be!*

Go to the east and, with your athame, cut across the lines of the Circle. Say:

*This Circle is now open.*

All may now leave the Circle if they wish. It is no longer closed and consecrated.

This ritual should be done during the week immediately preceding the New Moon. It is best done on a Tuesday. After the ritual, take out the dish of ashes and let the wind blow them away. If you can do this on top of a hill (or leaning out of an upper-floor window), it would be especially helpful.

## TO BE NOTICED BY ANOTHER

*Note:* Since we do not try to alter other people to make them do something they would not normally do, you must work on *yourself* so that you will be noticed, rather than working to make the other person notice you. But one way to come close to a specific person is to work with his astrological sun sign. For example, if he is a Virgo, then work on being noticed by a Virgo. It may well turn out that the very one you had in mind is the one affected, but there might well be another Virgo you hadn't even known about who suddenly comes on the scene, "noticing" you and being attracted to you. He may well turn out to be even better than the Virgo you first had in mind!

Caste and consecrate the Circle in the usual way, lighting all the candles, consecrating salt and water and yourself. On the altar, along with the regular altar items, place two apples and a long nail (the Gypsies would use a horseshoe nail). If you can't find a good long nail, a short (about four to six inches) piece of dowel wood, like a wooden skewer, will do. Place these alongside your athame in the center of the altar.

Ring the bell three times.

With your athame, cut one of the apples *crosswise* (not down from the stem). This will reveal the hidden pentagram of seeds within the apple. Take the top half (the half with the stem) and, with the tip of your athame, scratch your name in the pulpy flesh. Set it down to your right, the lower half of it off to your left.

Take up the second apple and do the same thing, cutting it crosswise. Set the top half of that off to the left and work on the lower half. In the fleshy pulp of this, scratch the astrological sign of the type of person you would like to notice you. Try not to think of any specific person; think of the *type* of person—interests, likes and dislikes, eye and hair coloring, and so forth.

Take up your top half (the one with your name in it), from where you placed it on your right, and put the two halves together. Push the nail, or wooden skewer, through from top (stem) to bottom, holding the two halves together. Now pass the assembled "apple" through the smoke of the incense and say:

*Lord and Lady, let me be noticed by another, if it is right for us. Let me share my love and joy with another. Help me display all that is worthy in myself; my inner and my outer love and beauty. So mote it be!*

If there is someone else in the Circle who wishes to do the same rite, they may use the other two apple halves. Otherwise, those two halves will be given to the gods in libation after the Circle.

Lay the assembled apple in the center of the Circle. Stand and raise your athame in salute. Say:

*Thank you, Lord and Lady, for this time spent in your presence. We came together in love and friendship; so let us go our separate ways. My thanks for watching over me, for guarding me, and for guiding me. Help me spread the love of the Craft throughout all lives I may touch.*

If several coven members are in the Circle, they walk around the Circle to pass the HP or HPS, kissing as they pass. When all are back in their places, say:

*Merry did we meet, so merry may we part. And merry may we meet again. So mote it be.*

Everyone should repeat:

*So mote it be!*

Go to the east and, with your athame, cut across the lines of the Circle. Say:

*This Circle is now open.*

All may now leave the Circle if they wish. It is no longer closed and consecrated.

This ritual is best performed on a Friday just before, and as close as possible to, the full moon. After the ritual, take the assembled apple and bury it in the ground beneath an oak tree or a rosebush.

# Finding Others With Similar Interest

Many young Witches form covens with schoolmates. This can be a good idea, but caution should be exercised. As I have mentioned, many are attracted to Wicca for the wrong reasons. Take your time forming a coven, if that is what you want to do. Really get to know the other members; know why they want to join and what they expect from the group.

The best way to start is to let it be known (discreetly) that you are starting a study group. You don't even have to make it a Witchcraft study group; it can be a New Age group, a folklore group, an astrology group, or anything similar. You can simply talk about your interests with one another (and in this way find who is especially attracted to the Craft, and why), or you can take a book or books (see the bibliography) for study and discussion.

Don't make your group bizarre, or you will attract all the wrong people. I have been a guest on many television talk shows, and I always make a point of wearing a suit and looking as "normal" as possible. Other "Witches" appear on shows wearing robes—usually black! Robes are for ritual use, not for public appearances. So try to be ordinary, and you will find others who are as sincere in their search for the Craft as you are.

As I've said, don't try to rush into forming a coven. But do know that you can start a coven with as few as two people. A single person is a solitary, but more than that makes a coven. At the other end of the scale, you don't want more than about a dozen people in a coven, or it will be too large and unmanageable. If you do happen to have a really large number of good people wanting to become Witches, then start two covens, or more. As we've covered in this book, start with one person performing a Self-Dedication, then go on to initiate the others.

There are Web sites on the Internet put together by teenage Witches. As might be expected, some are good and some are not. Make up your own mind about what other people have to say. Where the Internet is concerned, do not give out your real name and address. From many of these sites you can find what others are doing and get ideas. To be on the safe side, stick to your own circle of friends, at least at the beginning.

## A Teen's Prayer for Guidance

*Eternal parents, my dearest Mother and Father, I pray that you guide me through these confusing times and help me to make the wisest decisions in order to better my life. I pray that you help me to understand my parents and help them to understand me. Let my parents respect my opinions and understand that I am different from them and will not always agree with their views on life. I want to respect and love my parents on this earth, as I do you, my eternal Mother and Father, so I ask that you lead me in the right direction. Blessed Be.*
—Sasha Lovejoy, in *The Wiccan Prayer Book* by Mark Ventimiglia

# ~ 9 ~

# Witchcraft in the Office

There is no more reason for Witchcraft to be present in the office (or absent from it) than there is for Christianity, Judaism, or any other religion. Normally, religious beliefs do not come into play as a part of everyday office business. But as in so many other aspects of life, the fact that you are a Witch can make a subtle difference to your chances of success or failure in business. Back in 1971, Max Gunther, a freelance writer who contributed to many of the major magazines of the time, wrote a book called *Wall Street and Witchcraft*. In it, Gunther examined a wide variety of solitary Witches and Wiccan covens that played the stock market and came out ahead . . . *far* ahead! Although Gunther's appreciation of Witchcraft, if we may call it that, was rather flippant, he did reveal a number of facts. These included profiling groups who doubled their money every three years while basing their investments on astrology, and quadrupled savings in six months going strictly by the tarot. I'll have a look at these approaches later on.

---

*I've made about thirty grand on the market in 1970 alone. I know the Tarot is responsible because now my hunches feel right. I mean, I feel secure in them, I feel safe following them up. In the old days I never had this feeling. Whenever I'd buy a stock I'd feel miserable for days after, afraid I'd made another damned-fool mistake. The market was always a wild gamble for me. But now it's—well, it seems to be nearly a sure thing.*

—Max Gunther, *Wall Street and Witchcraft*

---

# The Office as a Temple

It is not necessary to actually cast a Circle in your office to achieve this sort of success. In fact, you don't even need to have an altar, a deity figure, or a single candle in order to conduct rituals that can lead to prosperity.

Several chapters back, I brought up the fact that Witches believe in a threefold return: Do good and you get back three times the good, but do harm and that, too, will come back in triples. This works just as much in the business world as anywhere else.

But what about the ethics of Witchcraft? The only Wiccan law is, "An it harm none, do what thou wilt." So as long as what you do brings no harm to anyone, you can play the stock market all you like and do magic to promote yourself in the business world.

In fact, I did just that myself, back in the 1960s, when I had not been long in the United States. At the time, I worked for an international airline as a lowly reservations clerk. The department in which I worked had lost its supervisor, who had been transferred to another department and was not replaced. I began to take on the responsibilities of that position myself, simply because someone had to take charge in order to get things done. But I found that the more I did, the more it was taken for granted, and soon I began to feel used. I was doing supervisory work while being paid a low clerical salary. To actually be promoted to the supervisor position would mean a pay increase which, with a wife and two small children to support, would have been more than welcome. So I did some magic to get the job. There was no one else apparently capable at the time, so I wasn't working against anyone. I just did the magic and waited. Within a week, I got the promotion and the raise.

No one who had been working at the airline for as short a time as I had, had ever been promoted to such a position so quickly. The skeptic would say that the promotion was coming anyway, and perhaps it was. But the point is, I did not hesitate to use magic to try to bring it to me when I felt I deserved it, and without trampling on anyone else to do so.

In this case, I did the magical ritual at home, not in the office. There are few times that you would need to do magical work in the office, even if you were able to, since the effects are not immediate. Your home, temple, or sacred Circle is the obvious place to work: You have the ideal surroundings and necessary tools. But if it is really necessary, magic can be done right there in your office.

# The Power of Suggestion

I very much believe that we can create our own realities. In fact, this has been borne out for me throughout my life. In simplest terms, we can say that to think positive will lead to positive results. In business, it is often necessary to think positive! But most people, most *cowans* (non-Witches), will think in terms of such as, "Oh, God, please let this happen!" Usually, they are not asking the god in whom they believe for help; they are using the term more as an expletive. As I mentioned in chapter 7, when you are working magic you need to think of the desired result having been *obtained*. Rather than asking for something to happen, you should give thanks that it *has* come about—even though, at this point, you don't know that it has. Let's look at an example.

If Charley Cowan is hoping for a contract to be offered to him, he may well spend most of his time worrying about what will happen if it doesn't materialize, and what the chances are of it happening or not happening. He will be on tenterhooks until he hears one way or the other.

On the other hand, in the same situation Diana Hunt—who happens to be a member of the Old Religion—would spend her time thinking about exactly *what* she wants to be included in the contract and focusing on the contract actually being signed. In her mind's eye, she will see it being offered to her and see herself signing it, with the subsequent celebration. Nine times out of ten, it is the Diana Hunt who gets the contract and the Charley Cowan who does not. The reason is simply the positive thinking of the Witch.

For really important work, a Wiccan will not hesitate to do a simple ritual right there in the office, if there is the privacy to allow it. This might be no more than lighting a candle or burning some incense as you meditate and concentrate on what is to be achieved. Many Witches, by the way, have burned incense in their offices under the pretext of getting rid of smells such as someone else's cigarette smoke! But unless you are in the position of having your own private office, where you can make yourself unavailable if you wish, you are unlikely to be able to do any true rituals at work. This need not be important, for there are other things you can do, even if you only have a desk in a small partitioned area.

> *The usual mistake made by beginners is to set aside any form of apprenticeship, to tackle the most difficult problems right away and to get discouraged at the first failure. A little modesty is always a good thing. The discredit unjustly suffered by capable radiesthetists is often due to foolhardy beginners.*
> —Abbé Mermet, *Principles and Practice of Radiesthesia*

# Pendulum Power

The use of a pendulum is known as radiesthesia. It is an ages-old practice often used by Witches with very good results. It is not so much magic as it is drawing on your inner awareness, tuning in to a greater consciousness through your Higher Self. In business, it can be used for a variety of things, including choosing worthwhile investments, picking career-enhancing employees or employers, finding the most propitious time for contract signing, and so on.

A pendulum can be any object suspended from a chain, ribbon, string, or the like. Commercially produced pendula are available in a wide variety of styles, but it is quite possible to make your own. A temporary pendulum can be made by simply suspending a ring on the end of a length of thread or ribbon. Or you can use a pendant necklace on its own chain. I have—in an emergency, in an office situation—actually made a temporary pendulum by connecting a number of paper clips and hanging a staple remover from the end!

The best length for the chain or thread will be determined by the length of your arm. Hold the end of the thread and, resting your elbow on a table, allow the pendulum to hang down. Hold the chain between your thumb and forefinger only. The pendulum itself should hang just off the surface of the table. This generally gives a length of about nine to twelve inches. Some Witches say the length should be exactly nine inches, since nine is a number with magical connotations.

Holding the pendulum in this way, and trying to hold it still, you will find that in fact it will start to swing gently backward and forward when you ask a question of it. If the answer to the question you ask is "Yes," then it will swing toward you and away from you. If the answer is "No," it will swing across you. If the question you ask is ambiguous in any way, or the answer is indefinite, then it will either not swing at all or swing in a circle.[19]

You can use an answer card if you wish, to be certain as to how it is swinging. Sometimes the arc of the swing is very small, and a card can help you see it. You can also use different answer cards for different things. For example, if you are asking about the passage of time you can either ask directly, "Will it be one hour?" and go on to ask about a variety of other

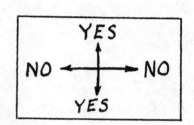

times until you get a "Yes," or you can use a card with a variety of times marked on it and see along which line the pendulum swings.

The pendulum can be very useful in making a decision between two or more possibilities. It can also be good for finding something that has been lost. You can draw a sketch map of the area where the item was lost and slowly move the finger of your left hand over the map while holding the pendulum with your right hand and asking if the object is where you are pointing.

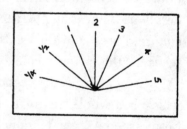

Another use of the pendulum in the office is in choosing investments. There are several ways of going about this. You can list the companies in which you are interested, or use a listing from a newspaper or elsewhere, and start with the point of the pendulum over the name of the company. If the listing has the names very close together, simply point to the name with your left hand (or with a pen or other pointer in your left hand) and hold the pendulum over the answer card with your right hand. Ask pertinent questions about the company, from the perspective of whether or not you should buy stock. Make all your questions such that they can be answered "Yes" or "No."

If you're considering a number of companies and don't know which one would

19. If you are left-handed, hold it in that hand. You may find the swings are the opposite of those for a right-handed person. You may have to experiment to find out how it swings for you.

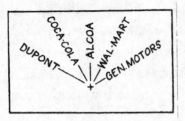

be best, write their names on a card, hold the pendulum at the bottom center point, and ask which would be the best one in which to invest. The pendulum should swing along the line of one name. In the same way, the pendulum can also be used for determining the best times or dates for business transactions. When it comes to determining schedules, however, most Wiccans turn to astrology.

## Astrological Timing for Business

The planets have a definite influence on our lives and on our businesses. You don't have to be an accomplished astrologer to work out many of the simpler decisions in business life. Of the ten planets used in astrology—sun, moon (not actually planets, of course), Mercury, Venus, Mars, Jupiter, Saturn, Uranus, Neptune, and Pluto—Mercury in particular is connected with merchants and merchandise. However, several others have some connection with particular aspects of the business world. For example, Jupiter is connected to the wine harvest; the sun to agriculture, herds, and flocks; Neptune to sailors and ships; Saturn to the sowing of seeds. As the various planets pass through the twelve houses, they exert influences.

It is not within the scope of this book to cover all the intricacies of astrology, which is a whole art in itself, but there are some things worth knowing. Many businesspeople, incidentally, do strongly believe in astrological forecasts and employ professional astrologers to work with them and their companies.

> *Nothing exists nor happens in the visible sky that is not sensed in some hidden moment by the faculties of Earth and Nature: these faculties of the spirit here on Earth are as much affected as the sky itself.*
> —Johannes Kepler (1571–1630), *De Stella Nova*

It appears that the movements of the three largest planets, Jupiter, Saturn, and Uranus, affect major, long-term economic markets. Movements of the smaller planets—Earth, Mars, Mercury, and Venus—produce smaller variations in the markets. Jupiter-Saturn conjunctions, which occur only about once every twenty years, signal a stock market downturn. But when Jupiter and Uranus are 120 degrees apart (known as in trine), the stock market climbs. Trines by Jupiter and Saturn are also worthwhile.

*THE CONSTELLATIONS AND THE STARS — ALBRECHT DÜRER (1515)*

Many astrologers place strong emphasis on the "natal" chart, as it were, of the individual company—the chart based on the company's date of incorporation. There are various directories that will give you this date for the company in which you are interested—Standard & Poor, or Thomas's Register, for example. From these you can learn not only the day that the company was incorporated but also the place, which is important in astrology.

The third thing you need to know is the hour that it was "born." This is seldom recorded. Some astrologers therefore use a general time of noon, while others employ the start of the next business day—9 A.M.—since this is when the business really started to function. With these three pieces of information, it is possible to draw a natal horoscope for the company in which you are interested.

Using this chart as you would an individual's, you can see the potential ups and downs to come. Buy when the company is at a low, knowing—from the chart—that a high is coming. Look particularly for favorable relationships among Jupiter, Uranus, and Venus, together with the sun, for the company.

> Once [the astrologer] has drawn his chart—a map of the sky as it looked, for example, from your place of birth in the hour you were born—he has what he believes is a kind of cosmic-energy map, showing what types and intensities of energy were impinging on your body's electronic system when you drew your first breath. This particular bundle of energies, he believes, has much to do with shaping your character and eventual destiny. He calls this your natal chart. By comparing your natal chart with a sky-map (or bundle of energies) on any future day, he thinks he can tell you in general terms what will happen to you on that day.
> —Max Gunther, *Wall Street and Witchcraft*

## It's in the Cards

Using the tarot to gain insight into stock market fluctuations and business in general can also be useful and accurate. I recommend sticking to simple layouts of the cards. One I have found useful for short-term investing is as follows.

Shuffle the cards while concentrating on the stock or stocks in which are you are interested. Cut the cards to the left with your left hand into three piles. Pick them up from the center pile first, so that they fall into a different order from that you laid down. Count down seven cards from the top and lay out this seventh card. Continue to count another seven, laying this to the right of the first card. Count down seven more and lay that below the other two.

The first card is an indication of the short-term outlook for that stock. The second is the long-term outlook. The third card is the probable result for you, personally, of investing in that stock.

The key here, of course, is in the interpretation of the cards. Rather than going by the traditional "meaning" of the card given in many books, and usually in the little handbook that comes with the deck you buy, consider what the card seems to say to you. Turn over the card and see what, in the picture, strikes you first.

The cards of the Minor Arcana can give you a good general feel for a situation. The pentacles suit ties in with money and is frequently a harbinger of profit, unless the card is reversed (upside down). In this case, it is still not a bad card; it just means that there will be delays and unforeseen glitches along the way. The degree of profit can be gauged by the number of the card (with ace being equivalent to one). The swords suit can be an ominous one, frequently indicating a downturn in the market. Here, though, if it is reversed, the fall will not be as bad as at first feared. The cups suit (whether upright or reversed) signals a smooth market with few fluctuations. The wands suit shows that you are going to have to stay on top and do a bit of juggling to come out ahead. Taking the ace as the lowest card, the lower numbers indicate minor forces at work in the market; the higher numbers show more intense activity.

The real core of the information from the tarot cards comes from the Major Arcana, though these cards can be much more difficult to interpret. They all have their meanings, but none of them are specific except in the context of the particular reading you are doing. In other words, the Hermit (for example) can show a dozen or more different things at different times for different people. Taking a popular deck such as the Rider-Waite deck, the first thing you might notice when you turn over the hermit card is the staff on which he leans. This you might interpret as indicating that the stock you are considering needs support or it is likely to fall. But if, when you turn over the card, you are most struck by the lantern and its shining light, then you might interpret this as indicating that the stock is throwing out brilliance, rising to a new height. You might be struck by the face of the Hermit looking downward, or the fact that he seems to be standing on a mountaintop.

There are, then, many different things that could strike you as you turn over each card, so it is not possible to simply say that such-and-such a card means so-and-so. It is what it means to *you*, at that particular moment, that is pertinent.

Use a tarot deck that has full pictures for every card. I have mentioned the Rider-Waite deck and would also mention my own Buckland Romani Tarot Deck. There are many out there; look at them and see which seems to attract you most. Go with your feelings.

> *The [tarot] cards are reflections of the mind. If there's nothing in your mind, there won't be anything in the cards.*
> —Stuart Kaplan

## Treasure Maps

A magical technique used by many Witches is the making of a treasure map. This is basically a means of focusing your energies on that which you desire. Making one is a ritual in itself, which you could well do at your desk in your office. I describe various such maps in my book *Practical Color Magick*, but here I'll just focus on the astrologically based form, which can easily fit right into the office atmosphere.

The basis of a treasure map is acknowledgment of the source of all things—God/Goddess/All-That-Is. In the Craft, we think generally in terms of the Lord and the Lady, from whom all things are possible. To start drawing your treasure map, place the God and Goddess in the center. You can either draw representations of them or use symbols such as a pentagram, sun and moon, yin-yang, or something similar. As you draw the figure(s) or symbol(s), see the Lord and Lady in your mind's eye and send them a silent prayer. Throughout the construction of this

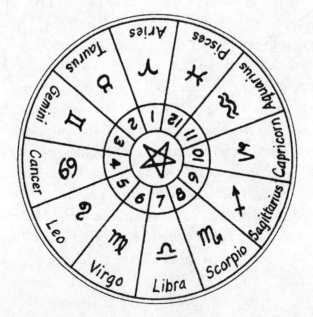

map, I strongly urge you to draw everything yourself, rather than cutting out pictures and sticking them on the map. It doesn't matter how poor an artist you are; what is important is the power or energy you put into doing the drawing. (In chapter 20, I'll be talking about making talismans, and I'll again emphasize the need to put your energies into that which you create.)

You are going to be drawing an astrological wheel, divided into the twelve houses of the Zodiac. The God/Goddess symbols are in the center, as the "Source." The houses start on the left, with Aries, and run counterclockwise. Each house is equated with particular things, as follows:

FIRST HOUSE—Appearance, health, outward behavior, temperament.

SECOND HOUSE—Financial condition, possessions.

THIRD HOUSE—Brothers, sisters, communication, mental aptitudes, perceptive abilities.

FOURTH HOUSE—Beginning and end of life, domestic affairs, the home, real estate, one of the parents.

FIFTH HOUSE—Creative expressions, love affairs, pets, sexual urges, speculation.

SIXTH HOUSE—Employer-employee relationships, hygiene, servants, sickness, veterinarians.

SEVENTH HOUSE—Business partners, contracts, marriage partners, obvious enemies.

EIGHTH HOUSE—Attitude toward life and death, gifts, partner's money, surgery.

NINTH HOUSE—Foreigners and foreign countries, long journeys, psychic development, publishing, religious and philosophical outlooks.

TENTH HOUSE—Employment, the other parent (from the one in the Fourth House), reputation, social status, standing in the community.

ELEVENTH HOUSE—Financial condition of the employer, friends, income from business when self-employed, social alliances.

TWELFTH HOUSE—Clandestine affairs, isolation, large animals, hospitalization, secret enemies, service to others.

Suppose you wish to (a) invest in a telecommunications company, (b) obtain backing for business expansion, (c) take a trip to Europe, and (d) sign a particular contract. These would fall into (a) the third house, communication; (b) the second house, financial condition; (c) the ninth house, long journeys; and (d) the seventh house, contracts.

On your blank treasure map, draw small pictures to represent each of these things. For example, in the third house, draw a picture of yourself alongside a picture of a telecommunications satellite, or the logo of the company in which you are interested. In the second house, draw yourself surrounded by money—coins and bills. In the ninth house, draw yourself and the Eiffel Tower, or the like (depending upon where you might want to go). In the seventh house, draw yourself holding up a signed contract.

All of these little pictures can be very simply drawn but, as you draw them, *see the thing you desire flowing from the source* (from the God and Goddess) to you. See yourself actually in possession of what you want. As you draw yourself and the money in the second house, for example, see the God and the Goddess directing money to you; see yourself getting that financial backing for the expansion you have in mind.

It helps to use a variety of bright colors when doing these drawings. Also color the background of the houses. Traditional colors are:

First House—Red.
Second House—Yellow.
Third House—Violet.
Fourth House—Green.
Fifth House—Orange.
Sixth House—Violet.
Seventh House—Yellow.
Eighth House—Red.
Ninth House—Purple.
Tenth House—Blue.
Eleventh House—Indigo.
Twelfth House—Indigo.

You don't need to color all the houses, just those in which you are working. When you have finished your treasure map, hang it in a place where you will constantly see it. If you have a glass top on your desk, slide it under the glass. Tape it on the side of your filing cabinet. Hang it on the back of your office door. Put it on the side of your computer. By doing this, you will come into contact with it a number of times a day, and each time you will be reminded of your goals. Each time you will revitalize the energy you put into making the treasure map and so bring about that which you desire. You will "cause change to occur in conformity with Will."

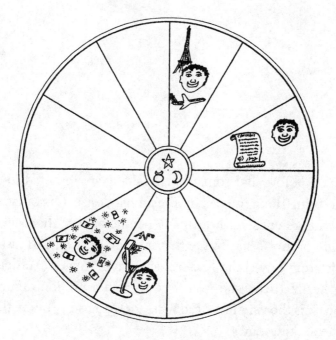

TREASURE MAP

# ~ 10 ~

# Witchcraft for Romance

Such is the draw of love and romance that many are tempted to use Witchcraft and magic to bring them the person they most desire. Of course this is not possible. You have only to consider how many people believe themselves to be madly in love with a film or music star to see that it could not work. If just a tiny fraction of the people desiring (say) Julia Roberts were able to work sufficiently powerful magic to bring her to them, she would be torn in a million different directions! (Though perhaps it is the very fact of so many desiring so strongly that all these energies cancel one another out.)

Remember the main tenet of Witchcraft: "And it harm none . . ." You must do nothing that will interfere with the free will of another. You *must not*, therefore, use magic to force someone to love you.

## Where to Direct Your Energies

This is not to say that you cannot use magic in the field of love and attraction. You most certainly can. It is all a question of where you direct your energies. And where better than on yourself?

Through magic you can give yourself an allure—an attraction that will draw others to you. And those so drawn to you may well include the particular person you desire without your having actually directed your power at him or her. In other words, rather than reaching out magically to grab hold of that person and force her to you, you will have caused her to be attracted to you and to come to you of her own free will. This is important.

Work on yourself, therefore, to make yourself attractive. There are several ways of doing this, the most effective being to pay attention to your appearance, hygiene, speech, manners, disposition—all these areas that many people just let slide. But the most simple yet effective magical way of working is through candle burning.

> The pleasure of the soul appears to be found in the journey of discovery, the unfolding revelation of expanding insight and experience. —Anthony Lawlor

## GLAMOUR SPELL—TO MAKE YOURSELF ATTRACTIVE TO OTHERS

The traditional glamour spell was one of deception. It was used to create an illusion—to make an old person appear young, or vice versa, for example. It was usually done to camouflage something or someone, so that they would not be noticed. Here, however, I am using it in the sense of truly making someone more glamorous and hence more desirable.

This ritual should be started on a Friday and repeated every day until the following Friday. This final Friday should be as close to (before) the full moon as possible.

In the center of your altar, place a candle to represent yourself—the petitioner. This should be carefully prepared. Use a candle of your own astral color (see the appendix), depending upon your birth date, and anoint it with oil. Extra-virgin olive oil is good for this, though a scented oil such as lavender or rose will also work well. Rub the oil on the candle from its middle outward toward the end. Work first from the middle to the base and then from the middle to the top of the candle until it has been completely anointed. As you rub on the oil, think of yourself as extremely attractive to others. In your mind's eye, see other people wanting to be with you, enjoying your company, and admiring you.

In a circle around your candle, stand up six pink candles. These should also be anointed with oil. As you anoint the pink candles, think of the qualities that you want in yourself. Think of your physical appearance and how you might like to improve it—your complexion, hair color and quality, teeth, deportment, and so on. Also consider qualities such as your sense of humor, intelligence, personality, and generosity. You can concentrate on a different quality for each candle if you wish, and you can use more than six, if necessary. These pink candles should stand in a circle, a distance of at least six inches from your petitioner candle.

As with any ritual Circle, stand properly prepared before the altar. The candles beyond the Circle should be lighted, but not the four quarter candles around the Circle, the altar candles, or the glamour candles on the altar. Proceed with the usual opening of the Circle, as for any Esbat or other ritual work. Then ring the bell three times and kneel before the altar.

> *Lord and Lady, I am here with a personal plea. I desire to bring a special love into my life. To do so, I wish to improve myself in all ways, both within and without. Work with me as I use these candles to draw to me that which I desire. Let everything I do be for the good of all and let none be harmed by anything I do. So mote it be.*

Ring the bell seven times, then light the central petitioner candle.

> *Here I stand, represented by this candle. Let my light shine forth as does this candle flame. Let me be ready and able to absorb all those things that I desire for myself. So mote it be.*

Light each of the pink candles. As you do so, concentrate on the qualities which you would like to see in yourself. See these qualities emanating from the candle flames, reaching out toward the candle in the center, which is you. When you have lighted all the pink candles, take up the incense and move the censer around so that the smoke drifts across all the candles on the altar. Replace the censer and then sit or kneel and meditate on what it is you want to achieve. See yourself as a new person, with all these qualities you want. See others coming to you, smiling and obviously happy to be with you. See yourself as popular and sought after.

After several minutes of this, move the pink candles one by one inward about an inch toward your own candle. You will be repeating this ritual every day for a week; judge the distance they need to be moved so that they will finally all touch your candle in the middle at the end of that period.

When you have moved each of the candles, ring the bell three times, then stand and raise your athame in salute. Say:

*Thank you, Lord and Lady, for this time spent together. We came together in love and friendship; so let us go our separate ways. My thanks for watching over me, for guarding me, and for guiding me. Help me spread the love of the Craft throughout all lives I may touch.*

If several coven members are in the Circle, they walk around the Circle to pass you, embracing and kissing you as they pass. When all are back in their places, say:

*Merry did we meet, so merry may we part. And merry may we meet again. So mote it be.*

Everyone should repeat:

*So mote it be!*

Go to the east and, with your athame, cut across the lines of the Circle. Say:

*This Circle is now open.*

All may now leave the Circle if they wish. It is no longer closed and consecrated. Extinguish the petitioner and pink candles; the pink ones first, and then the petitioner.

On the last day that you do this ritual, when you move the pink candles in to finally touch your petitioner candle, feel all the qualities you desired bursting forth within you. Feel and *know* that you are a changed person.

Although you may have been working on improving yourself so that you will be attractive to a particular person, when you have succeeded with your magic you may well find that there is another person you had never considered before who is actually far more suitable for you than the one you originally had in mind.

> *Playing is a basic animal instinct. We are at our most appealing when at play.*
> —Ilse Crawford

# Discovering Your Future Mate

There are many old methods used to find out who will be your future spouse. Among them is the following: Take an apple and hold it up in the light of a full moon. This should be the pure light, so if you are indoors, open the window and let the unobstructed light of the moon shine on the apple. Taking your athame, carefully peel the apple, trying to keep the peel in one long unbroken length. When you have done this, throw the peel over your left shoulder while asking the gods to indicate who will be your true mate. Look, then, at where the peel has landed. It is said that it will land in the shape of the initial letter or letters of the one who will be your true love.

It is also said that if you count nine stars in the sky at night, and repeat this for nine nights in a row, you will have a dream of your future spouse. If you are in a hurry, you can simply stare hard at the brightest star in the sky and blink nine times. This, it is said, will ensure that you dream of your future spouse that same night.

A more accurate method, I find, is to skry. "Skrying" is crystal gazing, or gazing into any reflective surface. If you don't have a crystal ball, you can use a clear glass of water. Place a glass tumbler, filled to the brim with fresh water, on a piece of black cloth on a small table. You can, of course, do this on your altar if you prefer. The black cloth is there so that as you gaze down into the water, your eyes will not be distracted by anything around it. It helps to have incense burning while you do this. I recommend myrrh or sandalwood.

Have just one candle burning for illumination and place it behind you, so that you do not see it reflected directly in the crystal ball or glass of water. Sit comfortably and build the white light around you, as described in chapter 3. When you have erected this protective barrier, turn your concentration onto the subject of your future partner in life. Don't try to picture anyone in particular; just think about seeing who it will be.

Open your eyes and gaze down into the tumbler of water. You can blink if you have to; there's no need to gaze fixedly. Gradually, you will see a face or figure appear. It may be that prior to this appearance, the water will seem to cloud over or fill with smoke. Just continue gazing, and the smoke will slowly clear. It will leave a picture of the one who will be your future partner in life.

Sometimes the picture you get is not specific. It is quite often symbolic. Make a note of everything you see, even if it seems to have no bearing whatsoever on what you are looking for. Later, when you review your notes, you will see the clues and (hopefully) make the connections. For example, you may see not a person but a bridge or several bridges over a river. Later you realize that someone you know, and who could possibly be "Mr. or Ms. Right," is named Bridges.

A Romani custom is to burn frankincense while skrying and to say:

*Skry, skry, skry for me.*
*Bring the face that I must see.*
*Let me gaze on my future mate*
*To know which lover will be my fate.*

---

**Prayer to Find a Compatible Spouse**

*Dearest Mother, I want to marry but I have not met the right person. Please lead me to someone who will love and understand me, and whom I can love and understand; someone with whom I can share the joys of a Wiccan life. Thank you, Mother, for I have faith that you have heard me and will answer my prayer. Blessed Be.* —Mark Ventimiglia, *The Wiccan Prayer Book*

---

# To Encourage Someone Who Is Shy

There is an old spell to give courage to a lover who is shy about presenting him- or herself. For this you need to obtain a piece of clothing belonging to the person, preferably something that has been next to the skin. Failing this, a handkerchief will do. Fill the cloth with seven acorns that you have found in the woods. For those who live in the city, there is usually a park within easy distance where you can find acorns. If all else fails, have someone else get them for you or, as a last resort, buy them.

Wrap the acorns in the cloth and bind it around with red ribbon or wool. Place the bundle under your pillow and sleep with it there for three nights in a row. Then take the bundle and bury it under a rosebush. Starting in the east, walk about the bush three times, *deosil*, calling out the person's name. Within a moon's time (a month), it is said that the person will gain the courage to approach you.

> If a girl has quarreled with her lover, she may get him back by taking a needle and drawing a little blood from the third finger of the left hand. Using the needle as a pen, she writes her initials and his in blood on an ironwood chip, draws three circles around the letters, and buries the chip in the ground. The recreant boyfriend will be hanging round again in three days or less.
> —Vance Randolph, *Ozark Superstitions*

# Discouraging Someone Who Doesn't Interest You

Many times you find someone is attracted to you when you are not in the least attracted to them. It can often be hard to get rid of such a person. There is an old country spell to do just that, however, and many Witches have made use of it. The trick here is not to simply get rid of the person, but to find someone who is better suited for him and whom he will find much more attractive.

This should be started on a Sunday, if possible in the waning cycle of the moon (but see below for the best timing). On a white sheet of paper, write your own name on the left-hand side and that of your unwanted suitor just below it. Write these names in black ink. Leave room on the right-hand side of the paper. Draw a red circle around the two names and then roll up the paper. Tie it with a blue ribbon and place it in the bottom drawer of a chest of drawers.

The following Friday, undo the paper and, with a green pen, scribble around the red circle, canceling it out. Then draw a large red heart on the right-hand side of the paper. Again roll it up, tie it with the blue ribbon, and place it in the middle drawer of the chest of drawers.

The following Thursday, undo the paper. With the black pen, scratch out the name of your admirer and rewrite it inside the red heart. Draw red, black, and green circles around the heart. Roll up the paper, tie it with the blue ribbon, and place it in the top drawer of the chest of drawers. Leave it there for a full moon's time (one month). During this time, your admirer will find someone else he thinks is more attractive and will leave you alone.

The timing for this magic may be a little tricky. You want to finish on a Thursday that is as close as possible to the new moon—in other words, in the waning cycle of the moon. Mark this on the calendar, then count backward from it to the previous Friday, and then to the Sunday before that. It may well mean that the start of the ritual, on the Sunday, falls into the waxing cycle of the moon. What is important is that it *terminate* in the waning cycle.

## To Develop True Love

When you have found the right person for you, it can be reassuring to magically ensure that the love will only grow and not diminish over time. Here you are not going against anyone's free will, for your lover has already declared his or her love for you. You are merely reinforcing what is already there.

Make a placket out of two pieces of cloth. Felt is best, though cotton or silk can be used. The placket should be about three or four inches square, depending on the size of the photographs that you are going to use (see below). One piece of felt should be pink, and the other blue; the thread used to join them should be red. Sew the pieces together along three of the sides, leaving the fourth side open.

Set up your altar with the placket lying in the middle. Beside it place a photograph of yourself and one of your lover. If you have just one photograph of the two of you together, then this will do, but make sure there is no one else in the picture. Have needle and red thread available on the altar also.

This ritual should be done on a Friday prior to the full moon. Start your ritual in the usual way. As with any ritual Circle, stand properly prepared before the altar. The candles are alight beyond the Circle, but not the four quarter candles around the circle, nor the altar candles. Proceed with the usual opening of the Circle, as for any Esbat or other ritual work. Then ring the bell three times and kneel before the altar. Say:

*I am here to request of the Lady and her Lord that the love shared between myself [name] and my love [name] be ever present, only growing in intensity over the years. We have come together through the agencies of the gods and would remain in that sublime state for all time.*

Take up the placket and hold it in the smoke of the incense. Make sure the smoke gets inside the placket as well as all around the outside. Lay it down and pick up the photographs. Cense those also. Then hold the placket in your left hand and the photographs in your right. Say:

*Here are representations of myself and my love. I place them safely and securely inside this sacred placket . . . [Do so, face to face] . . . in the knowledge that I am symbolically placing them inside the security of time watched over by the gods. Let our love blossom and grow in this womblike environment, developing a strength and unity that is unbreakable.*

With the threaded needle, sew up the open side of the placket, sealing the photographs inside. Ring the bell seven times and hold the sealed placket over the smoke of the incense, then lay it down again on the altar top. Sit and meditate on the two of you together. See your love growing and blossoming. See yourselves as two flowers whose stems intertwine. Know, in your heart, that nothing can come between the two of you. Pour libations to the gods and drink to them. Ring the bell three times then stand and raise your athame in salute. Say:

*Thank you, Lord and Lady, for this time spent together. We came together in love and friendship; so let us go our separate ways. My thanks are watching over me, for guarding me, and for guiding me. Help me spread the love of the Craft throughout all lives I may touch.*

If several coven members are in the Circle, they walk around the Circle to pass you, embracing and kissing you as they pass. When all are back in their places, say:

*Merry did we meet, so merry may we part. And merry may we meet again. So mote it be.*

Everyone should repeat:

*So mote it be!*

Go to the east and, with your athame, cut across the lines of the Circle. Say:

*This Circle is now open.*

All may now leave the Circle if they wish. It is no longer closed and consecrated.

It is even better if both you and your lover do this ritual together. You can each place your own photograph in the placket and speak all the words together.

# ~ 11 ~

# Witchcraft in Marriage

*Marry in white, you have chosen just right.*
*Marry in blue, your man will be true.*
*Marry in brown, you'll live out of town.*
*Marry in green, ashamed to be seen.*
*Marry in yellow, you've got the wrong fellow.*
*Marry in gray, you'll be a widow someday.*
*Marry in red, wish yourself dead.*
*Marry in black, better turn back.*

—Old folk rhyme

In the Craft, Beltane, the Witch Sabbat at the start of May, is traditionally a time for weddings known as "Handfastings." It is the time of the Sacred Marriage between the God and the Goddess. In a Wiccan Handfasting, the bride represents the Goddess and the groom, the God. The two are not two individuals coming together but two halves that go to make up a whole, complementing and completing.

The foundations of a good Wiccan marriage are mutual respect and support and encouragement for each other's interests and accomplishments. In a Wiccan coven, it is said that each of the coven members is like the spoke of a wheel; none is either first or last. All are necessary to make up the whole.

So it is in marriage. Neither one is first nor last; both are of equal importance. Ideally your marriage partner is not just your wife or husband but also your best friend. Perhaps this has become something of a cliché—but in Wicca, it is true.

> *The marriage means the two that are one, the two become one flesh . . . if you are acquiescing constantly to it instead of to individual personal whim, you come to realize that that is true—the two really are one.*
>
> —Joseph Campbell, *The Power of Myth*

# A Wiccan Wedding

Witches may or may not wish to go through a legal marriage ceremony. If they do, it will be before a justice of the peace or appropriate local official, or it may be at a Unitarian-Universalist church with a ceremony of their own devising.

But what really matters to them is the ritual of Handfasting performed in the sacred Circle. If the High Priest or High Priestess performing the ritual holds the requisite ministerial credentials, this ceremony is sufficient for all things. If not, then the couple may choose to have a simple legal ceremony at some time in addition to the one in the Circle.

In the old days, there was a ritual procession that honored the bride and groom. This was a large, joyful group that traveled the boundaries of the village, stopping at all farms and houses along the way for the couple to receive good wishes and gifts. The couple would either be carried by their coven members or would ride in a small cart, pulled by the coveners, a pony, or even a goat. Flowers, a sign of fertility, would be plentiful both on the cart, carried by the processioners, and strewn along the way.

The procession will end up at the site of the Wiccan Circle. This is decorated with flowers, fruits, and nuts—again, signs and symbols of fertility. The Circle may well be cast in a larger diameter than usual to accommodate the Handfasting activity. The High Priest and High Priestess will be waiting at the east entrance to the Circle, ready to anoint the Witches as they come into the sacred space. Any non–coven members will assemble outside the confines of the Circle itself, as a circle beyond the Circle.

The dress of the couple depends upon their tradition. Some wear white robes, some go skyclad (usually with the whole coven skyclad), some will wear traditional *cowan* dress such as a white wedding gown for the bride and a white tuxedo for the groom. The actual Handfasting rituals vary considerably, depending upon the tradition of the Wiccans involved.

Here is a typical one that could be used by a new hereditary coven, for any family member wishing to expand the family group. It is written with both a High Priest and a High Priestess officiating, but can be easily adapted for just one without the other.

# Wiccan Handfasting Ritual

This ritual should be performed in the waxing cycle of the moon. The Circle is suitably decorated with flowers; all the outside candles are alight. The High Priest (HP) and High Priestess (HPS), properly prepared, greet the bride and groom at the east portal and anoint them with oil—HP anointing the bride and HPS the groom. As they draw the cross within the circle on the forehead and pentagram over the heart, they salute and say:

**HP/HPS:** **Here I do consecrate you in the names of the Lord and the Lady. Be here in peace and love, with honor to all life.**

The bride and groom enter and stand facing the altar, leaving room for HP and HPS. Other coven members enter, are similarly anointed, and stand around the Circle.

HP and HPS move to stand in front of the altar, which has all the tools on it. Along with the regular tools is a three-foot length of red silk ribbon and, if the couple wish to exchange rings, the wedding rings. The candles beyond the Circle are alight, but not the four quarter candles around the Circle itself, or the altar candles. The wine goblet is full.

HP rings the bell three times. HPS takes up her athame, kisses the blade, and holds it high in salute.

**HPS:** **Hail, Lord and Lady. Here I do build a temple of life in which to honor you. Assist me as I lay down the foundation stones on which I will build my cone of power.**

HPS lowers the blade and walks over to the east point in the Circle. She points the tip of the blade at the line drawn on the ground and slowly walks around the

Circle, directing energy as she goes. She continues until she returns to the point where she started. There she raises the athame in salute and describes a pentagram in the air. She kisses the blade and returns to the altar.

HP now walks over to the east point in the Circle, taking with him a lighted taper. He lights the east candle.

> **HP:** **Here is light at the east, where the life-giving sun rises each day. Here is erected the Watchtower of Air, standing guard over this temple of the gods.**

He moves on around to the south and lights that candle from the taper.

> **HP:** **Here is light at the south, where fires rise up to warm and illuminate the earth. Here is erected the Watchtower of Fire, standing guard over this temple of the gods.**

He moves on around to the west and lights that candle from the taper.

> **HP:** **Here is light at the west, where waters move gently to give the moisture of life to the earth. Here is erected the Watchtower of Water, standing guard over this temple of the gods.**

He moves on around to the north and lights that candle from the taper.

> **HP:** **Here is light at the north, where the earth forms a solid foundation for all life. Here is erected the Watchtower of Earth, standing guard over this temple of the gods.**

HP returns to the altar and lights the altar candle(s).

> **HP:** **Here is light that I bring into the temple. Let it light the way through the darkness of ignorance to the world of knowledge. Light to life, in all things.**

HPS again takes up her athame and dips the tip of the blade into the bowl of salt.

> **HPS:** Salt is life. Let this salt be pure and let it purify our lives, as we use it in this rite dedicated to the God and Goddess in whom we believe.

She takes three pinches of the salt and drops them into the water. Moving her athame blade across to the water dish, she dips it in there.

> **HPS:** Let the sacred salt drive out any impurities in this water, that together they may be used in the service of these deities, throughout these rites and at any time and in any way we may use them.

She mixes the water and salt with the athame blade, stirring in a clockwise direction three times around, then lays down the athame and picks up the dish of salted water. She goes to the east point of the Circle and raises the dish.

> **HPS:** I use this sacred liquid now in the building of this, our sacred temple. I dedicate it to the gods, in love and light.

Lowering the dish, HPS starts once again to walk slowly *deosil* around the Circle, dipping her fingers into the water and sprinkling it along the line of the Circle. She returns to the east point and raises the dish briefly in salute, then returns to the altar. She puts down the salt dish. HP takes up the censer and goes to the east point, where he raises it in salute.

> **HP:** The fire of this censer, with the fragrance of its smoke, serves to cement the foundation of this our temple, dedicated to the Lord and the Lady.

HP lowers the censer and again passes along the line of the Circle, swinging the censer so that the fumes and smoke pass along it. When he returns to the starting point, he again raises the censer in salute and then returns to the altar.

HP replaces the censer and both he and the HPS take up their athames. They raise them in salute and describe the pentagram over the altar. All Witches raise their athames also.

**HPS:** Lord and Lady, God and Goddess, I invite you to enter into this temple constructed to venerate you. Be with us here and witness these rites held in your honor. Here today are two who would be made one, in your eyes. Witness their promises to one another and stand beside them throughout the life they wish to lead together. So mote it be.

**ALL:** So mote it be!

All kiss their athame blades and then set them down or replace them in their sheaths. HPS dips her forefinger into the water and marks a cross within a circle on the forehead and a pentagram over the heart of HP.

**HPS:** Here I do consecrate you in the names of the Lord and the Lady. Be here in peace and love, with honor to all life.

HP does the same, dipping his fingers in the salted water and consecrating the HPS.

**HP:** Here I do consecrate you in the names of the Lord and the Lady. Be here in peace and love, with honor to all life.

HPS rings the bell three times three or nine times in all.

**HPS:** Welcome, my brothers and sisters. And doubly welcome to you who come to this sacred place to be joined in the time-honored Handfasting rite.

**HP (to bride):** What is your desire?

**BRIDE:** To be made one with my soul mate, [name], in the eyes of the gods and of my brothers and sisters of the Craft.

**HPS (to groom):** What is your desire?

**GROOM:** To be made one with my soul mate, [name], in the eyes of the gods and of my brothers and sisters of the Craft.

| | |
|---|---|
| **HPS:** | Do you both wish this in the names of the Lord and the Lady, God and Goddess of the Craft? |
| **BRIDE and GROOM:** | We do. |
| **HP (to bride):** | What do you bring with you to this marriage? |
| **BRIDE:** | I bring love and respect. I love [name] as I love myself, honoring and respecting him in all things. I will always support him in everything he does and join with him in love and praise of the gods in whom we believe. I will defend his life before my own. May the gods give me the strength to keep these my vows. |
| **HPS (to groom):** | What do you bring with you to this marriage? |
| **GROOM:** | I bring love and respect. I love [name] as I love myself, honoring and respecting her in all things. I will always support her in everything she does and join with her in love and praise of the gods in whom we believe. I will defend her life before my own. May the gods give me the strength to keep these my vows. |
| **HPS:** | Lord and Lady, here stand two of your folk. Witness now that which they have to declare. |

HP rings the bell seven times.

The bride and groom face each other. They grip right hand to right hand and left hand to left hand. HP binds the hands together with the red ribbon. HPS holds the censer under their hands, censing them. She then holds her athame over the tied hands while the HP holds his athame under them.

| | |
|---|---|
| **BRIDE and GROOM:** | We come into this sacred Circle of our own free will, to join together as one in the eyes of the Ancient Ones. We are no longer two individuals but are now two halves of one whole. Each of us is incomplete without the other. Be with us in all things, dear Lord and Lady, and |

help us cleave together throughout this life and beyond. All this we ask in your names. So mote it be!

ALL:        So mote it be!

HP and HPS replace their athames and untie the hands. HP gives the bride the groom's ring and HPS gives the groom the bride's ring. The bride and groom put the rings on each other's fingers. They then hold hands.

HP:        As the grass of the fields and the trees of the woods bend together under the pressures of the storm, so too must you both bend when the wind blows strong.

HPS:        But know that as quickly as the storm comes, so equally quickly may it leave. Yet will you both stand, strong in each other's strength.

HP:        As you give love, so will you receive love. As you give strength, so will you receive strength. Together you are one; apart you are nothing.

HPS:        Know that no two people can be exactly alike. No more can any two people fit together, perfect in every way, no matter how hard they may try.

HP:        There will be times when it will seem hard to give and to love. But see then your reflection as in a woodland pool: When the image you see looks sad and angered, then is the time for you to smile and to love (for it is not fire that puts out fire).

HPS:        In return will the image in the pool smile and love. So do you change anger for love and tears for joy. It is no weakness to admit a wrong; more is it a strength and a sign of learning.

HP:        Ever love, help, and respect each other, and then know truly that you are one in the eyes of the gods.

HPS:        So mote it be!

ALL:        So mote it be!

The bride and groom kiss each other, then salute HP and HPS. They turn and move around the Circle, saluting and embracing all within.

Then follows the ceremony of Cakes and Ale followed by celebrations and the Closing of the Circle.

There are many variations on the Handfasting rite. If the ritual can be performed out in the open, with plenty of space, then it is not unusual to have a small fire burning at the east entrance and for the couple to leap over the fire at some point. This was an ancient fertility rite enacted at fire festivals in many areas across Europe and elsewhere. Similarly, a "besom," or broomstick, might be laid down and the couple jump over that, also promoting fertility.

Much celebrating follows the rite, of course, and in the old days it would invariably end with many couples slipping away to make love together. This was as much a form of sympathetic magic as anything else, the intent being to help bless the couple with children.

> Beltane is the celebration of the Sacred Marriage, as it has been down through the ages, a celebration of the union of the God and the Goddess, of male and female, of spirit and matter. It has been celebrated by the priestesses of Ishtar in the wedding chambers atop the ziggurats of ancient Sumer, and by ecstatic dancers around the Maypole, the venerated phallus image entwined with ribbons and adorned with flowers, as it was symbolically plunged into the sacred wells of the Earth Mother.      —Pauline Campanelli, *Pagan Rites of Passage*

## A Clean Break

Witches do not take their marriage vows lightly, yet they realize that, no matter how idyllic a relationship may seem at the start, people do change. Over the years, the heat of passion can die and the spark of love be extinguished, no matter how much we may fight against it. When this happens, Witches believe that no good is served by chaining together the couple until such time as they come to almost hate one another! Far better to make the break and let them each go their separate ways, perhaps to find love and happiness again with someone else.

Toward this end there is a Wiccan ritual of Handparting. In it, the couple agree to part and to do so in love and with honor toward one another. It is seldom that a

Wiccan couple, finding that love has died, end their relationship in bitterness and animosity.

The couple will meet with the Elders of the coven and decide upon a fair division of property, plus provision for the support of any children of the marriage. Everything is put in writing and signed by both partners. Neither should be coerced into signing what he or she does not feel is fair. When this settlement has been signed, then the ceremony of Handparting can be performed.

## Wiccan Handparting Ritual

The Circle is cast in the usual way, as at the start of an Esbat or any other ritual. The husband stands before the High Priestess and the wife before the High Priest, all four in front of the altar. An Elder, whom we will call the scribe, is present with the written agreement. As many coven members as possible should also be present. A length of red ribbon lies on the altar.

| | |
|---|---|
| **HPS:** | **What matter is it that brings you both before the gods, in this our sacred Circle?** |
| **HUSBAND:** | **I desire to be Handparted from [wife's name].** |
| **WIFE:** | **I desire to be Handparted from [husband's name].** |
| **HP:** | **Do you both desire this of your own free will?** |
| **HUSBAND and WIFE:** | **We do.** |
| **HPS:** | **Has a settlement been reached between you, regarding the division of your property and the care of your children [if appropriate]?** |
| **HUSBAND and WIFE:** | **It has.** |
| **SCRIBE:** | **That agreement I have here, duly recorded, signed, and witnessed.** |

The scribe presents the document to HP and HPS, who examine it and then lay it on the altar.

| HP: | You are both certain that this is the step you wish to take? |
|---|---|
| HUSBAND and WIFE: | We are. |
| HPS: | Then let us proceed. But be mindful, both of you, that you stand here in this sacred Circle in the presence of the Mighty Ones. |

The husband and wife join right hand to right hand and left hand to left hand. HP loosely loops the red ribbon around their hands. The couple repeat the following line by line, said by the High Priestess:

| HPS: | Together repeat after me: "I, [name], do hereby most freely dissolve my partnership with [spouse's name]. I do so in all honesty and sincerity, before the Lord and the Lady and with my brothers and sisters of the Craft as my witnesses. No longer are we as one. Now we are two individuals free to go our separate ways. We release all ties, rights, and obligations to one another, yet we will ever retain respect for one another as we respect and love all our fellow Wiccans. So mote be it! |

HP pulls the ribbon away and the couple release their hands.

| HP and HPS: | Handpart! |

The couple remove their wedding rings, if they have them, and give them to the High Priest. He sprinkles and censes them.

| HP: | I hereby cleanse these rings, in the names of the Lord and the Lady. |

HP returns the rings to the individuals, to do with as they may.

| HPS: | Now you are Handparted. Let everyone know that you are so. Go your separate ways in peace and love. |

**HP:** Let there be no bitterness between you. Go in the ways of the Craft, as brother and sister. So mote it be.

**ALL:** So mote it be!

The couple kiss one another, then kiss the HP and HPS. The ceremony of Cakes and Ale follows, and the Closing of the Circle.

> *It has been said that marriage is an outmoded institution and that marriage is just too difficult to carry through. Hopefully, in the Pagan world, love, power, and magick can still be gained through handfasting, for in the larger society, we find near indifference to the marital union's spiritual significance.*
> —Jeff Charboneau-Harrison, in *Modern Rites of Passage*,
> edited by Chas. S. Clifton

# ~ 12 ~
# Witchcraft at Home

There are any number of ways to incorporate Witchcraft into your everyday life at home—and, generally speaking, a Wiccan home is a very happy home. Apart from the regular Esbats and Sabbats, you can use the regimens of meditation, affirmations, candle magic, poppet magic, color magic, feng shui, healing, and a host of other disciplines (all of which are covered in this book) to make your life better and decidedly more pleasurable.

> We are surrounded by unseen, non-physical energies that are naturally produced by other human beings. Most of these energies are benevolent, or at least neutral, in their effects. Some, however, can be disturbing to poor psyches and health. Others (negative thoughts or energies deliberately sent our way) can be harmful. We also face the possibility of physical dangers to our bodies, minds, emotions, and possessions. This is a fact of life.
> —Scott Cunningham, *The Magic in Food*

## Enhancing the Energies of Your Home

In a Wiccan home—be it the home of a hereditary family of Witches or the covenstead for a coven—the whole atmosphere is tangibly different from that of a *cowan* home. This may well be due to the buildup of energies from having Circles in the home, but it is also very much a result of the natural love and mutual respect among all Wiccans.

Many Wiccans make use of the ancient Chinese art of feng shui to consciously create harmony in the home, as I mentioned in chapter 6. (Many more create this harmony naturally, without realizing that they are incorporating feng shui principles.) There I spoke of using the art to create harmony in a room shared by two teens, but it can be equally effective when applied to the whole house.

The principle behind feng shui is pretty much the principle behind a comfortable Wiccan home—energy should flow freely throughout. The Chinese call this energy *Ch'i*. *Ch'i* should be able to flow freely from room to room, and within any room, without obstruction. Within your own body, your personal *Ch'i* should also flow freely. When it does, you feel good, with lots of energy. When you are sick, it is because there is some obstruction to the body's *Ch'i*.

When you enter a room and you feel uneasy for no apparent reason, it is probably because the room's *Ch'i* does not match your own. This is what is felt by psychics when they "read" the vibrations of a particular room or house. Wiccans are good at sensing good or bad vibrations in this way. The *Ch'i* of a Wiccan temple or Circle room is usually wonderful, and perhaps this is largely due to the constant clockwise movement of the coveners around the Circle in the rituals. The ringing of a bell in the rites would also add to the *Ch'i*, since sound energy is an important ingredient of feng shui. The fragrance of incense, oils, and perfumes is another plus.

> *We do not think of the compass as the only essential tool for reading Feng Shui. We note the directions of objects, but emphasize their Mouth of Ch'i [the primary point where energy comes into your home] and relative positioning.*
> —Professor Lin Yun, world authority on feng shui

Along with the actual movement within the house or room, such factors as location, shape, color, and arrangement of furniture can affect things. In chapter 6, I showed a *bagua* map—a breakdown of the room, or house, into sections with indications of what is governed by each section.

*Bagua* literally means "eight sign" and is usually drawn as an octagon with the various areas marked in it. The center section is known as the belly of the dragon and is also equated with health. You do not necessarily have to align everything with the points of the compass, but you should align things according to the *bagua*.

To do so—and to find out what rooms correspond with what—the front or main entrance to your home should be aligned with the knowledge/career/helpful people side. (It doesn't matter, therefore, whether the entrance is exactly in the center or to one side.)

Examine the way your own home is set up compared to the *bagua*; it can be very revealing. A Wiccan couple I know worked hard to get ahead, but could never catch up with themselves financially. Then they realized that the wealth and prosperity area of their home was an attached storeroom with no door to the outside, so that no matter how hard they worked, symbolically everything could just float out and away! Another writer friend of mine had a hard time coming up with material for his books and articles. Then he found that the creativity area of his apartment was loaded up with *blank* paper—boxes of reams of paper for his computer printer and his copier.

The colors equated with the areas of the bagua are as follows:

| | | |
|---|---|---|
| Knowledge | Front left corner | Blue |
| Career | Front center | Black |
| Helpful people | Front right corner | Gray |
| Family | Middle left side | Green/Blue |
| Health | Center | Yellow |
| Children | Middle right side | White |
| Wealth | Back left corner | Purple |
| Fame | Back center | Red |
| Marriage | Back right corner | Pink |

These colors could be incorporated into the rooms in those areas of the house, either in the actual wall colors or in the upholstery or the like, to promote the home's *Ch'i*.

One of the most important areas of a home is that aligned with family in the *bagua*, the middle left side. If at all possible, let your family room be in this area. Let it be where you gather together whether to watch television, listen to music, talk, read, or sit and relax. This would also be an ideal area to have your temple or Circle room, since the coven is your family.

Along with color, there are other ways of enhancing these different areas. One way to work on the family area is to have a metal chime hanging there. A red ribbon that's nine inches long (or a multiple of nine) is also supposed to be good for the *Ch'i* there, as are many green plants.

Speaking of plants, I have noticed that nearly all Wiccan homes have a wealth of plants, both indoor and outdoor. Closeness with nature is an integral part of being Wiccan, of course. Bird feeders, birdbaths, window boxes, kitchen gardens, flower beds, potted plants, and the like are all part and parcel of being Wiccan and of building that wonderful natural energy that becomes part of the home.

> *The first principle in the Feng Shui philosophy is that every person, place, and thing is alive with the vital energy we call Ch'i. This concept is all-inclusive, changing our physical existence from a world "that" is largely inanimate to a world "who" is completely alive.*
> —Terah Kathryn Collins, *The Western Guide to Feng Shui Room by Room*

# Magical Protection of the Home

You would think that a Wiccan home, by virtue of being so much equated with nature and all that is good in life, would be immune from any negativity of any sort. Regrettably, the opposite is frequently the case. Whether from ignorance, fear, or jealousy, there are individuals and groups who target Wiccans and Wiccans' homes for both physical and magical attack. For physical attack, of course, there are channels that can help. The ACLU is an excellent champion of Wiccan rights, and the police in most areas are generally sympathetic. But magically, there are a number of things we can do to protect ourselves.

I have spoken of building an all-encompassing ball of white light around you as a personal psychic protective barrier. This can be extended to larger areas. It is a good idea to create a coven protective barrier for every covener's home.

In every home, cast a consecrated Circle. Then, all should sit within it and do the meditation work described in chapter 7.

As the white light builds and fills your body, having pushed out all grayness and negativity, see it expanding even beyond your body to form a ball, or egg, of white light all around you. Then see it expanding to fill the area in which you are working; see it meeting and joining up with the similar white light coming from the others in the Circle, then growing to fill the whole Circle itself. Now all of you in the Circle concentrate to expand the light even more, until it fills the room and finally the whole house.

This, as I say, should be done in the home of everyone in the coven. Anytime one of the group moves into a new house or apartment, get together and do it. Once the white light has been established, the individual can reinforce it every morning. Lying in bed, breathing deeply, and going through the same process, you can reenergize the light filling the whole home.

There are some old folk charms that are said to reinforce the white light treatment. One of these is European mandrake root. If you can obtain one of these, or even a piece of one, then you should either bury it at the front entrance to the house or place it in a container that can be attached over the doorway. Walking all around the property sprinkling salt and water and swinging the censer will also help cleanse the area spiritually. Use the consecrated salt and water that have been used in a ritual.

> Trying to perform magic in a place which is often in use will cause problems and make the magic less successful because the different vibrations from other people will linger in the atmosphere. You would then need to spend a lot of time and energy re-setting the balance in that place. Your objective is to create an atmosphere of serene concentration. Anything that disturbs you, for whatever reason, has to be removed. . . . Look around and consider every object with this in mind. If it is disturbing to your peace, remove it. —Marina Medici, *Good Magic*

## The Covenstead

*Covenstead* is the name given to the regular home of the coven. For a hereditary coven, it is the home of the family, of course. For any other group, it is usually the home of the High Priestess or wherever the Circles are usually held. As I mentioned earlier, the ideal place to hold your meetings would be in a room that could be kept just for this purpose.

If you do have a separate room you can use for the meetings, set up the altar and Circle permanently. You can paint a circle on the floor, but I would recommend having the Circle area carpeted if possible, just for comfort. You can always obtain an old carpet and cut it into a circle that will fit within the ritual area.

It is preferable to have a lockable closet in the room in which to keep all the coven ritual tools. You will also need somewhere to store the spare incense, charcoal, candles, wine, and so forth. Remember that entering and leaving the Circle takes place in the east, so mark your Circle, or lay your carpet, to leave as much room as possible in that section.

Lighting can be fun. I have seen some beautiful temples in which the lighting can be lowered or raised by a control under the altar. I have seen others lit entirely by candles. Both have their appeal. Subdued lighting certainly seems preferable for rituals, with the main illumination coming from the ritual candles, but it is certainly useful to have full lighting for setting up the altar and for clearing away after the ritual.

One temple I saw had the eastern corner of the room sectioned off, with a piece of wood with a door in it across the corner like a small corner closet. At an Initiation, it made an excellent waiting room for an initiate to stand in while the preliminary ritual work was done. Another I have seen was in a basement next to a secondary bathroom. The coveners had the luxury of stepping directly from their ritual bath into the Circle room. Some are elaborately decorated with murals around the walls. One I have seen has a reproduction of the Initiation murals from Pompeii. Certainly if you have the room you can have fun and create a very special temple for yourself and your coven. But even if you don't have the room, you can still have fun.

---

### To Remove Negative Energies From a Home

*Cut a large onion into as many slices as rooms in the house. Place each slice in a dish and cover with cider vinegar, then put one of the dishes in every room of the house. After a week, dispose of the vinegar and onions in running water. (You can also use the garbage disposal to get rid of these. If you decide on this method, quarter a whole lemon and toss it into the disposal afterward.) This seals the house from further negativity.* —Dorothy Morrison, *Everyday Magic*

# A Private, Solitary Temple

A solitary Witch I know turned a built-in closet into a beautiful ritual area. It was a typical clothes closet with two sliding doors across the front. Inside the door, across the right-hand wall, she created a built-in altar extending the full width of the closet. The floor was covered with a thick, deep green carpet. Before the altar stood a *seiza* bench—the traditional Buddhist kneeling bench. It could just as well have been a *zafu* cushion, or any small bench. She painted the walls with stars, flowers, fairies, and little people; the ceiling with clouds and stars.

There was no room to dance or even move around the altar, of course, but for everyday prayer, meditation, and even magic working, it was ideal. The joy was that, with the doors closed, it gave no hint as to what lay behind. Perfect if you share a room or apartment with someone non-Wiccan.

---

*In the end, all that really matters is that we approach wherever we live with full attention and an open heart . . . a bouquet of flowers, a song, the smell of freshly baked bread, an affectionate embrace, such things can transform any place into a happy, heartwarming abode.*                              —Thomas Bender

# ~ 13 ~

# Witchcraft for Plants and Pets

One of the original roles of the Witch was that of herbalist for the local community. She had to understand the healing powers of medicinal plants and herbs, including a good knowledge of poisons, so that she could recognize a case of poisoning and apply the correct antidote. Most modern Witches have a garden whenever possible, or at the very least a window box or collection of potted plants. There is a Wiccan affinity with nature of which I have spoken repeatedly, but there is also mutual need between plants and humans.

Plants and trees absorb the carbon dioxide produced by humans and their machines. In return, they produce the oxygen we need in order to live. This is a demonstrable balance of nature, and it is important that we do not damage it.

Some Witches specialize in herbs and grow them almost to the exclusion of other plants. Yet the Witch gardens of old were a plethora of all types of flowers, herbs, and even vegetables. The contrived, artistic herb gardens frequently found attached to larger homes were a later development, as much for decoration as for the cultivation of the herbs themselves. That is not to say, of course, that you should not have some order to your garden, if you so desire.

## Eye of Newt

The colorful, local names of many plants were given to them because of their appearance or because of their use. Sunflower is an obvious one, from its appear-

> *The witches' knowledge of nature is far better charted than is their allegiance to this or that world of religious ideas. Both witches and monks carried on the ancient practice of herbal medicine. . . . The medicinal plants which were mainly cultivated were those which had been used as long ago as in the time of Hippocrates and Galen. . . . The witch of the fairy tale and her surroundings never really existed except in the realm of fantasy. Witch and peasant lived side by side in the village. She dared not, like the old monks and herbal doctors, plant a garden where she could systematically cultivate her herbs. Instead, she secretly gathered the plants she wanted to use, either where they grew wild, or where she cultivated them unseen in out-of-the-way places.*
> —Harold A. Hansen, *The Witch's Garden*

ance. Coltsfoot (also known as bullsfoot), cat's eye, lamb's-tongue, snake's-head, and goatsbeard are all obviously so called because of their appearance. Sleepwort, feverfew, pleurisy root, and boneset are examples of names given for the properties of the plants.

It is from this that the early Christian church took ammunition for its propaganda against the Old Religion. To say that Witches threw donkey's eyes, toads, horse tongues, bloody fingers, catgut, and the like into their cauldron's made the actions of the wise ones sound disgusting! In fact, these ingredients were all ordinary herbs. Today, we can specify what we are talking about by using the Latin name of the plant, but in the old days it was only the colorful common name that was used, at least by the country folk.

Many a Witch of old was accused of having a "familiar," or an imp of the devil to do her bidding, in the shape of a toad. The reason for this was that most wise ones did indeed keep a toad in their gardens to keep down the populations of insects that attacked the flowers and plants. Many of the plants and herbs were very aromatic and attracted all forms of insect life. A toad was therefore almost a necessity.

Today's Witches grow many herbs for their aromatic properties, to use them in mixing incense. Other herbs and plants are used for medicinal purposes and in magical spells. (For a full listing of the magical properties of herbs, see the appendix.) These are often chosen by the planetary signs that govern them. For example:

*Sun* Angelica, bay, carnation, celandine, chamomile, chrysanthemum, eyebright, goldenseal, heliotrope, lovage, marigold, peony, rosemary, rowan, St.-John's-wort, sesame, sunflower, and witch hazel.

*Moon* Adder's-tongue, aloe, bladderwrack, cabbage, calamus, chickweed, club moss, cucumber, gardenia, grape, Irish moss, jasmine, lettuce, lily, moonwort, poppy, potato, turnip, willow, wintergreen.

*Mercury* Agaric, bean, bittersweet, bracken, caraway, celery, clover, dill, fennel, fenugreek, fern, flax, goat's rue, horehound, lavender, lemongrass, lemon verbena, lily of the valley, mandrake, marjoram, mayapple, mint, mulberry, parsley, peppermint, pimpernel, wax plant.

*Venus* Alder, alfalfa, apple, aster, avocado, bachelor's-button, barley, bedstraw, birch, blackberry, bleeding-heart, blue flag, buckwheat, burdock, caper, cardamom, catnip, coltsfoot, columbine, corn, cowslip, crocus, cyclamen, daffodil, daisy, elder, feverfew, foxglove, geranium, goldenrod, groundsel, heather, hibiscus, hyacinth, iris, lady's-mantle, larkspur, lilac, magnolia, maidenhair, mugwort, myrtle, oat, orchid, orris, passionflower, pea, pear, periwinkle, persimmon, plum, primrose, ragwort, raspberry, rhubarb, rose, rye, spearmint, spikenard, strawberry, sweet pea, tansy, tomato, tulip, valerian, vervain, violet, wheat, willow, wood aloes.

*Mars* Allspice, anemone, basil, bloodroot, briony, broom, cactus, carrot, chili pepper, coriander, cumin, damiana, deer tongue, dragon's blood, garlic, gentian, ginger, gorse, hawthorn, High John the Conqueror, holly, hops, horseradish, hound's-tongue, leek, mustard, nettle, onion, pennyroyal, pepper, pine, poke root, prickly ash, radish, shallot, sloe, snapdragon, thistle, tobacco, Venus' flytrap, woodruff, wormwood.

*Jupiter* Agrimony, anise, betony, borage, chestnut, cinquefoil, clove, dandelion, dock, endive, fig, honeysuckle, horse chestnut, houseleek, hyssop, linden, liverwort, maple, meadowsweet, nutmeg, sage, sarsparilla, sassafras, witchgrass.

*Saturn* Beech, beet, belladonna, boneset, buckthorn, comfrey, datura, elm, hellebore, hemlock, hemp, henbane, horsetail, ivy, knotweed, lady's-slipper, mimosa, morning glory, pansy, poplar, quince, skullcap, skunk cabbage, slippery elm, Solomon's-seal, wolfsbane, yew.

From the above it can be determined, in general terms, which herbs are best used for what purposes. For example, the sun is associated with beauty, creativity, hope, money, self-expression, and victory. Therefore, any herbal magic you intend to do for any of these purposes should make use of one or more of those herbs listed under the sun, previously. Here are the associations for the other planets:

*Moon* Childbearing, dreams, healing, memory, theft, virginity.

*Mercury* Business, communication, debt, fear, loss, travel.

*Venus* Beauty, family life, friendship, fruitfulness, growth, harmony, love, nature, pleasures, sexuality, strangers, youth.

*Mars* Courage, enemies, exorcism, lust, matrimony, protection, sexual potency, war, wealth.

*Jupiter* Clothing, desires, legal matters, oaths and treaties, prosperity and riches.

*Saturn* Building, endings, freedom, exorcisms, gifts, longevity, real estate, sowing, tenacity, visions.

## Herbs and Plants

| COMMON NAME | LATIN NAME |
| --- | --- |
| Adder's-tongue | Erythronium americanum |
| Bear's ear | Primula auricula |
| Bird's-eye | Adonis vernalis |
| Bloody fingers | Digitalis purpurea |
| Calf's snout | Linaria vulgaris |
| Cat's foot | Asarum canadense |
| Chicken-toes | Corallorhiza odontorhiza |
| Cockscomb | Rhinanthus crista-galli |
| Donkey's eyes | Mucuna pruriens (seeds) |
| Dove's foot | Geranium sylvaticum |
| Flesh and blood | Potentilla erecta |
| Frog's foot | Ranunculus bulbosus |
| Horsetail | Equisetum hyemale |
| Jew's ear | Peziza auricula |
| Lizard's-tail | Saururus cernuus |
| Mouse-ear | Hieracium pilosella |
| Old-man's-beard | Chionanthus virginicus |
| Shepherd's heart | Capsella bursa pastoris |
| Snake milk | Euphorbia corollata |
| Swine snout | Taxaxacum officinale |
| Toad | Linaria vulgaris |
| Wolf's foot | Lycopus virginicus |

For example, if you are doing magical work to ensure the best outcome of a lawsuit, then you would look for herbs ruled by Jupiter (for legal matters). Sage is one of these, so you could burn sage as your incense for this ritual. When doing magic for protection, you would use an herb of Mars, such as garlic or High John the Conqueror.

## Flower and Herb Drying

Dried flowers and herbs are very useful for decorating altars, making potpourris and incense, scenting oils and candles, and various other uses. Do keep in mind when drying herbs or flowers that they will continue to mature during the drying process. For this reason, it is best to pick them before they have actually bloomed (also after the dew has dried).

For lavender, pick when the bottom flowers are just beginning to open, then air-dry for three or four days in an empty vase. Roses are best dried in silica gel, though they can be air-dried early in bloom by hanging them upside down in a dark room for about ten days.

There are two main ways of drying plants: air-drying and employing desiccants, or sprays. The latter is used mostly for cultivated flowers. Air-drying is the older, more traditional method and is best for wildflowers, grasses, weeds, and especially those plants that grow in dry or even sandy soil.

Most herbs can be air-dried by hanging them upside down in bunches, out of the sun. Don't make the bunches too big or they will mildew. And tie them with a rubber band rather than string. As they dry, they tend to shrink; if you have tied them with string, they will fall out of the bunch and spread across the floor! The rubber band will contract with the plants and keep holding them. When they're dry, store the plants in containers, away from direct sunlight.

---

*Among other herbs which are poisonous and harmful, Henbane is not the least, so that the common man, not without fear, should spit at that herb when he hears its name spoken, not to mention when he sees it growing in great quantity where his children are running at play.*  —Simon Paulli, *Flora Danica,* 1648

# Outdoor Altar or Shrine

Many Wiccans place an altar in their gardens, where the libations from the rituals will be poured. For others, it is not so much an altar as a shrine, with representations of the God of the Greenwood and the Earth Mother peeping out from among the foliage. Some use actual statuary; others, perhaps a large rock or two. It can certainly be a wonderful place to go to meditate or even to do some magic, surrounded by the plants you have cultivated yourself.

If there are trees or bushes in your garden, hanging wind chimes from them can add immeasurably to the ambience of the area, as can the burning of incense or sage. (Stick incense can be ideal here, since it is so easy to stick it into any piece of ground.) A small water garden is also a perfect addition.

Many Wiccans will dedicate their gardens, consecrating them at some stage of development. This can be as simple as walking a garden's boundaries pouring wine, while calling upon the gods to bless all that grows within those boundaries and to watch over the garden and guard it from sickness and disease. Walk *deosil* when you do this, and do it in the waxing phase of the moon.

I have seen some wonderful decorative stepping-stones and altar stones made by Witches. All that is needed is a mold such as a large plastic plant tray for a round stone, or even a pizza box for a square stone. Poke a few small drainage holes in the bottom of whichever you use. Mix some mortar, such as Quickcrete, making sure it is fairly firm and not too runny. Pour it into the round or square mold and smooth the top with a trowel. (Do use gloves when doing this work.) Now press in any design objects you like. I have seen marbles used, unusual stones, tile chips, old keys, and even actual ferns and other pressed plants.

Don't push too hard—just enough for the objects to sink level with the surface. If they sink down too fast, your mortar mix is too watery; you'll have to start over. Then simply leave it for enough time to dry thoroughly and harden. This can be a few hours.

When it is set, simply turn it over and drop it out (with a pizza box, you can simply tear off the cardboard). You can color the mortar mix initially, if you wish, by adding stain to the water that you will add to the dry mortar. Also, you can reinforce a large stone by laying a fine chicken wire mesh, or something similar, in the mortar about halfway through the thickness.

# Indoor Gardens

Not all are lucky enough to have an outdoor garden, but this does not stop the average Witch! Houseplants can add tremendous energy to a house or apartment, and to the well-being of the inhabitant(s). Window boxes, potted plants, and even whole tabletops of indoor plants and herbs are possible and recommended.

Here are some typical houseplants that can be easily grown and maintained and yet have good magical properties.

*African violets* Governed by Venus. This is a plant of protection that continuously gives off peaceful vibrations conducive to harmony and spirituality.

*Aloe vera* Governed by the moon. It is a protective plant and also a barrier against intruders. Medicinally, it is excellent for the (external) treatment of burns.

*Bird's-nest fern* Governed by Mercury. It is a bringer of luck and of riches; it is also protective. Dried and thrown on a fire, it will exorcise evil entities. It is said that if you bite into the first frond of springtime, you will not suffer from toothache for the next twelve months. When dried and placed in an open jar, it will attract money into the house.

*Cactus* Governed by Mars. This is a plant of protection. It will keep you from bodily harm and also protect the house from burglars. It absorbs negativity. It is a good idea to place one or more in each of the four corners of the house: east, south, west, and north.

*Catnip* Governed by Venus. Catnip has powers of love and happiness, and enhances beauty. It is used in love sachets. It attracts good spirits and good luck.

*Chrysanthemum* Governed by the sun. It protects from evil spirits.

*Crocus* Governed by Venus. The crocus will bring love to the grower. It will also promote visions.

*Cyclamen* Governed by Venus. If kept in the bedroom, it will protect you while you sleep. It is a cleanser, ensuring that no negative magic can come near. It will also help remove grief and can raise passion.

*Daffodil* Governed by Venus. This is a flower of love and luck. It increases fertility and brings abundance in all things.

*Foxglove* Governed by Venus. It keeps evil out of the house.

*Heather* Governed by Venus. It is a bringer of good luck. It aids in seeing spirits of the dead. When burned with fern, heather will cause rain to fall. It is a guard against rape and other violent crimes.

*Ivy* Governed by Saturn. It drives out all negativity. It is also used in love charms and is traditionally worn by brides for good luck. It guards against negativity in all forms.

*Lavender* Governed by Mercury. This is frequently used in love spells and charms. It protects against spousal abuse. It can induce good sleep, longevity, peace, and happiness. It is also a protection from the evil eye.

*Orchids* Governed by Venus. They are used in love spells. They can help induce trance states and develop psychic powers.

*Palms* Governed by the sun. A palm is a tree of fertility and for regaining sexual potency. If placed near the main entrance to the home, it will protect that home and its occupants from all harm.

*Rose* Governed by Venus. This is a love flower, also useful in healing, divination, luck, calming stress, and protection. A rosebud tea will help induce prophetic dreams.

*Succulents* Governed by the moon. They bring an abundance of love and worldly wealth and are good for psychic development.

*Tulip* Governed by Venus. This will keep you from poverty. It is used in many love spells.

*Venus' flytrap* Governed by Mars. It is a bringer of love and a protector. It will also bring luck and money into the house.

---

*If you want to have a corner of your garden which is especially magical, plant there the exquisite little flower called Solomon's Seal, with its waxy white blossoms. Plant also the iris, or fleur-de-lis, the "flower of light," the symbol of inspiration; and, if you can get it, plant the true vervain (verbena officinalis), and the rue or "Herb of grace." The last two plants are the favorites of Italian Witches. . . . You cannot possibly have a magical garden unless you have some plants there which honour the moon goddess, the mistress of magic. Most plants with pure white flowers are ruled by the Moon, especially those which give forth their perfume in the evening.*
        —Doreen Valiente, *Natural Magic*

There are as many qualities, if not more—both medicinal and magical—for herbs. Witches grow as many herbs, both in and out of the house, as they do other plants and flowers. One of the best books on the use of herbs in magic is *Cunningam's Encyclopedia of Magical Herbs* (see the bibliography). There are also many of the old herbals that contain a wealth of information, such as *The Herball, or General Historie of Plants* by John Gerard, originally published in 1597 but now available from Dover, New York. *Culpeper's Complete Herbal,* by Nicholas Culpeper, originally published in 1652 but again recently reprinted, is also a classic, though much of the material is now outdated.

There is a whole library of modern books on herbs for both medicinal and magical purposes. I recommend *The Herb Book* by John Lust (Bantam, New York, 1974), *The Herbalist* by J. E. Meyer (1960), *Planetary Herbology* by Michael Tierra (Lotus Press, Twin Lakes, WI, 1988), *Rodale's Illustrated Encyclopedia of Herbs* (Rodale, Emmaus, Pennsylvania, 1987), and *The Reader's Digest's Magic and Medicine of Plants* (Reader's Digest, Pleasantville, New York, 1986).

---

A recent study by NASA has shown that approximately fifteen plants will fully cleanse the air in an eighteen-thousand-square-foot home, removing the off gases such as formaldehyde, benzene, trichloroethylene, and more. The plants used in the NASA tests (which was conducted over a two-year period) included Chinese evergreen (*Aglaonema* spp.), peace lily (*Spathiphyllum* spp.), arrowhead vine (*Syngonium podophyllum*), English ivy (*Hedera helix*), corn plant (*Dracaena fragrans*), and devil's ivy (*Scindapsus* or *Pothos* spp.).

---

## Communing With Nature

The gardens of Witches are invariably lush and full, with beautiful flowers, perfect herbs, and large, delicious vegetables. The main reason for this is simply that Witches talk with the plants and with the nature spirits who look after the plants. Witches believe that all living things have spirits, or souls, including animals and plants. Some Christian and other sects preach that only humans have souls. Imagine an afterlife without birds, animals, and plants! Yet the Reverend Franklin Loehr, director of the Religious Research Foundation of America, was able to show in a study that seeds that had been prayed for developed much faster than those that had not. The results of the study were published in the best-selling book *The Power of Prayer on Plants*. More than that, Dr. Marcel Vogel has conducted ongoing experiments that show that plants can even think! In *The Secret Powers of Plants*, author Brett L. Bolton says:

> Love is the strongest force in the world, the most powerful means of communication, because love needs no verbalizing. It has its own level of understanding. Loving is man's primary responsibility and when we release love to a plant, it responds electrically in a rhythmic movement because it somehow perceives and receives. Dr. Vogel feels if we can learn to love so simple a thing as a plant, we can develop our ability to love on higher levels, and ultimately transcend the selfishness with which we love people.

But more than the visible living things, there are what we might term "the fairy folk," for want of a better name. They are the invisible spirits who also inhabit this earth, albeit perhaps in a different dimension. Sometimes it is possible to make contact with them . . . to bridge the gap between the two worlds.

Back in the 1960s, a man named Peter Caddy founded a community known as Findhorn with his wife, Eileen. It was situated in the barren, windswept wilds of Scotland, along the coast from Inverness on the shores of Moray Firth. It was a truly inhospitable area, with sandy soil bearing sparse desertlike life. Yet, in a few short years, the Caddys and those who went to join them had turned the place into a lush paradise brimming with a multitude of beautiful flowers, huge vegetables (forty-two-pound cabbages and sixty-pound broccoli plants, it was reported!), twenty-one types of fruit, forty-two herbs, and sixty-five different vegetables. Over the years, many articles were written about Findhorn and its founder, with writers going and living in the community for a year or more. The secret of this incredible gardening, according to Caddy, was "love." But more than that, the residents worked with the spirits of the land; with fairies and elves. The word *deva*, a Hindu term meaning "a being of light," was used for these beings.

---

*Love, hate, joy, fear, pleasure, pain, excitability, stupor, and countless other appropriate responses to stimuli are as universal in plants as in animals.*
—Sir Jagadis Chandra Bose

In the same way, many Witches work with the spirits of the vegetation, watering, composting, planting, and relocating plants and bushes according to directions they receive. Not all have as spectacular success as did the Caddys, but invariably their gardens are far healthier than those of their neighbors.

The way to do this work is simply to talk quietly to the plants and to be open to any thoughts and feelings that come to you as a result. Encourage them as you would a child. Praise them and look after them.

> There can be little doubt that the plant kingdom is truly man's best friend. He benefits from it in thousands of ways beyond his creature comforts and daily sustenance. But even more important than what man gets from the plant world should be his realization that there is a relationship between plant, man, and animal.
> —Brett L. Bolton, *The Secret Powers of Plants*

## Pamper Your Pets

In the same way, it pays to speak to your pets. Most people are close to their pets and talk to them a lot anyway. But there is a difference between "saying things" to them and actually talking to them. When you talk to them, you need to also listen for an answer. If you do, you will soon reach the point where you do actually hear this answer. At first it may just seem to be an impression that comes into your head, but you will quickly find that it does indeed relate to, and even respond to, what you have said or asked.

Most Witches can tell when a pet is unwell and, more than this, frequently know what needs to be done to help the animal. Some put it down to "intuition," but it is more than that. It is an understanding; an attunement between human and animal.

As I mentioned earlier, some of the Witches of old were charged with having a "familiar." This was thought to be a spirit or servant of the devil that would do the witch's bidding. In fact, it was simply a pet that the witch had and spoke to. And when I say "pet," it wasn't necessarily what we would classify as a domestic pet today. It might have been a mouse or rat that habitually came into the cottage, or a rabbit that made regular raids on the vegetable garden. But it was second nature for the people to speak to these creatures, and to speak quite naturally as though to another person.

As you work with animals, you will find that they each have their own personalities, just as humans do. Some are mellow; some are very active. Some are inquisitive, while others are suspicious and cautious. By patiently working with any animal—even a wild one—you can win its confidence and reach the point where you understand one another and communicate.

My wife was, for many years, a herpetologist, owning a variety of snakes. Every one of these reptiles had his or her own personality. This may seem strange to say about snakes, but it is true. Some were affectionate, while others were inquisitive and active. One—a corn snake—was an excellent healer and would naturally move to the part of our bodies that needed healing. This was proven time and again. And by speaking, and *listening*, to them, a great deal was learned and shared.

> *If you talk to the animals they will talk with you, and you will know each other. If you do not talk to them, you will not know them, and what you do not know you will fear. What one fears one destroys.*   —Chief Dan George

# ~ 14 ~
# Witchcraft in the Bedroom

The Old Religion was originally tied in closely with the need for fertility—of the crops, of animals, and of humans. The Witches of old did not hesitate to use sexual magic to promote fertility. It should be no surprise, therefore, that modern Witches have a very open and liberal view of sex. They have not been brainwashed into believing it to be something "dirty" and shameful, but know it is a beautiful thing and very much a part of all life. This is not to say that Witches are promiscuous. Quite the contrary. Witches in general are far more constant and faithful to their partners than are most of their contemporaries.

Regrettably, many of us have had a more traditionally religious upbringing and have certainly been tainted by the Christian notions of sex. From this, we have absorbed what might be termed the Victorian forbearance of coition. We have been taught that it is almost "unnatural," when in fact the reverse is true.

> *Witches do not have any hang-ups about sex—we worship the forces of life and as such sex is sacred and can play a very important role in some ritual work.*
> —Fiona Horne, *Witch: A Magical Journey*

## The Power of Sex

In working magic, the main ingredient is the power that is raised, by the individual or by the group. I spoke of this in chapter 7. Without such power, no magic can be performed. There are many ways of doing this power raising: chanting, dancing, awakening the kundalini, drumming, scourging, and the sex act. Sex magic is the art of using the sexual experience, and especially the orgasm, for magical purposes.

Dr. Jonn Mumford, in *Sexual Occultism*, says that the most important psychophysiological event in the life of a human is the orgasm. This orgasm is achieved following much the same pattern as any magical working and power raising. It starts slowly and very gradually builds to a climax.

> *Sex magic is the art and science of utilizing sexual experience for the concrete materialization of desire and the expansion of the inner life.*
> —Swami Anandakapila

During sexual excitation, all aspects of extrasensory perception are heightened. You become much more sharply attuned to the psychic realm than in your normal state. Immediately before, during, and after climax the mind is in a state of hypersensitivity, which can be especially useful when working magic. During orgasm, many people have experienced timelessness, accompanied by subjective sensations of being "absorbed" by their partner. Successful sex magic involves an interplay of all of these factors.

When working sex magic, the magical process can be broken down into the following steps. First is the planning stage, when the exact details of how to proceed are worked out and agreed upon. This includes what "goal" to aim at, what methods of arousal will be used, what to visualize during the act, and—especially at the climax—what to set your sights on during the release of the power. Then comes the actual practice: the magical, sensual, and sexual foreplay that develops into the serious buildup of power. There is a connection, in the case of coital working, and the gradual building of power leading to the aiming and the final release.

Let us look at the working of a couple first. Then we'll examine how sex magic is performed both by solitaries and by whole covens.

> *Sex magick can be a very potent way of achieving results. In the first place, sexual power is tightly connected to psychic energy; both run up the central spine (the kundalini force) and it is easy to mistake one for another when you are in circle. . . . Sex magick utilizes the process of building energy through sexual excitation, the orgasm releases it.* —Yasmine Galenorn, *Embracing the Moon*

## One, Two, or More

The literal climax of sex magic is the orgasm. As I pointed out in my *Buckland's Complete Book of Witchcraft*, just how this is achieved is unimportant; sex magic can thus be done by the solitary, by a couple, or by a whole coven. All that matters is that the orgasm be the time of directing the power generated to the target selected.

A couple would start by kneeling facing one another. Perhaps with eyes closed, they gently caress each other's bodies, not especially trying for arousal. At this point the breasts and genitals are best avoided, concentrating more on the hair, face, arms, and legs. Thoughts can be on one another at this time, since arousal will eventually need to come about. At some point they begin to kiss and hug, pressing their bodies close together and caressing backs and buttocks. On moving apart again, the caressing will continue but may now include breasts and genitals, the aim being definitely toward awakening the kundalini. Here the mouth, tongue, and lips may be brought into play as much as the hands. As the couple become totally aroused, the male may sit back and allow the female to sit astride his legs, with his phallus entering her. At this point it is necessary to focus the mind on the object of the magic.

The couple proceed by gently rocking back and forth, each focusing on the person to whom the power will be directed; as always in magic, seeing in their mind's eye the result of a successful working. Both should try to hold off the orgasm as long as possible while they work on the visualization. When he can hold off no longer, the male should let the female know, by prearranged signal, when he is about to ejaculate (or vice versa, if the female is likely to be the first to climax). The female should try to arrive at orgasm as close to the same time as possible, which she can do by working her clitoris with her fingers. At the moment of orgasm (whether together or one after the other), they should see the power shooting out from them to the target, like a bolt of lightning. One Witch has described the release as a force "that pulses from my lower chakras, surging up through the others before blasting out of my crown chakra, at the top of my head."[20]

The couple should try to stay joined for as long as possible, though if they wish the male may gently fall backward to lie on his back with the female on top of him. (If the male has trouble holding off his ejaculation for sufficient time, he may lie on his back from the start with the female on top of him, and control the movement of them both.)

As I've said, the method of achieving orgasm is unimportant. For this reason it is quite possible for such sex magic to be performed by couples of the same sex, through mutual masturbation. In fact, any variety of sexual stimulation methods may be employed, whether by homo- or heterosexual couples, including mutual masturbation and oral stimulation.

For the solitary, the obvious answer is masturbation. This type of magic has been performed by solitary Witches for generations; probably the majority induce the power release with their hands, but some Witches certainly use such magical items as priapic (phallic) wands and, these days, such seemingly nonmagical items as dildos and vibrators.

> *So potent is Sex magick that even when practiced half-heartedly or by the inept, there is always some result.* —Louis T. Culling, *A Manual of Sex Magick*

Sex magic by whole covens is unusual, in the sense of being rarely performed. There is absolutely no reason why it should not be done—with the coven working in pairs or solitary—but to many modern witches it carries connotations of an orgy, and this, of course, is an image we are trying to avoid. So much depends upon the makeup of the coven—the relationships, ease, and comfort among members. It is also not easy to arrange an orgasm for all members at, or even close to, the same time, so the benefit of group working is mostly lost. This is yet another reason why it is more common to find sex magic done by single couples and solitaries rather than by covens. Donald Michael Kraig, in his excellent book *Modern Sex Magick*, details the methodology of working with a group—not as individuals or individual

20. Fiona Horne. *Witch: A Magical Journey*. Thorsons, New York, 2000.

couples, but as a whole group—that would work well but would also need very mature participants.

One thing does need to be emphasized where sex magic is concerned: No one should be coerced into doing it. Sex magic is simply one method out of many, and it is definitely not for everyone. If you encounter a group that claims that this *has* to be done, turn and walk away!

> *Although the persecuting Inquisitors may have tortured some of the (Knights) Templars into telling about Sufi secrets of Sex Magick, nevertheless all of this meant only "sex perversion" to the Inquisitors. To this day it is the same. Although the ideals and practices of Sex Magick are far more idealistic and spiritually inspiring than the ways of common sexual relations, it is not an uncommon thing for restricted minds to yelp. "Sex Magick! That's immoral sex perversion!"*
> —Louis T. Culling, *A Manual of Sex Magick*

# Witchcraft in the Bedroom

An adjunct to sex magic is the simple relationship of Witches to one another in the bedroom. With liberated minds and acceptance of sex as part of the whole pattern of nature, Witches enjoy a wonderful relationship in bed. They are not afraid to explore one another's bodies, to try a variety of sexual positions, to accept the spirituality of sex, for they view the body as a temple. The woman is viewed by the man as an earthly representation of the Goddess, and the man is seen by the woman as an earthly representation of the God. To join together in sexual intercourse is to enact the *Hieros Gamos*, the Sacred Marriage, of the ancient mysteries. Even on a relatively mundane, domestic level, Witches retain this concept in their unconscious, or even conscious, minds, giving them a respect for the act while still being able to enjoy it at a deep, chthonic level.

# Male and Female Energies

It must be remembered that we all have both male and female within us. We are all both God and Goddess. In this respect there is no negativity projected by true Witches toward homosexuals. In fact, historically, homosexuals were frequently venerated as instruments of the deities. Siva, or Shiva, is sometimes depicted as a hermaphroditic god, having divided himself into male and female, as did another Hindu god, Brahma. The Greek Janus was not only double headed but also of both sexes. Hermes was androgynous, as was the ancient Syrian god Baal. Even Zeus, the father of the gods, had his moments of homosexuality (though he was not androgynous), being attracted to Ganymede and seducing him. So all life, and all forms of sexuality, are revered in Wicca.

## Salutes

This might be an appropriate place to speak of what are known in Wicca as salutes. A salute is nothing more than a kiss. When a ritual says "they salute," it simply means "they kiss." Again, hugging and kissing are a natural part of life for humans who are close to one another, as coven members are.

There are also certain ritual kisses, known variously as the threefold salute, the fivefold salute, and the eightfold salute. The threefold salute traces the outline of a triangle and is done on mouth, breast, breast, and back to the mouth (to close the figure). The fivefold salute describes a pentagram and is genitals, right foot, left knee, right knee, left foot, and genitals. The eightfold salute is both of these salutes, one after the other. In some traditions, there is an inverted threefold salute: genitals, breast, breast, genitals.

Kissing these parts of the body is an acknowledgment of the sacredness of the body and of life. It is also an honoring of the God or Goddess within each of us. In the rituals given in this book, I include these salutes, but if anyone is uncomfortable with them—being new to the Craft—then it is appropriate to simply kiss.

## The Great Rite

At the Sabbat rites (see chapter 19), there is the enactment of the Great Rite. This is the *Hieros Gamos* I mentioned previously; the sacred marriage of God and Goddess. As the earthly representatives of the Lord and the Lady, the High Priest and High Priestess of a coven will have ritual coitus as part of the Sabbat rite. Enacting the Great Rite at Samhain is a reaffirmation of life necessary when entering

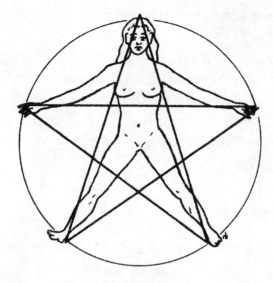

the dark half of the year, with all of nature seemingly dying. It is a similar celebration at the opposite turn of the wheel, at Beltane, as a celebration of the return of life.

There is much discussion in Wicca as to whether or not the Great Rite should be enacted "in token" (symbolically) or in reality. In my formative years in Wicca, I was taught to believe that not to do it in reality was something of a slight to the gods. I still feel this way. However, I understand that there are those for whom this is too big a leap from their non-Pagan upbringing, and I would not attempt to pressure them. Even for those who agree that it should be done in reality, many feel that the rest of the coven should leave the Circle for this rite, returning when it is completed. Again, I disagree. In the early days of the Craft, the people were attuned to fertility and the naturalness of sexuality; I cannot believe that these early Witches would have dutifully tramped out of the Circle just because their leaders were performing ritual coitus. Indeed, it is the fact that this is *ritual* coitus that, to my mind, makes it acceptable. But again, I would not force my opinion on others.

So the Great Rite is performed at the Sabbats. In some traditions, it is also performed at other times, such as when a Witch is taken to the Third Degree in a degree-oriented tradition. In my *Ray Buckland's Magic Cauldron*, speaking of the Great Rite when performed at the Third Degree, I say, "There *is* sex involved in the Great Rite, then. But, of course, it is not sex for its own sake. It is a very sacred, holy, union which is the culmination not only of that particular ritual, but of the whole journey the initiate has traveled through the degrees (over a period of several years)."

The symbolic version of the rite is found in the Cakes and Ale ritual (and there I would not argue with its "in token" appropriateness). The High Priest's athame represents the male phallus, and the goblet of wine the female vagina. In the words of that ritual, "As the athame is to the male, so the cup is to the female, and conjoined they bring blessedness." The High Priest then lowers his athame into the wine held by the High Priestess.

## THE GREAT RITE

HPS lies on the ground before the altar, her head to the east, with arms and legs outstretched to form a pentagram. HP kneels between her legs.

> **HP:** **I am here to adore thee, at the sacred place, the center of the most revered altar of life. That center is itself the origin of all things, and so I do adore it.**

HP salutes HPS on the genitals.

> **HP:** **I worship at this altar, this cup of joy and beauty, by the power of the raised sword.**

HP again salutes HPS.

> **HP:** **By seed and root, by stem and bud, by leaf and flower and fruit, I invoke thee, Lady of Light and Beauty, to lift me to the stars.**

HP gives HPS a threefold salute.

> **HP:** **Lovely Lady of Life, I am your servant in all things. I adore you.**

HP gives HPS an eightfold salute.

**HP:** As the Lord of Life and Death welcomed and embraced his Lady, so do I welcome and embrace you. As the God joined with the Goddess, so do I join with you. As our Lord became one with our Lady, so do I with you.

HP lies forward on HPS, touching his phallus to her genitals as he salutes her on the lips. He then returns to kneeling.

**HP:** By moon rays' silver shaft of power,
By green leaf breaking from the bud,
By seed that springeth into flower,
By life that courseth in the blood.
Altar of mystery manifold,
The sacred Circle's central point.
Thus do I join thee as of old,
With kisses of my lips anoint.

HP salutes HPS' genitals, then gives the eightfold salute.

**HP:** Open for me the secret way between the gates of night and day. Here where sword and cup unite in infinite joy and love.

HP then lies on the living altar, and the Great Rite is enacted.
HP and HPS kneel facing one another. Both speak together:

**HP and HPS:** Bear witness, Lord and Lady, to this rite of love and devotion enacted by your faithful servants here today. It was done in your honor and in witness to your life-bringing power and beauty. Blessed be!

*Come forth, under the stars, and take your fill of love. I am above you and in you. My ecstasy is in yours. My joy is to see your joy. I am divided for love's sake, for the chance of union. And the sign shall be my ecstasy, the consciousness of the continuity of existence, the omnipresence of my body. Be not animal; refine thy rapture. If thou drink, drink by the eight and ninety rules of art: if thou love, exceed by delicacy; and if thou do aught joyous, let there be subtlety therein. But ever unto me—unto me.* —Aleister Crowley, *Liber 31*

# ~ 15 ~

# Witchcraft for Protection

In chapter 5, I described how to consecrate the whole house in preparation for a new child coming in. But whether a child is expected or not, it is a good plan to consecrate a house or apartment to give maximum psychic protection to those who live there. Slander, gossip, psychic attack by ignorant people of other religious persuasions, verbal abuse, magical attacks—all can be kept at bay by thoroughly consecrating the house. The following ritual will not only keep out all psychic negativity but also help protect the property from intrusion by burglars, rapists, and other such abusers and undesirables.

However, I would like to point out that true psychic attack, especially by anyone knowledgeable and powerful in such matters, is rare, and few have actually had a curse placed on them. I say this because I get letters from any number of people saying that a tarot card reader, or someone similar, told them they had been cursed; they want to know how to get rid of it. Any card reader or self-proclaimed psychic who tells you something like that is invariably going to follow up by saying ". . . but for so much money I can remove the curse." Yes, it's usually a come-on to get money out of you. And if you pay, guess what? "It's a stronger curse than I thought. It's going to cost a whole lot more money to get rid of it!"

Forget it! The likelihood of your having been cursed in the first place is remote, to say the least. Psychic attack can happen, but it's rare. Let's look at it in more detail.

# Bell, Book, and Candle

The old protection rite popularly known as "Bell, Book, and Candle" has been in use for generations by people of all persuasions. It is best done by the leader of the coven High Priest or High Priestess—but can be done by the owner or renter of the property alone if necessary. The rite gets its name from the fact that it starts and ends in the consecrated Circle—where, of course, you find the bell, the Book of Shadows, and candles.

The Circle should be cast in the usual way. (All the coven may participate in this, or just the principals. It is written here for all participants, but feel free to adapt it for the number available.) Once the Circle has been cast, HPS will take up her athame and the salted water, HP the censer, the homeowner the bell, and a covener the altar candle. HPS leads the way around the Circle to the east. There she cuts the Circle with her athame and lets everyone pass out. She follows and then turns and closes the Circle, describing a sealing pentacle with her athame. HPS then leads the group, going first to the front, main entrance to the house. At the entranceway, the candle is placed on the floor, in the middle of the opening. The bell is rung three times. HPS dips her fingers in the salted water and sprinkles it on the door itself and all around the door frame. HP holds the incense so that the smoke censes the door and frame, as he moves it slowly all around the perimeter. HPS holds up her athame in salute.

> **HPS:** **Lord and Lady, guard this entranceway, cleansing all who pass through it. Keep out any and all impurities, that those within this house may be protected by your light and love.**

She describes a pentagram. The bell is rung seven times.

The candle is picked up. All proceed to the next door, if there is one (moving clockwise around the house), and do the same thing. When all outside entrances have been consecrated, the group will proceed to the rooms. Start with the room immediately to the right of the main entrance. There the group stands in the center of the room. The candle is placed on the floor and the bell rung three times.

HPS leads the way to the first corner of the room. There she sprinkles the water, and the HP censes with the censer. They do every corner of the room, and every corner of every closet that may be in the room. Then, returning to the center of the room, the bell is rung seven times.

**HPS:** Lord and Lady, guard this room, cleansing all who come within it. Keep out any and all impurities, that those within this house may be protected by your light and love.

The bell is rung nine times.

Proceed to the next room and on through the house, doing the same cleansing in each and every room. Don't forget any cellar, basement, or attic. When all rooms and all closets within them have been cleansed, HPS will lead the group back to the Circle and, opening it, will allow them to pass in. She will follow and close it behind her, sealing it with a pentagram.

All tools are returned to the altar. All raise their athames in salute.

**HPS:** Lord and Lady, let your light and your energy remain in all corners of this home, guarding it from any and all negativity. Protect all who dwell in here at all times.

This is a good house cleansing and may be done any time you feel it is needed. I recommend doing it once a year. I also recommend concluding, after the Circle has been closed, by walking all around the outside of the house (or the whole apartment building, if it is an apartment), sprinkling and censing.

## Personal Protection

The best personal protection is to build the ball of white light around you *every* morning, when you first wake up. This will keep any negativity at bay all day long. But you can—and I think you should—also make a Witch's bottle.

There are two kinds of Witch's bottles. In much of the early literature on Witchcraft (written by Christian commentators), it is described as a bottle to protect *against* Witches and Witchcraft! Often made of metal, it would be filled with urine and thrown onto a fire. When the temperature rose sufficiently, it would burst. It was said that this would cause black magic to be thrown back on the "Witch"—and as the stories go, frequently an old woman in the village would be found with burns on her body the next day. Ergo, she was the Witch who had cast the evil spells!

The true Witch's bottle is that made *by* a Witch for his or her own personal protection. Take a small bottle or jar and fill it half to three-quarters full with sharp objects such as pins, needles, nails, screws, broken glass, broken mirrors, and so on. The metal can be old and rusty or new and shiny; it doesn't matter. Then urinate into the bottle, to fill it. If a woman can get menstrual blood in there also, this is supposed to be especially efficacious.

Cap the bottle, seal it with wax, and bury it at least seven inches deep in a spot where it will not be disturbed. So long as it remains undisturbed, it will protect you, returning to the sender any negativity directed at you. In fact, following the Wiccan belief, anything directed toward you will actually return to the sender threefold.

The bottle is buried at least seven inches deep so that it is below the frost line, if there is one. So long as it stays there, it will keep on working. However, many Witches make up a new bottle every year, in case it accidentally gets broken.

> By the power of the Goddess
> Within me,
> Whom I serve
> With all my body,
> With all my heart,
> With all my strength,
> I encompass me about
> With the Divine Circle of Protection
> Across which no human error dares set its foot.
> —Prayer for protection from The Book of Shadows

## Curse Protection

I've said that it is extremely unlikely that you will be the object of a curse. A curse is very specific and, if sent, would be directed by someone powerful in the arts of magic. But the term *curse* is often applied to any sort of harmful magic sent your way, including negative thoughts of fundamental Christians, who are fearful of anything outside their narrow requirements. So, looking at this loose definition, let's examine some of the remedial prescriptions available.

First is a simple ritual such as candle burning. If you really feel someone is or has been working against you, do this ritual.

## PURIFICATION RITUAL

This should be done during the waxing cycle of the moon, on a Monday, Tuesday, or Friday. You will need four stones: jade, opal, rose quartz, and amethyst. (You may use one of each, four of any one of these, or any combination.) You will also need four white candles and either a large candle in your primary astral color (see the appendix) or a poppet of yourself that you have made, stuffed with basil, dill, and plantain.

Place the poppet (or astral candle) in the center of the altar and the four white candles around it in the east, south, west, and north. Place the stones between the white candles.

Open the Circle in the usual way, then stand before the altar and raise your athame in salute. Say:

*I am here to cleanse and purify myself, to obliterate any negativity directed at me, that I may enjoy the peace, love, and joy that lie around me.*

Sprinkle the poppet with the salted water and hold it in the smoke of the incense. If it is the astral candle, then anoint it with oil, rubbing from the center outward and concentrating on yourself, seeing it as representing yourself, then hold it in the smoke of the incense. Say:

*Here is a poppet [or candle] of myself. All that I do to this, I do to myself. I acknowledge that I have the strength and healing powers within myself to overcome any and all negativity that is directed toward me.*

Anoint the four candles in the same way. Sprinkle them and then hold them in the smoke of the incense for a moment. Put them back down and light them, east first, then south, west, and north. Say:

*I surround myself with the white light of love and protection. It protects me from all directions: east, south, west, and north. As these flames burn bright and strong, so does the light of love and life burn bright and strong within me, keeping me from any harm.*

Take up the stones one at a time, first the one between the east and south, then on around clockwise. Anoint each stone with the oil; then hold it in the smoke of the incense for a moment before replacing it on the altar between the candles. Say:

*Surrounding me, I build a barrier of protection to support that barrier of light projected by these candles. Together may they guard me from any and all negativity now present or at any time in the future directed toward me. I ask this in the name of the Lord and the Lady, knowing that in their love I am blessed. So mote it be!*

Sit quietly for a few moments, giving thanks to the gods for all that they do for you. When you close the Circle, leave the four white candles to burn down, if at all possible. If they must be extinguished, then do so after the Circle has been closed, pinching them out in reverse order to the one in which they were lit.

# Baths, Mirrors, and Washes

Taking a bath that contains salt is the usual way of preparing the body for the ritual Circle. But many Witches make a habit of regular consecration and purification by taking baths into which they have put specific herbs for spiritual cleansing. This is a good practice, especially if you live in a community where you face pressures from outside groups and individuals.

Such ritual baths should be taken at specific times, if possible. For example, a bath for love should be taken on a Friday, one for money on a Sunday, one for riches on a Thursday, and so on (see chapter 7, or the appendix, for the planetary rulers of the days).

For protection, the best day is a Saturday, ruled by Saturn. Take your bath regularly every Saturday. It is best taken in the hour of Saturn, though most Witches don't get into the finer details of planetary hours. It is sufficient if you simply do it on a Saturday, but try to take it at the same time of day or night every time.

Into the bath, throw a bundle of herbs tied up in a muslin bag or piece of cheesecloth. For protection, use basil, bay, dill, fennel, and rosemary—about the same amount of each. Instead of this an even better, more concentrated, form is to steep these herbs before your bath in about three cups of boiling water for fifteen minutes. Then pour the strained water directly into the bath.

When you are in the bath itself, focus your mind on your body absorbing the protection of the gods. The herbs come from Mother Earth, so their essence is being absorbed into your body from her . . . strong protection!

Mirrors have always been regarded as protective devices. They are used a great deal in feng shui as well as in Witchcraft. Hang a mirror near any outside doorway, facing out. In fact, you can fasten it to the back of the door, with the reflective side against the door's surface. Better yet is to have it on the outside of the door, reflective side out. Hanging small mirrors in trees and bushes close to the doors is also effective. They serve to reflect any negativity directed toward the house or its occupants.

In feng shui, hanging wind chimes from the trees and bushes has the same effect. Bells can also work in similar fashion to mirrors and wind chimes.

Washes can also be useful, though they are found and used more in Voodoo than in Witchcraft. For protection, steep the same herbs—basil, bay, dill, fennel, and rosemary—in a pint of fresh water. Let them sit for three days, shaking them three times a day. Keep them in a cool, dark place while the wash is working. Every time you shake them, concentrate on the fact that they are for the purpose of protection. At the end of three days, strain the water and use it to wash down the front and rear doorsteps to the house, plus any other entrances. As you wash the steps, say:

*Lord and Lady, bless this entranceway that no negative forces may enter. Let in only that which is good and positive and keep out any who would do harm. Protect all those who are within. So mote it be!*

> Wash is a term given for an herb mixture usually steeped in water and used to sprinkle on or wash down the floor of a home, business, mailbox, etc. It is designed to attract or dispel certain influences.
> —Ray T. Malbrough, *Charms, Spells and Formulas*

Folklore contains a large number of charms and spells for protection. They include keeping an onion on your windowsill to attract and absorb negativity; circling the house with acorns; keeping a piece of mandrake root over the doorway; and leaving a bowl of salted water in the center of the floor of the main room of the house.

## Amulets and Talismans

Talismans are tools that have been specifically made for magical purposes. Amulets are natural items adopted for magical use. Examples of amulets are rabbits' feet, four-leafed clovers, acorns, pieces of quartz or other stones, a bear's claw, and so on. One powerful amulet held in high regard by Witches is a stone that has a natural hole through it. This is a representation of the vagina and, as such, has been honored for thousands of years around the world, especially as a fertility charm. In India, it is referred to as a *yoni* (the male counterpart being a *lingam*). Since an amulet is a natural object, it is not possible to make one, merely to adopt one for magical use. It should be duly consecrated before being employed magically.

A talisman *is* handmade. There are many different types, some simple and some very complex. They can be made of wood, metal, paper, bone, ivory, stone—virtually anything. The easiest is one made of paper or, more traditionally, parchment. Parchment is not easy to come by these days, so many Witches make talismans on parchmentlike paper, just to give it a more ancient appearance.

The best day on which to make your talisman depends on those planetary rulers we've already looked at (chapter 7 and the appendix). For protection, just as with the ritual bathing described previously, the best day is Saturday. The metal of Saturn is lead, so the best talisman for protection would be made of lead. However, parchment paper will work very well.

### Ruling Planets for Talismans

| | | | |
|---|---|---|---|
| MONDAY | Moon | *Silver* | Merchandise, dreams, theft |
| TUESDAY | Mars | *Iron* | Matrimony, war, enemies, prison |
| WEDNESDAY | Mercury | *Mercury* | Debt, fear, loss |
| THURSDAY | Jupiter | *Tin* | Honor, riches, clothing, desires |
| FRIDAY | Venus | *Copper* | Love, friendship, strangers |
| SATURDAY | Saturn | *Lead* | Life, building, protection |
| SUNDAY | Sun | *Gold* | Fortune, hope, money |

In its simplest form, you could ritually write PROTECTION on the paper, consecrate it, and carry it with you to serve you as a protective talisman. What we are going to do is just that, but in a more effective way—you actually put power into the word, helping the unconscious mind take much greater note of it.

First of all, rather than just writing PROTECTION on the parchment, you could write the word in one of the so-called magical alphabets (see the appendix). These are alphabets that have been used for centuries in magical works.

There were two reasons for using them. The first was simply secrecy. If a Witch was writing out spells and charms in a Book of Shadows, he or she wouldn't want anyone else who might obtain that book to be able to use them. It's similar to ensuring that, if an adult item falls into a child's hands, the child cannot use it and harm him- or herself. So this was partly to protect any unauthorized dabbler. But the other, and far more important, reason for using a magical alphabet was to put power into the item.

For example, if you are writing the word PROTECTION on a piece of paper, you will do just that—write it without thinking too much about it. But if you are writing the word using letters, or symbols, with which you are not familiar, then you have to concentrate on what you are doing; every little twist and turn of every symbol for each and every letter requires effort and attention. In so doing, you are putting your energies, your power, into the writing. Some novice Witches and Witch "wannabes" think it is clever to learn some of the magical alphabets, such as Runic or Theban, and then show off by writing letters and notes in them. In fact, they are defeating the whole purpose of the writings. The point is to *not* be familiar with the letters. To take a piece of parchment, about three inches by three inches, and laboriously write PROTECTION on it in one of the alphabets is to really put power into that piece of parchment.

If you then sprinkle and cense it and, in a ritual held in the Circle, state what its purpose is, then you have made a magical talisman that will work. But for protection, you want it to be as powerful as possible. Let us look at ways to enhance your talisman even more!

A form of magical working used by ceremonial magicians was the magical square. (I show a couple of simple ones in chapter 8.) There were magical squares for just about every purpose, some simple and some complex. Some were made up of numbers and others of letters.

You are going to construct a magical square of numbers and then, from that, produce a magical *sigil* that by itself represents the whole word PROTECTION. This you will put on one side of your talisman, and the magical alphabet version of the word, together with personal data, on the other.

Start by finding the numerological value of PROTECTION. Back in chapter 3, when you were finding your Witch name, we looked at this. Again, it is set up as follows:

| 1 | 2 | 3 | 4 | 5 | 6 | 7 | 8 | 9 |
|---|---|---|---|---|---|---|---|---|
| A | B | C | D | E | F | G | H | I |
| J | K | L | M | N | O | P | Q | R |
| S | T | U | V | W | X | Y | Z |   |

From this table, you can see that protection is $7 + 9 + 6 + 2 + 5 + 3 + 2 + 9 + 6 + 5 = 54 = 5 + 4 = 9$.

Now, construct a magical square that contains all nine numbers, but is set up so that they add up to the same total no matter which way you add them—horizontally, vertically, or diagonally—as follows:

| 4 | 9 | 2 | = | 15 |
|---|---|---|---|---|
| 3 | 5 | 7 | = | 15 |
| 8 | 1 | 6 | = | <u>15</u> |
| 15 | 15 | 15 | = | 45 |
| 45 | ... 4 + 5 = | | | <u>9</u> |

On this pattern of numbers, draw a square over the total number of your word, which is 9. Then, to indicate the start of the word, draw a small circle over the number 7 (the P of PROTECTION). From there, you will draw lines connecting the numbers, following the numbers of the letters: 7-9-6-2-5-3-2-9-6-5. Use another small circle at the ending number 5. It will look like this:

| 4 | 9 | 2 |
|---|---|---|
| 3 | 5 | 7 |
| 8 | 1 | 6 |

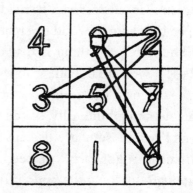

If we now take this geometric figure off the square full of numbers, it will look like this:

This final figure, known as a *sigil*, has all the properties of protection, filled with the power you have put into it from your construction and artistry.

Draw the *sigil* on one side of your piece of parchment. On the reverse, write the word in one of the magical alphabets; it doesn't matter which one. Then, under the word, write your own name in that same magical script and add your birth date.

In a ritual Circle (which can be done at any Esbat meeting, or at a special ritual just for this), consecrate the talisman by sprinkling it with the salted water and holding it in the smoke of the incense, saying:

> *Here is my talisman, constructed by me to protect me in all things. Let it be the focus of the love of the Lord and the Lady so that their goodness will keep me from all harm. So mote it be!*

Keep this talisman with you at all times. Some people make a small bag of silk or linen to put it in, and hang it from a cord around the neck.

This talisman is for protection; follow the same process whatever your need: for love, matrimony, money, health, knowledge, or specific abilities. Change the words you say when consecrating it appropriately.

A similar talisman can be made on metal, engraving the *sigils* and words. It can also be burned into wood or etched into stone.

The important thing is that the talisman should be made by the person who will use it. You are the one who will put all your energy into the talisman because it is for your own protection (or other purpose). Someone else would not have the same measure of intensity, so the talisman would not be as effective.

As I've said, similar talismans can be made for love, health, wealth, matrimony, or friendship. For each, you need to see which day is pertinent and build an appropriate *sigil*. In doing the *sigils*, if the word you are using has a double letter, or two letters with the same number, so that you should be on the same square twice consecutively, there is a "stop-and-go" symbol to use, which consists of two small triangles:

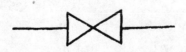

An example would be the *sigil* for MATRIMONY, where there are two 9s together:

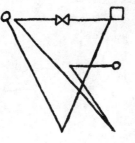

> By utilizing an uncommon form of writing . . . you can direct your energies, your power, into what you are working on. Magicians would use this method for charging (with power) everything they needed: their sword, censer, wand, athame, bell, trumpet, trident, etc. They would even write Words of Power on their robes and on a parchment hat.—Raymond Buckland, Buckland's Complete Book of Witchcraft

# Binding Spell

Another protective measure is a "binding spell." This is something that—while it does go against someone's free will—is not actually negative if done for protective purposes. What it does is stop the person from doing something that would harm you. For example, perhaps you don't want it known locally that you are a Witch—but someone finds out and is about to spread the word. It would be quite all right for you to stop them from doing this. It would not *harm* the person, merely restrict them in that particular field.

For this, you will make a poppet to represent the person. Take two pieces of white cloth and, laying one on top of the other, cut out a rough gingerbread-man shape. Sew all around the figure but leave an opening at the top. Turn the figure inside out, so that the sewing edge is on the inside. Stuff the figure with any three of the following herbs: anise, asafetida, bay, bloodroot, broom, chamomile, fennel,

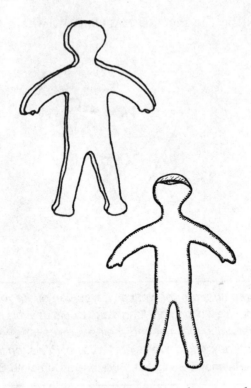

hyssop, lavender, parsley, peppermint, rosemary, thyme, valerian, or vervain. Also, put a walnut inside the figure.

When it has been stuffed, sew up the top of the figure and then mark it to show who it represents. Embroider, paint, or use Magic Markers to put on a face and facial hair (if there is any); add wool of an appropriate color for the hair. On the body, mark the person's name, if known, and her astrological sign also, if known.

As an alternative, you can make the figure of wax, clay, or the like, chopping the herb(s) finely and mixing in. The personal details can then be scratched onto it. In simplest form, you could just cut out a flat figure from cardboard and mark or paint it to represent the person. But the making of a figure by modeling or sewing and stuffing puts far more power into it, because far more time and energy were spent in making it.

In a consecrated Circle, lay the poppet on the altar. Beside it have a length of brown or black ribbon, wool, or thread. Touch your athame to the poppet and say:

*Here is [name]. It is her [him] in every way. What I do to this figure I do to her.*

Pick up the poppet and sprinkle it with salted water and hold it in the smoke of the incense. Then take up the thread and slowly and deliberately bind it around the poppet, making sure you cover the mouth to start. It is even better if you use thread and a needle and actually sew up the mouth of the poppet before continuing with binding around the body. When you have sufficiently bound the figure, lay it down on the altar again and, touching your athame to it, say:

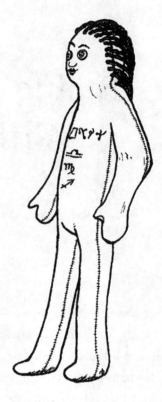

*Now is this person [name] bound by these actions. Now will she be unable to speak and demonstrate in any way against me or to cause me any problems by the spreading of gossip or by any action that would bring harm to me. Let her be free to speak and act on any other matters but not those that concern me and my well-being. So mote it be!*

After closing the Circle, carefully wrap the poppet in a piece of white linen and put it away in a place where it will not be disturbed.

# ~ 16 ~
# Facing the Unexpected With Witchcraft

The unexpected comes to almost everyone, at some time. It might be news of a death, an illness, financial problems, an auto accident, or whatever. Different people are affected in different ways by such sudden, unexpected news. How do Witches handle it?

The first step is to know, and to acknowledge, that everything that happens, happens for good reason. The gods know what they are doing and, even if we cannot share their long-range vision, at least we can trust in them. We, as Witches, can respect that there is a larger plan than we may or may not be aware of that is taking place.

An example in my personal life was when my first wife unexpectedly left me after eighteen years of marriage. I was devastated and could not believe that there was any justice in the world! Hindsight is always so much clearer. It took a year or more to see that in fact there had been good reason for what happened. We had gone through an essential period together, but had finally reached a point where it was necessary to go our separate ways in order for each of us to advance. It turned out that my life was better for the break, as I hope hers was, and has continued to go from strength to strength. But at the time, I could not see the wisdom of the gods.

We are all here to go through certain experiences and to learn certain lessons. Some of these experiences and lessons can be painful, but in the broad scheme of things they are extremely valuable and take us forward in the syllabus of this particular lifetime.

The second step for the Witch is to try to remain calm and to view the larger picture. How will this affect life as you have known it so far? What are the short-term effects? What are the long-term results? What changes, if any, will need to be made?

To do this, it is best to meditate. Meditation has the immediate action of calming you and distancing you from what has been reported or taken place. In sudden, unexpected circumstances, it is actually possible to meditate in the midst of chaos. Simply close your eyes, breathe deeply, center yourself, cut off your mind from everything going on around you, and try to focus your mind on nothing at all. This won't be easy, especially under these circumstances, but you need to place yourself in a void where you are untouched by anything, especially feelings. If you are unable to focus on nothing, no matter how hard you try, then focus your mind on some calm woodland scene. Perhaps study a large tree, or a wide vista, or a tumbling waterfall, in your mind.

Deep breathing is the key. Go through the entire deep-breathing routine—taking in the white light, exhausting the negative. As you do so, you will find your pulse drop, your breathing come easier, your mind relax; you will be able to place things into perspective.

From thinking of nothing at all, you can then ease into what has happened. Look at it as unemotionally as you possibly can, as though you are an outsider looking in. From there, you can consider what immediate actions need to be taken.

> Sometimes a thing that seems bad when it happens turns out to be the proverbial blessing in disguise. The Goddess, as we all know, works in mysterious ways. More practically than that, though, some of the things we call bad could be called something else: an inconvenience, a challenge, an opportunity, a change of plans. Although it can be difficult to find purpose and inspiration in everything that happens, it is a worthwhile undertaking.
> —Ashleen O'Gaea, The Family Wicca Book

# Wiccan Novena

One item we might adopt and adapt from Roman Catholics (and why not, since they have taken so much from us!) is the idea of the novena. For them, this is basically a nine-day devotion—a prayer that is repeated over a period of nine days. In Wicca, we can take a prayer or affirmation and repeat it over a number of days, or hours, or even minutes, as necessary. In effect, it is a calming tool that gives us time to collect ourselves and to, again, get things back into perspective.

The words can be a prayer of comfort, asking the Lord and Lady to be with you and to help you through this crisis. If necessary, it can be a short prayer that can be repeated over and over again, until you begin to calm:

*Lovely Goddess, powerful Lord, be with me now in my hour of need. Comfort me and calm me that I may see your greater plan for what has happened here.*

Something as simple as this can be repeated as many times as it takes to calm you. If you are able to light a candle and sit, stand, or kneel before it, all to the good. You can then go on to repeat this every morning or evening for the next eight days, and it will slowly ground you and bring you back into manageable touch with the realities of what has happened.

In affirmation form, you could say:

*I am calm and secure in the hands of the Lord and of the Lady. I am calm and secure in the hands of the Lord and the Lady. I am calm and secure in the hands of . . .*

Repeat as much and as often as necessary. You can write these prayers and affirmations for yourself, or give them to someone who suddenly is in need of one.

---

### Prayer in Times of Stress and Confusion

*O dearest Goddess, Mother of the green earth, blue waters, and the silver moon, please be with me now in my time of need. Stress and confusion have taken hold of my life, and I feel the weight of life's burdens suffocating me. I am truly afraid, but I know that you in all your loving kindness hear me now, and I feel the heavy weight getting easier to bear. O dearest God, Father of the dark forests and shimmering mountains, grant me your spiritual strength so that I can come through this time of crisis and get back to my normal life once again. Blessed Be.*
—Mark Ventimiglia, The Wiccan Prayer Book

# Preparation for Possible Bad News

When there are signs that bad news may be in the offing—when an elderly relative is taken into the hospital, for example—it may be worthwhile to try to divine the probable outcome. This can be done in various ways: with tarot cards or runes, by using the pendulum, by skrying, by meditating, and so forth. If you can get an idea of what is likely to happen, then you will be less surprised and emotionally upset when and if it actually does happen. You will have time to adjust to the idea of the coming situation.

With the pendulum, you can ask specific questions such as "Will [name] recover from this setback?" "Is this a terminal illness?" "How long does [name] have?" With the tarot or other divination tools, you can cast various spreads to see what the future holds, both for you and for the person involved. An astrological chart can tell you a lot, if you know how to interpret it properly (though this does require an expert). I have personally found skrying, which I described in chapter 10, to be one of the best tools for seeing the future, especially under the sort of circumstances we are discussing.

# Extra Strength From the Coven

But despite all of the above, there are times when even a Witch, with all his or her knowledge and understanding, is devastated by some news or happening. This is the time when the coven, and the High Priest and High Priestess especially, make their presence felt. Coven is family, and family is there for comfort. A Circle should be held and everything done to comfort and show love to the one who is the recipient of the bad news.

One of the comforting and energizing techniques is for the covener—we'll call him the recipient—to sit in the center of the Circle, against the altar. The rest of the coven will then dance around him, building up energy as though they were going to do magic. When the climax is reached, this energy is directed toward the recipient, filling him with strength, warmth, and love.

A talisman for acceptance and comfort is a good idea, as is doing the candle-burning ritual "To Accept a Situation."[21]

---

21. Raymond Buckland, *Advanced Candle Magick.*

## The High Priestess's Love

*You may come to her for a few seconds then go away and do whatever you will.*
*Her love is unchanging.*
*You may deny her to herself or to yourself, then curse her to any who will listen.*
*Her love is unchanging.*
*You may become the most despised of creatures, then return to her.*
*Her love is unchanging.*
*You may become the enemy of the gods themselves, then return to her.*
*Her love is unchanging.*
*Go where you will; stay however long you will, and come back to her.*
*Her love is unchanging.*
*Abuse others; abuse yourself; abuse her and come back to her.*
*Her love is unchanging.*
*She will never criticize you. She will never minimize you.*
*She will never fail you. Because, to her, you are everything and she herself is*
    *nothing.*
*She will never deceive you. She will never ridicule you. She will never fail you.*
    *Because, to her, you are God-Nature to be served and she is your servant.*
*No matter what befalls; no matter what you become; she awaits you always. She*
    *knows you. She serves you. She loves you.*
*Her love for you, in the changing world, is unchanging.*
*Her love, beloved, is unchanging.*

—Lady Olwen, Gardenerian Book of Shadows

# ~ 17 ~

# Witchcraft and Death

*To every man upon this earth*
*Death cometh soon or late,*
*And how can man die better*
*Than facing fearful odds,*
*For the ashes of his fathers*
*And the temples of his gods?*
    —Horatius, Lays of Ancient Rome

Witches are probably better equipped than most other people to deal with news of terminal illness and death. We have been brought up in the Craft with the knowledge of reincarnation, knowing that each and every one of us is here on this earth for a certain time, to learn and experience certain things. We know that when this time is over—and it will vary from one person to the next—it will be time to move on toward the next incarnation. Each life has been previously planned by the spirit, or soul, before coming into this world. We knew what the circumstances would be and we knew when we would have to move on.

The hard part is always for those left behind . . . those others who have grown to know and to love us. But Witches, being aware of this planned pattern, are more inclined to celebrate a death as a "graduation," rather than to mourn it.

*Death borders upon our birth, and our cradle stands in the grave.*
    —Bishop Hall (1574–1656)

# Crossing the Bridge

The death ritual is known by various names. I prefer *Crossing the Bridge*, since it conjures pictures of the spirit literally crossing over a bridge between this world and the next. And with a bridge, it is possible to come back the other way. There is, then, the possibility of being able to communicate with the dead. This is something I'll look at shortly.

Around the world, lights are associated with the dead. Traditionally, they are there to light the way of the departed spirit to the netherworld. The jack-o'-lanterns of Hallowe'en were originally used for this. In Japan, paper lanterns are used. In ancient Egypt, candles were lit. The Day of the Dead, in Mexico, features a candlelight procession to the cemetery.

In the myths of many countries, the land of the dead is located across a river or sea. The bridge of Wicca stretches across such a river, though it has no name. The Afterworld, however, is known by the majority of Wiccans as *Summerland*—this thanks to Gerald Gardner, who actually took the name from one used by Spiritualists.

A Gallup poll found that three out of four Americans believe in an afterlife. How we view this world, this Summerland, depends greatly on our upbringing and spiritual training. Christianity holds to a heaven aspect and a hell aspect (with Roman Catholics throwing in purgatory as a bonus!). Which one you go to depends on how well you have lived your life, they say.

Wiccans disagree. We believe that everyone goes to one place (which, for convenience, I will call Summerland). We don't have to wait until death to get our rewards and punishments; we get them during life, according to how we live it. (In the beginning of this book, I spoke of this belief in a threefold return.)

Summerland is, as we might expect, a beautiful place. What we know of it is what we have gleaned from people who have returned from near-death experiences, and from accounts obtained by genuine mediums who communicate with the dead.

I personally believe very strongly that such communication is possible. In fact, I wrote extensively about it in my *Doors to Other Worlds*. "Many records of near-death experiences speak of leaving the body, going toward a bright light—oftentimes down a sort of tunnel—and seeing deceased loved ones there. In these experiences these loved ones often told the spirit to return, that the time had not yet come to pass completely over."

> *When I awoke in the spirit-life and saw that I still had hands and feet and all the rest of the human body, I can't say what feelings took hold of me. I realized that I had this body . . . a spiritual body, but a body. Imagine being re-born, free from the decaying flesh. I gazed on weeping friends with a saddened heart, mingled with joy, knowing that I could still be with them daily, though unseen and unheard. Then I felt a light touch on my shoulder and turned to find many loved ones who had long since departed life on earth; all there to greet me and help me move on.*
> —A departed spirit, speaking through a reputable medium

Pauline Campanelli, in *Pagan Rites of Passage*, suggests that the passageway to the light might be analogous to the original birth canal bringing us from the darkness of the womb into the light.

There is no pain in death. On the contrary, death is freedom from pain and suffering, which disappear at the moment the spirit slips out of the physical shell.

According to shamanism, what we see as a rock, or a tree, or a bird is in fact just the outward manifestation of that rock, tree, or bird. Similarly, what we see as a human being is just the outward manifestation of a human being. The inner spirit is in all things. It is this spirit that survives bodily death. For this reason, there are rocks and trees and birds and all animals in the afterlife. What a dull place it would be without them!

So when we die, we find ourselves in Summerland—which, outwardly, looks much like this land where we lived and breathed. We are probably all ethereal beings there, so the "appearance" of these things is only in our spiritual minds. Because of this, we are able to change what we perceive to what we wish to see. If we die old and deformed, we can be young and vibrant again in the afterlife. We see ourselves there as we most wish to see ourselves. It is only when communicating with someone still on the earth plane that a spirit would temporarily assume the appearance by which the living person would recognize him or her. It should also be remembered that there is no such thing as time in the afterlife. Time is a human-made concept.

The Wiccan belief is that we spend a certain amount of "time" between lives. It is a rest period, like a school vacation between semesters. During this period, we review our previous life and plan the next one. Presumably we do this with the aid of the gods. We plan where, when, and to whom we will be born and what lessons and experiences we will undergo. But before we get too far ahead of ourselves, let us have a look at the ritual of death; the ending of the physical life.

## CROSSING THE BRIDGE RITUAL

This rite may be performed at any of the other rituals or as a rite in itself, preceded by Casting the Circle and followed by Cakes and Ale. If done with another ritual, it should be done just before the Cakes and Ale.

There should be an extra white candle standing unlit in the center of the altar. Flowers may be arranged around it. The bell is rung thirteen times.

HP: We hear the bell of remembrance, rung today for [Name], who has moved on across the bridge to Summerland.

HPS: That [Name] is not with us in body, here today, is our loss and saddens us all. Yet although we sorrow we also rejoice, for she [he] has left this plane to move on toward the next lifetime. She has completed the lifework that had been planned and now moves forward, through the light, to that which lies ahead.

HP lights the central candle on the altar. Touching her athame to it, HPS says:

HPS: Here we send our love and our energies to help you pass across the bridge, into the light and into the arms of the Lord and the Lady. May your spirit burn as brightly as does this candle flame. You have touched many hearts in your time with us and we will miss you. Blessed be!

ALL: Blessed be!

HP and HPS sit with the rest of the coven. Anyone who now wishes to say anything to the deceased, or about the deceased, may do so. If it is only "I love you," or "We'll miss you," or whatever, it may be said. The coven should reminisce about the deceased, preferably remembering the good times; laughing and joking is encouraged. Laugh and send love to the one who has gone. When all have said what they need to say, rise and join hands. Slowly the coven dances *deosil* around the circle, keeping hands together. They may chant the name of the one gone, or may simply chant "I love you."

The bell is rung seven times.

All take their athames and point them at a spot behind the altar, imagining the deceased standing there smiling at them. In fact, she may appear. The coveners should concentrate on sending love and joy, projecting their feelings along the line of their athames. When HPS feels enough has been done, she says:

**HPS:** **We wish you all the love and happiness we may. We will always remember you with love. You are always welcome at our Circles. Do not forget us. We will meet again. So mote it be.**

**ALL:** **So mote it be.**

Then follow with the Cakes and Ale, followed by Closing the Circle.

*Note:* This ritual may also be done upon the death of a pet.

## Communicating With the Dead

There are many ways of communicating with the dead. One of the easiest, yet most effective, is through meditation. Meditation is actually "listening." By making yourself quiet and settling your mind, you can open up to hear what may be sent to you, whether from the gods themselves or from someone near and dear to you who has crossed the bridge. In your mind you may ask questions, if you need to, and you will receive answers.

Skrying (see chapter 10) can also be effective, as can automatic writing. In the latter, you sit quietly after doing the ritual white light cleansing (which *must* be done before any and all psychic exercises such as this) and rest your hand, holding a pen or pencil, on a sheet of paper. Do not look at your hand; meditate on the person you are trying to contact. Send thoughts or questions to him, if you wish. After a while, you may feel your hand start to twitch and even to start scribbling on the paper. Do not look at it. Give it plenty of time to settle down. Eventually you will be aware of it moving across the paper and writing something.

When it stops, look at the paper; you will probably see that actual words have been formed. Sometimes there is a lot of scribbling before you get actual writing. Do not try to force it—in fact, it is best not to look at it as it is working. You can watch television, have a conversation with someone, or read a book while your hand is writing! It is recommended that you not watch the paper, to prevent yourself from influencing what is written. You may go through a lot of paper, so be ready to flip over the sheet when your hand gets to the bottom.

One recommendation is to use large sheets of construction paper, or wrapping paper, so that you have plenty of space. I have even obtained old rolls of wallpaper and written on the back! Eventually, when you get used to automatic writing, you will be able to watch what is being written as it writes without consciously influencing it, and can ask questions that will be answered immediately.

The Ouija Board, or Talking Board, is another useful item, but be careful with it. Again, by doing your white light work ahead of time, you will be protected. But it seems there are always many spirits wanting to come through, and they are not always the ones you want to hear from. If what you get from a Talking Board is not right or upsetting in any way, simply stop using it, if only for a week or so. If it tells you to do things you would rather not do . . . don't do them! Again, my *Doors to Other Worlds* looks at many of these methods in detail.

# Burial or Cremation

There is no set directive on what should be done with a Wiccan body after death. The majority of Witches do seem to favor cremation, but there is nothing against burial if that is the preference. If the deceased has left instructions or has, in life, stated a preference, then that should certainly be honored. Rather than have a grave and erect a gravestone on precious land, many Witches will plant a tree, or trees, as a memorial to the deceased.

Wiccans believe that the body is merely a shell for the spirit, so what becomes of the shell after death is unimportant, since it is now empty. It is the spirit that will go on to inhabit another, different, shell for the next lifetime.

Some Witches suggest donating money to a worthwhile charity, rather than spending it on flowers for a funeral. Many believe that the funeral should be a celebration—with much good food, drink, and merriment—to send the "graduated" deceased upon his or her way.

*My involvement with paranormal phenomena has convinced me that the whole experience is simply an extension of our natural awareness and mental abilities. The phrase "life after death" presupposes a following event, when it seems to me to be a parallel existence which is continual. The before, after, and during is purely relative to the observer. We mustn't forget that we invented time as we conceive it.* —Michael Bentine, *The Door Marked Summer*

# ~ 18 ~

# Witchcraft and Other Religions

*There's naught, no doubt, the spirit calms*
*As rum and true religion*

—Byron, *Don Juan*

It has been said that Witchcraft is the fastest-growing religion in America today. No one can actually give any figures, however, since there is no central body for Wicca. We have no Wiccan "pope" or the like; no one leader of all Witchcraft. There is no "Queen of All the Witches" or "King of All the Witches," though from time to time publicity-seeking individuals lay claim to such titles.

The truth is that all covens are autonomous. In other words, they are self-governing. Some have had other covens grow off from them over the years in degree systems, making the original High Priestess a "Witch Queen" or "Queen of the Sabbat" (*a* Witch Queen, not the Queen of All Witches!).

Basically all covens look after themselves and are not governed by a higher authority. And since most covens and traditions do not publicly declare themselves, it is impossible to say how many there are. We can only estimate, based partly on sales of books such as this, and that estimation puts Witches in the hundreds of thousands in the United States alone.

In a handbook put out by the U.S. Department of the Army for use by chaplains,[22] Wicca is listed alongside Christian Heritage Groups, Indian Heritage Groups, Islamic Groups, Japanese Heritage Groups, Jewish Groups, Sikh Groups,

22. Department of the Army Pamphlet 165-13, *Religious Requirements and Practices of Certain Select Groups: A Handbook for Chaplains.*

and "Other" Groups, which include Baha'i Faith, Church of Scientology, and the Native American Church. So Wicca is accepted as a religion by the federal government, as it should be.

Yet still many other religious groups regard Witchcraft as anti-Christian, anti-good, antipositive, even synonymous with Satanism (despite the fact that Witches do not even believe in Satan, let alone worship him!).

Such misconceptions of Witchcraft come, of course, largely from the distortion of history promoted by the early Christian Church. For so many centuries, Witchcraft was presented as the enemy of Christianity, with its followers worshiping the devil, that this concept has remained even in today's otherwise enlightened society. The major problem was that printing came into being when the persecutions were at their height. Consequently, anything published on the subject of Witchcraft, right from that very beginning of printing, was from the church's point of view. Not unnaturally, it was heavily biased. Later writers used these early books as their only sources of reference, so this misrepresentation of the Old Religion was passed along for generation after generation. Only in the last fifty years has the true story of Witchcraft been presented. It is no wonder, then, that so much misinformation still persists.

> At its simplest, a religion is the word used to describe a group of people who all subscribe to the same basic beliefs about a god, and have a common or similar way of worshipping that god. But in many ways that is too simplistic . . . there are some features common to all religions, there is enormous diversity among religions, and sometimes within what is commonly thought of as one religion.
> —Chris Richards (editor), *The Illustrated Encyclopedia of World Religions*

# Straightening Out the Misconceptions

All we can do to straighten out these misconceptions is educate the masses. It is a long, uphill struggle, but we have come a long way in the last fifty years. Today, more and more, Witchcraft is being presented as, and accepted as, a religion in its own right. The media, in the form of movies and television series, is starting to present Wicca in a more or less accurate manner. True, we still have to put up with inaccuracies, stereotypes, mixing of fact and fiction, but on the whole the message is getting out. And we can all do our bit to increase that accurate awareness.

In school and in the office, there should be no religious discrimination. For example, if crucifixes and Jewish stars are allowed to be worn, then so should pentagrams. Nor should there be enforced prayers. Many times at such gatherings as Rotary Club functions—which promote businesses in communities—and other such, there are dinners or lunches where the local minister is asked to give the blessing. Why should a Christian blessing be accepted? In such circumstances the witch should insist upon referring to "the Gods" (or the God and the Goddess) rather than to "God." "Blessed Be" or "So Mote It Be" is as appropriate as "Amen." The sign of the Pentagram should be as acceptable as the sign of the Cross.

Pledge allegiance? Sure, but "... one nation under *the gods*, indivisible ..." The phrase *under God*, incidentally, was added to the pledge by an act of Congress in 1954. The original pledge, written in 1892 by Francis Bellamy, contained the phrase *my flag*.

If we think we are having a hard time getting accepted, think of the struggle of the Jews and others. In fact, there are many parallels between Judaism and Witchcraft. Both have been severely persecuted in the past and seen millions put to death because of their religious beliefs; both are still struggling to be accepted for what they are, not for what others see them as.

# The Comic Approach

A Fundamentalist Christian group publishes and distributes hate literature in the form of little comic books. These tracts attack not only Witches but Catholics, Hindus, Mormons, Jews, Baha'is, Muslims, Freemasons, and more. They are published by Chick Publications, Life Messengers, World Missionary Press, and others. They are a wealth of misinformation, alarmist statements, and downright nonsense. They are left littering public places such as bus stations, train stations, public restrooms and phone booths. Any Wiccan or pagan whose address becomes known will receive them in the mail—sent with no return address, of course!

In recent years one Wiccan church has been fighting fire with fire. Pathfinder Press[23] has put out some Wiccan and Pagan oriented booklets done in exactly the same comic book style, but presenting the true picture of what we do and what we

---

23. Pathfinder Press, P.O. Box 57, Index, WA 98256-0057

believe. With titles like "The Other People," these anti-tract little booklets explain why pagans do not have "original sin," don't have to be "saved," and don't acknowledge a Bible as any authority. Unlike the Fundamentalist versions, we do not litter with them. They are, however, very handy for handing out to those annoying people who come banging on the door and try to force their religious beliefs on you, feeling theirs are the only correct ones.

# Differences Within the Craft

Since there is no overall administration of Wicca, there are many differences found within the Craft. Earlier, in chapter 2, I spoke of this, noting that variety in Wicca is much like that found in Christianity and other religions. In Christianity, you can find Baptists, Episcopalians, Roman Catholics, Methodists, and many others. They are all Christians, holding the basic concepts of this religion, but they vary in their approaches to worship, in their rituals, in their hierarchies, and so on.

So it is in Wicca. There are many different denominations or "traditions." No one is any more right, correct, or authentic than another; all are valid. Some include more ceremonial magic than others, some more ritual, while others are very simple and basic. Some balance the God and the Goddess, while others emphasize one over the other.

The first visible form of modern Witchcraft was Gardnerian. This was Gerald Gardner's version of the old Celtic form that he had been initiated into in the 1930s. It was the first form made public and has become the basis for most forms since.

Sometime after its introduction—with the final repeal of the last law against Witchcraft in England—Alex Sanders began to promote his own version, called Alexandrian. This was made up largely of the Gardnerian rituals but with the addition of some ceremonial magic. Strangely for a Wiccan tradition, this latter contains a great deal of Christian material.

As the years passed, other forms of Wicca and of Paganism surfaced, including Druidism, Celtic Wicca, Saxon, Norse, Welsh, Scottish, American Celtic, Dianic, and a host of others. Many more groups had no specific label and were generally eclectic.

Virtually all Wiccan groups celebrate the same Sabbats, and most follow the

Esbat form established by Gardner. A variety of names are used for the deities, some mixing a God from one part of the world with a Goddess from a totally different part, which personally I find difficult to comprehend.

The very marking of the Circle can vary. One or two groups stipulate that it must be marked with salt, or with sand, or even sulfur, while most don't mind how it's marked.

The tools used are another indication of different thoughts. Some groups cast the Circle with a sword, while others will use a staff, a broomstick, an athame, or even just a finger. Some covens will include a wand in their tools, while others see it as unnecessary, since an athame can do all that a wand can do.

Some traditions scourge while others do not. Some use a pentacle, ankh, white-handled knife . . . there is a wide variety of tools. The bottom line is that anything used should be used for good reason. It should not be included just because it seems like a good idea or because you think that "all" Witches use it.

> *Various attempts have been made to classify religions, but with only partial success, and there is no generally accepted scheme. Every religion is a complex of many elements, and there is no one specific feature which adequately characterizes it.*
> —William Benton, Encyclopedia Britannica

# Eclecticism

More and more eclectic groups are appearing, making up their own rituals (which I think is good) and their own forms of ritual. There are so many different types of people in the world, and so many individuals; it is good that would-be Witches have a wide choice of tradition. Religion is such a personal thing that it is important to find that which is exactly right for *you*. You should not have to compromise.

But I do see a downside. Today the Craft seems to be getting so diluted, so "anything goes," that I fear there is a possibility of it washing itself away! Anyone can do virtually anything, claim it is their tradition, and call themselves Witches. And who is to say they are not? But I have seen insidious negativity creeping in.

A recent writer on the Craft (who should know better!) has recently endorsed another (non-Witch) author's suggestion of saying the Christian Lord's Prayer backward as part of a ritual. What can this possibly have to do with the Old Religion? Isn't this the very thing that so many of us have worked so hard to get rid of over the years? And I have seen acceptance of negative magic ... working against people, going against others' free will, even placing curses. All this is done in the name of modern Witchcraft.

This same writer has said: "I am one Witch who does not embrace the Wiccan concept of the Threefold Law. . . . In my opinion, if you psychically set yourself up to believe that you will receive a threefold punishment as a result of your spell work, as so many Wiccans have been taught to do, then chances are that this is exactly what you will get!"

Well, yes! That's the whole point. The writer continues, "It's the same if a healthy person convinces himself that he is sick or dying. Sooner or later his body will respond to his negative thought energies and begin to show signs of illness, pain may be felt, an actual disease may manifest, and the victim of his own fears may even die as a result of what he had physically set himself up to believe."

This is the whole point of the belief! It is by this belief that we are prevented from doing anything negative. If this writer can understand that we can bring illness upon ourselves, why can this writer not see that we can also bring incredible blessings by thinking positively? This stops a person from behaving negatively and promotes the positive way of life, which is the whole point of the Threefold Law.

Hopefully Wicca will survive in its true *positive* form, despite such manipulators of belief and such workers of negative magic.

---

*The writers against religion, whilst they oppose every system, are wisely careful not to set up any of their own.*
—Edmund Burke (1729–1797)

# ~ 19 ~

# Through the Year With Witchcraft

The Sabbats were always times for celebration in Wicca and have remained that way. Normally no "work"—magic or healing—is done at a Sabbat unless there is some emergency. Such work is done at the Esbats.

In the old days, the Sabbats were quite often a time when a number of different covens would get together to celebrate. These were the large gatherings of Witches, spoken about by ancient writers and depicted by artists.

The Esbats, in contrast, were always small, personal coven affairs. If a number of covens came together for the Sabbat, then the senior High Priestess, or Queen of the Sabbat, would officiate. Today, the celebrations become potluck feasts, every covener bringing a dish to add to the Sabbat table for the meal after the ritual.

## The Sabbats

There were four major Sabbats and four minor Sabbats. In the beginning of this book, I spoke of the two main deities, the God of Hunting and the Goddess of Fertility. The God ruled during the winter half of the year—sometimes called the "dark" half—when it was not possible to grow food and humankind had to rely on success in hunting. The summer months, or "light" half of the year, were ruled over by the Goddess, who looked after the crops. So the year was originally divided into two parts.

> *In Europe there were two main festivals, which fell exactly six months apart, and each half year was again bisected and marked with a minor festival. But the dates of these festivals were not everywhere identical; for whilst the non-Celtic peoples divided the year in accordance with the solstices and equinoxes, with Midsummer Day and Midwinter Day, or Yule, as their chief festivals, the Celtic peoples divided it in accordance with the entry of the seasons, their two principal festivals being Bealltainn (1 May) and Samhuinn or Hallowmass (1 November).*
>
> —F. Marian McNeill, The Silver Bough

The divisions came at Samhain and Beltane. Samhain fell at the end of October, Beltane at the end of April. These two halves were then split into quarters, with celebrations marking the midpoints of the dark and light halves. Halfway through winter was Imbolc, at the end of January. Halfway through summer was Lughnasadh, at the end of July.

Later in the development of humankind, the sun festivals were added to these agricultural ones as the minor Sabbats: the summer and winter solstices and the spring and autumn equinoxes.

**SAMHAIN** (November Eve)
Yule (December 21)
**IMBOLC** (February Eve)
Spring (March 21)
**BELTANE** (May Eve)
Midsummer (June 21)
**LUGHNASADH** (August Eve)
Autumn (September 21)

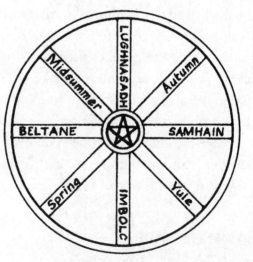

THE WHEEL OF THE YEAR

The Witchcraft year ends and begins at Samhain, the Witches' new year. *Samhain* is pronounced *SOW-n* (the *sow* part to rhyme with *cow*). There are variations on its spelling, as with many Wiccan names. For example, Scottish Witches call it *Samhuinn*. As with all of the old festivals, celebrations began the night before—the eve of the date. So Samhain is actually on November Eve (and Beltane on May Eve, Imbolc on February Eve, Lughnasadh on August Eve). Celebrations began that evening when the sun went down, and continued until the following sunrise.

Samhain, as the end of the old year and the start of the new one, was a time when it was believed the veil between the worlds was thin. This, then, was a time when it was relatively easy to communicate with the spirits of loved ones who had died the previous year. Many Witches believed that the dead came back to celebrate the Sabbat with them. (In fact, I have witnessed this myself, most notably at the 1964 Samhain Sabbat when I and the whole coven saw Gerald Gardner come and join us.)

It is from this idea that today there are stories of ghosts at Hallowe'en, the Christianized version of Samhain. It is also from this idea of communication with the dead that Samhain is an especially good time for divination about the future. And of course, in the old days, it would have been of critical interest to divine the nature of the coming winter.

The Samhain feast was always a big one. This was the time when the herds and the flocks had to be thinned, so that only enough sheep and cattle essential to survival would need to be fed over the harsh winter months. The rest would be put to the slaughter, their meat salted and stored. The Samhain feast therefore included plenty of freshly slaughtered meat, cooked on the sacred Samhain fire. Such fires blazed from all the mountaintops, marking visual lines of pagan association across the length and breadth of Britain. Bale fires burned at all the major Sabbat dates.

Since the emphasis has been on the Goddess through the summer and is now, at Samhain, shifting to the God, this turnabout is emphasized by the "crowning" of the High Priest in his role of God. He is crowned with a horned or antlered headpiece.

## SAMHAIN SABBAT

*Note:* These following rituals are written for full coven participation. Feel free to adapt them for smaller groups and for solitary work. Modify them, if you wish.

Better yet, write your own rituals. Have fun!

The Circle should be decorated with appropriate flowers, branches, nuts, fruit, pumpkins, and the like. Some decoration should also be on the altar. It is appropriate to use orange altar candles for this rite. A bale fire (contained within a cauldron, if working indoors) may be burning in the west, outside the Circle. On the altar sits a small dish or miniature cauldron with a small pad of paper and a pencil alongside it. The antlered or horned helmet is on the floor beside the altar.

The Circle is opened with the usual ritual. If it is or close to a full moon, this rite (see chapter 4) is performed next. Then the bell is rung three times. The High Priest moves to stand at the east entrance to the Circle.

> **HPS:** Come! Let's away to the Sabbat!
>
> **ALL:** To the Sabbat!

HPS leads the coveners around the altar and over to the east. HP opens the Circle and all, except HP, follow HPS out of the Circle. HP stays behind and closes the Circle after them. Coveners, led by HPS, dance all around the outside area, winding around, in and out, back and forth. Any small drums, tambourines, bells, or similar instruments may be piled outside the Circle to be picked up now and used during the dance. Any appropriate chant or song may be sung. (See the selection in the appendix, "Chants and Songs for Sabbats and Esbats"—but anything with a good, joyful beat will do.)

When HPS feels it is time, she leads the coven back to the east entrance, where they drop off their instruments. HP admits them and closes the Circle again, returning to his place beside HPS. The bell is rung seven times.

> **HPS:** Again the wheel of the year completes its turn and an end becomes a beginning. Let us look back on the joy and the laughter we have experienced over the past twelve months, but also let us not forget the sorrows and losses from that time.
>
> **HP:** Give thanks, now, to the Lord and the Lady for all that we have learned, all that we have experienced in that time now past.

There follows a few moments of silence while all in their own way give thanks for what has gone before, reflecting on the previous year. The bell is rung three times.

> **HPS:** Now we leave the light of the summer months and enter into the long dark days of winter. Now is the time to gather our pos-

> sessions about us, casting off those we no longer need that we
> may travel lightly through to spring. Think carefully about that
> of which you most desire to be rid. Then approach the altar and
> cast it from you, burning it in the holy flame of our altar's own
> bale fire.

One by one, the coveners approach the altar. They may stand or kneel, as they see fit, and write on a piece of notepaper what they would most like to be rid of. This could be a bad habit, an unhappy position, a lack of money, or any other burden. Then, taking the piece of paper, they light it from the altar candle flame and allow the ashes to drop into the dish or small cauldron. While each is doing this act, the rest of the coven dance around the Circle, *deosil*, chanting. This chant may simply include the names of the God and the Goddess used by the coven, or it can be one of the traditional chants (see the appendix). When all have written and burned their papers, including HP and HPS, then the circling comes to an end and the bell is rung seven times.

**HPS:** We are at the crack of time, for this day is in neither the old year nor the new. This is our opportunity to reach across the veil to touch once again the ones we have loved, who have passed beyond our everyday barriers. Reunite now, by reaching out with hand and mind.

**HP:** Life is a spiraling dance, and as we move we pass and repass, moving forward and moving back, yet ever moving on. The wheel of the year turns and we turn with it.

**HPS:** The veil between the worlds is thin. Here in the Circle, in that place between the worlds, we are able to communicate freely with those we know and love who have passed on. Let us sit and join hands with those loved ones, touching our hearts together and joining our love.

All sit and take hands. For as long as necessary, the coven remains together, enjoying any personal or group connections with loved ones who have died. At this time, some of those who have passed over may well make themselves visible again, to individuals or to the group, or they may whisper in the ears of those close to them. Memorable perfumes may be smelled. Notable songs may be heard. When sufficient time has passed, the bell is rung three times.

**HP:** Now let us enjoy a dramatic reminder of this season of the year.

One, two, or more of the coveners should have prepared a small play, mime, story, dance, or the like to enact the themes of Samhain: life–death–life; the turning of the wheel; the return of the dead loved ones; the gathering of the harvest and storing it for winter. These and many more themes can be used. Let the presentation be light yet earnest, so that everyone may enjoy it. At the end, the bell is rung seven times.

| | |
|---|---|
| **FIRST WITCH:** | **The old year ends!** |
| **ALL:** | **The old year ends!** |
| **SECOND WITCH:** | **The new year begins!** |
| **ALL:** | **The new year begins!** |
| **THIRD WITCH:** | **The wheel turns!** |
| **ALL:** | **The wheel turns!** |
| **FOURTH WITCH:** | **And turns again!** |
| **ALL:** | **And turns again!** |
| **HP:** | **Welcome to our Lord!** |
| **ALL:** | **Welcome!** |
| **HPS:** | **Welcome to our Lady!** |
| **ALL:** | **Welcome!** |

HP kneels before the altar, facing HPS. A Witch takes up the antlered helmet and passes it to HPS. HPS holds the helmet over HP's head.

**HPS:** Here do I hold the symbol of our Lord, God of Hunting, God of Death and All That Follows. Ahead of him lie the dark cold months of winter. We have done all that we are able to prepare both ourselves and the Lord for his journey. May he travel with our love in his heart, as we all live with his love in ours.

HPS places the helmet on HP's head. He rises and she gives him the eightfold salute. HP turns to face the coven. He crosses his arms in the God position (see chapter 4).

| | |
|---|---|
| **FIRST WITCH:** | **Now is our Lord among us. Blessed be!** |
| **ALL:** | **Blessed be!** |
| **HP:** | **I accept this mantle of darkness, knowing it to be but a necessary step toward life. Join with me as I thank our Lady for the bounteous fruits of the summer months now past. Join with me as I look through the dark tunnel that I must pass to the cold clear light of spring that lies ahead. Join with me as I accept the mantle of death and darkness that all of nature embraces. Help me to steadfastly move forward to the joys of rebirth that we will celebrate half a wheel from today. So mote it be."** |

HPS gives HP the threefold salute. One by one the coveners come forward and give him the threefold salute. The bell is rung nine times.

HP removes the helmet and replaces it beside the altar. There follows the Great Rite, then the Cakes and Ale rite; the Circle is opened. Games, dancing, and feasting end the celebration.

The winter solstice is Yule, from the Norse *Iul*, meaning "wheel." Some traditions recognize it as marking the end of the reign of the Holly King and the beginning of the reign of the Oak King. (For more on this splitting of the God, see the Farrars' *Eight Sabbats for Witches*.)

These two kings may be seen as two different aspects of the one God. The one, the Holly King, is the waning half of the year, up to Yule. The second, the Oak King, is the waxing half of the year, the change coming at Yule with its shortest day. Traditionally there is a battle between the two, with the Oak King killing the Holly King, symbolizing the death and rebirth of the year at its turning point, the longest night of the year. The Farrars point out the remnants of this belief are found in the traditional Yule Mummers play, performed across Britain.

A Yule log was burned at this time, preferably obtained from the land of the covenstead—never purchased. It was then ceremoniously carried in and placed in the fireplace (or the bale fire if at the Sabbat site), with just one end in the fire. Once lighted from the remnants of the previous year's Yule log, it would then be inched forward as it burned. The end of the Yule log was saved, however, and carefully kept through until the following year. It was believed that the Yule log would protect the house from fire and lightning throughout the year.

> The idea of purification by fire is universal. Burnt offerings and sacrifices are purified and there are numerous ceremonies connected with festivals in which both humans and their animals pass through fire which also fumigates and expels evil powers. Fumigation also imparts strength since smoke represents the energy of fire and it is also a preservative.
>
> —J. C. Cooper, *The Aquarian Dictionary of Festivals*

## YULE (LESSER) SABBAT

The Circle should be decorated with appropriate flowers, holly branches, mistletoe, ivy, and the like. Some decoration should also be on the altar. It is appropriate to use red or green altar candles for this rite. A bale fire (contained within the cauldron, if working indoors) may be burning in the south, outside the Circle. Two male witches are chosen to be Holly King and Oak King. They may wear appropriate crowns. On the altar, lay a number of short tapers, enough for each covener to have one when the time comes.

The Circle is opened with the usual ritual. If it is, or is close to a full moon, this rite is performed next. Then the bell is rung three times. The High Priest moves to stand at the east entrance to the Circle.

**HPS:** Come! Let's away to the Sabbat!
**ALL:** To the Sabbat!

HPS leads the coveners around the altar and over to the east. HP opens the Circle and all, except HP, follow HPS out of the Circle. HP stays behind and closes the Circle after them. Coveners, led by HPS, dance all around the outside area, winding around, in and out, back and forth. Any small drums, tambourines, bells, or similar instruments may be piled outside the Circle to be picked up now and used during the dance. Any appropriate chant or song may be sung.

When HPS feels it is time, she leads the coven back to the east entrance, where they drop off their instruments. HP admits them and closes the Circle again, returning to his place beside HPS. The bell is rung seven times.

The Oak King sits beside the altar. The Holly King starts to dance *deosil* around the Circle, fairly fast to start but gradually slowing.

| | |
|---|---|
| **HPS:** | **Now have the days lost their light. The nights have lengthened and the sun is at his lowest. The year winds down.** |
| **HP:** | **What can be done to aid our Lord, to bring the sun to its height once more?** |
| **HPS:** | **Turn, turn, turn the wheel.** <br> **Round and round; around it goes.** |
| **HP:** | **The flame that died, it now doth heal.** |
| **ALL:** | **Round and round; around it goes.** |
| **FIRST WITCH:** | **Return, return, return to life.** |
| **ALL:** | **Round and round; around it goes.** |
| **SECOND WITCH:** | **Welcome sunlight; farewell strife.** |
| **ALL:** | **Round and round; around it goes.** |

The Oak King rises and moves to stand in the south. As the Holly King comes around, the Oak King stops him. They have a mock battle, first one, then the other almost falling.

Eventually the Holly King is thrown to the ground. The Oak King then starts to dance around the Circle in his place.

| | |
|---|---|
| **HP:** | **The Sun Lord dies; the Sun Lord lives!** |
| **ALL:** | **Round and round; around it goes.** |
| **HPS:** | **Death opens hands and new life gives.** |
| **ALL:** | **Round and round; around it goes.** |
| **HP:** | **Turn, turn, turn the wheel.** |
| **ALL:** | **Round and round; around it goes.** |

**HPS:** The flame that died; it now doth heal.
**ALL:** Round and round; around it goes.

All except the Holly King, who returns to sit by the altar, join the Oak King in dancing around the Circle. After three times around, each Witch takes a taper from the altar and goes to his or her place.

**HPS:** Let us kindle fresh fire to light our Lord on the rest of his journey through to spring.

HP takes the altar candle and goes around lighting the tapers. All hold them high. HP returns the altar candle to its place on the altar.

**ALL:** Fire for strength! Fire for life! Fire for love!
**HPS:** Let this fire aid the Lord, giving him strength to finish his journey.
**ALL:** So mote it be!

HP places the antlered helmet on his head, takes the Oak King by the hand, and together they walk majestically around the Circle three times. The bell is rung seven times.

HPS gives threefold salute to HP. One by one the coveners come forward and threefold salute him. The bell is rung nine times.

HP removes the helmet and replaces it beside the altar. There follows the Great Rite, then the Cakes and Ale rite; the Circle is opened. Games, dancing, and feasting end the celebration.

---

*On the first night of February, the eve of Imbolc, gather together all of the greens that adorned the house throughout the Yule season, including a branch or two of the fir tree that was hung with holiday ornaments. Then, as a part of the Imbolc sabbat rite, add these greens to the Sabbat Fire (a little at a time, and carefully, because by now they are hazardously dry), dancing and chanting all the while with words like: "Now we banish Winter! Now we welcome Spring!"*
—Pauline Campanelli, *Wheel of the Year*

Imbolc, or Imbolg, is the quickening of the year, with the first stirrings of spring. The meaning of the term *imbolg* is "in the womb." Despite falling in the dark half of the year, Imbolc is actually a very Goddess-oriented Sabbat, many versions of it centering on the goddess Bride (pronounced *breed*), Christianized as Brigid.

It is a feast of lights and, hence, also known by Christians as Candlemas. In some Scandinavian countries, a young girl wears a crown of candles at the festival. In most Wiccan Imbolc rituals, the crown of lights is also worn. Care needs to be taken with this, since you don't want to set anyone's hair on fire or have hot wax drip on someone's head! A simple crown can be made from a circlet of copper (easily bent and formed) with thirteen candleholders (the number of moons in a year) attached to it.

I'd suggest small holders to take birthday-cake candles. These will burn for about fifteen minutes, which is quite long enough for the ritual use. Birthday candles don't drip much, but even so, make holders that will catch any drips that there might be (see chapter 20).

At the end of the harvest the previous fall, the last sheaf of wheat was kept, since the spirit of the grain was believed to have retreated to it. This would then become the seed for the next harvest the following year.

This last of the wheat was often shaped into a human figure, known variously as a corn dolly, harvest mother, or sheaf mother. It might even be dressed in woman's clothing and laid in a bed known as Bride's bed. A priapic wand—a phallic-shaped wand, often tipped with a pinecone—is laid in the bed with her, across the figure so that they form an X. Many modern Witches make such a corn dolly and keep it in the house through the winter. It can be used in the Imbolc ritual.

---

The Roman god of procreation, Priapus, gave his name to the phallic wand used in many Wiccan rites. He presided over the fecundity of flocks, herds, and the fields. He also protected orchards and gardens, where his phallic image was prominently displayed. The Witches' Priapic Wand is a representation of the phallus and may be a length of wood about 18 to 21 inches in length with the end carved like a phallus, or may be a wand with a pine cone attached to the end as symbolic of the organ. Its use is suggested in some rituals though a regular wand may be used in its place.

---

## IMBOLC SABBAT

The Circle should be decorated with appropriate flowers, evergreen branches, bay sprigs, mistletoe, and holly. Some decoration should also be on the altar. It is appropriate to use yellow altar candles for this rite. A bale fire (contained within a cauldron, if working indoors) may be burning in the north, outside the Circle. Just inside the Circle, in the north, is a small cauldron containing kindling for a fire (or a number of large candles, or the like, to give the semblance of a fire). The candle crown lies on the altar. The Bride bed, containing the corn dolly, and the priapic wand are beside the altar, as is the antlered helmet.

The Circle is opened with the usual ritual. If it is or close to a full moon, this rite is performed next. Then the bell is rung three times. The High Priest moves to stand at the east entrance to the Circle.

**HPS:** **Come! Let's away to the Sabbat!**
**ALL:** **To the Sabbat!**

HPS leads the coveners around the altar and over to the east. HP opens the Circle and all, except HP, follow HPS out of the Circle. HP stays behind and closes the Circle after them. Coveners, led by HPS, dance all around the outside area, winding around, in and out, back and forth. Any small drums, tambourines, bells, or similar instruments may be piled outside the Circle to be picked up now and used during the dance. Any appropriate chant or song may be sung.

When HPS feels it is time, she leads the coven back to the east entrance, where they drop off their instruments. HP admits them and closes the Circle again, returning to his place beside HPS. The bell is rung seven times.

| | |
|---|---|
| **HPS:** | **Now our Lord has reached the midpoint in his journey to meet the Lady. Ahead of him he sees her light.** |
| **HP:** | **Though apart, they are still as one. They are both light and shadow.** |
| **FIRST WITCH:** | **This is a time for lambs to be born.** |
| **SECOND WITCH:** | **For ewes to come into their milk.** |
| **THIRD WITCH:** | **Spring is in the distance.** |
| **FOURTH WITCH:** | **Our thoughts turn repeatedly to the Goddess.** |

The first Witch moves the Bride bed into the center of the Circle. The second Witch takes the priapic wand, kisses the tip of it, and lays it across the corn dolly in the Bride bed.

The bell is rung three times.

**HPS:** **Let us light the fire of the sun to carry our Lord on the rest of his journey.**

One of the Witches lights the fire in the small cauldron in the north. HP kneels, and HPS places the antlered helmet on his head. He rises and she gives him the threefold salute. HP dances away and around the Circle, *deosil*. As he comes to the cauldron in the north, he jumps over it. He dances seven times around the Circle, each time leaping over the cauldron, then returns to the altar. HPS kneels. HP takes up the candle crown and places it on her head. With a taper, he lights the candles on her crown from the altar candle, then helps her rise. HPS stands in the Goddess position, and he gives her the eightfold salute.

**HP:** **All hail to our Lady of Light, beautiful Goddess.**
**ALL:** **All hail!**
**HP:** **Mother of the Sun, Goddess of Fire, we welcome thee and invite thee in. All hail!**
**ALL:** **All hail!**

HPS walks slowly three times, *deosil*, around the Circle. She then stands in the Goddess position, and all the Witches come to her and give her the threefold salute. HPS kneels, and HP removes the candle crown, extinguishing the lights and replacing it on the altar. HPS gives HP the threefold salute. One by one the coveners come forward to give HP the threefold salute. HP removes the antlered helmet and replaces it beside the altar.

The bell is rung three times.

**HP:** **Now let us enjoy a dramatic reminder of this season of the year.**

One, two, or more of the coveners should have prepared a small play, mime, story, dance, or the like to enact the themes of Imbolc—the first stirrings of spring; the turning of the wheel; the bringing of light to aid the Lord. These and many more themes can be used. Let the presentation be light yet earnest, so that everyone may enjoy it. At the end, the bell is rung seven times.

HP and HPS perform the Great Rite beside the Bride bed. The bell is rung nine times. Then follows the Cakes and Ale rite; the Circle is opened. Games, dancing, and feasting end the celebration.

The days and nights are of equal length at the spring equinox. As with all the equinoxes and solstices, the exact date depends upon the calendar. They generally fall on the twenty-first of the month but can be a day or so before or after. The late Dr. Margaret Murray claimed that the equinoxes were never celebrated in Britain, but today's Wiccans include them in the Sabbats, making an equal division of the year. Many Witches call this festival Ostara, or Eostre, after the Teutonic goddess whose name was picked up by the Christians and applied to Easter.

At this time of year, and at the next Beltane Sabbat, the Great Rite is appropriate, if not necessary. As the Farrars state:

> Spring was a particular season in classical and pre-classical times for a form of the sacrificial mating . . . the *Hieros Gamos*, or sacred marriage. In this, woman identified herself with the Goddess, and man sank himself into the Goddess through her, giving of his masculinity but not destroying it, and emerging from the experience revitalized. The Great Rite, whether symbolic or actual, is obviously the witches' hieros gamos.

## SPRING (LESSER) SABBAT

The Circle should be decorated with appropriate spring wildflowers, branches, fruit, and the like. Some floral decoration should also be on the altar. It is appropriate to use yellow candles for this rite. On the altar is the priapic wand. Also on the altar is a large bowl filled with soil and a packet of seeds beside the bowl (these can be flower or vegetable seeds). A large bunch of flowers lies on the ground in front of the altar, together with the antlered helmet. Outside the Circle, in the east, lies a pile of poles, broomsticks, and pitchforks.

The Circle is opened with the usual ritual. If it is or close to a full moon, this rite is performed next. Then the bell is rung three times. The High Priest moves to stand at the east entrance to the Circle.

**HPS:**     Come! Let's away to the Sabbat!
**ALL:**     To the Sabbat!

HPS leads the coveners around the altar and over to the east. HP opens the Circle and all follow HPS out of the Circle. HP closes the Circle then follows after them. Coveners, led by HPS and HP, take up the poles, broomsticks, and pitchforks and, riding them like hobbyhorses, dance all around the outside area, winding around, in and out, back and forth, jumping and leaping up in the air as they dance. Any appropriate chant or song may be sung.

When HPS feels it is time, she leads the coven back to the east entrance, where they drop off their poles. HP admits them and closes the Circle again, returning to his place beside HPS. The bell is rung seven times.

**HPS:** **Blessings on all at this our springtime rite. Now is the Lady beginning to awaken. Now is the Lord almost at the end of his journey.**

**HP:** **Welcome, thrice welcome beauteous spring! Welcome to the time of planting the seeds and to a time of birth.**

**HPS:** **Celebrate! Celebrate all!**

All move around past the altar, picking up a flower or flowers as they go and dancing around, *deosil*, singing or chanting. They circle seven times and, on the last circling, lay down their flowers along the line of the Circle.

The bell is rung three times. HP places the antlered helmet on his head.

**HPS:** **Springtime is seed time. Now let us plant the seeds of our minds, that we may gather our future harvests.**

HPS takes the packet of seeds from the altar and moves around giving a seed, or seeds, to each Witch. All now sit, kneel, or place themselves comfortably, meditating on that which they would like to see manifest for them in the coming year. This is a time to plan ahead and install the confidence that may be needed to attempt all that you would like to attempt. You are not working magic here, but programming your mind for probable action.

After a suitable time, HP takes the bowl from the altar and passes it around. Each Witch digs a small indentation in the soil of the bowl, with his or her finger or athame, and plants the seed(s). When all have done this, HP returns the bowl to the altar. There he takes up the priapic wand and holds it between the palms of his hands, phallic end up, as he faces HPS. She kisses the tip of the wand then gives HP the eightfold salute.

**HPS:** **May the power of the raised wand find the seed within the furrow. Blessings be upon this handsome wand.**

HPS takes up the bowl of soil and holds it between her breasts, facing HP. He inverts the wand, holding it over the bowl and touching its tip to the soil.

**HP:** **Bless these seeds, Lord and Lady, that they may grow and flourish, even as the hopes and inspirations of your Wiccans here would do. Let the power, joy, and energy of the gods flow down through this wand into the bowl, causing all to be fertile. So mote it be.**

**ALL:** **So mote it be!**

HP and HPS place the bowl and wand on the altar and salute each other. One by one the coveners come forward and give each of them the threefold salute. The bell is rung nine times.

HP removes the helmet and replaces it beside the altar. There follows the Great Rite, then the Cakes and Ale rite; the Circle is opened. Games, dancing, and feasting end the celebration.

Scottish Witches call it *Bealltuinn;* the Irish call it *Bealtaine*. Falling opposite Samhain, Beltane is the second most important Sabbat of the year, marking the end of winter. The emphasis of Samhain was on death; the emphasis of Beltane is on birth, or rebirth. It is another of the festivals during which the bale fires would light the mountaintops of Britain, joining together the Pagans in their worship. A feature of the festival was jumping over the bale fire. Sometimes two fires were built; cattle would be driven between the two, to make them fertile.

This is the Sabbat best known for its joy and laughter and for the games played by all, including those games that lead couples off into the woods for their own personal celebrations of fertility. The traditional maypole was an unabashed symbol of the virile male member, danced around by young and old alike.

*Round and round the Maypole*
*Merrily we go,*
*Singing hip-a-cherry,*
*Dancing as we go.*
*All the happy children*
*Upon the village green,*
*Sitting in the sunshine,*
*Hurrah for the Queen.*
　　—Traditional English children's song when dancing around the maypole

## BELTANE SABBAT

The Circle should be decorated with appropriate May flowers, young oak leaves, and the like. Some flowers or hawthorn blossoms should also be on the altar. It is appropriate to use yellow altar candles for this rite. On the altar lies a crown of flowers for HPS. A bale fire (contained within a cauldron, if working indoors) may be burning in the north, outside the Circle, and in the east there should be a maypole.

This is a pole as tall as space will allow, decorated with ribbons and with a garland around its tip. Long colored ribbons hang from the top, so that they may be taken up by the dancers at a later stage of the ritual. Hanging from the pole, near the base, are two large balls, one gold and one silver. They represent the sun and the moon, but also represent the testicles; the pole itself symbolizes the penis.

The Circle is opened with the usual ritual. If it is or close to a full moon, this rite is performed next. Then the bell is rung three times. The High Priest moves to stand at the east entrance to the Circle.

**HPS:**　Come! Let's away to the Sabbat!
**ALL:**　To the Sabbat!

HPS leads the coveners around the altar and over to the east. HP opens the Circle and all, except HP, follow HPS out of the Circle. HP closes the Circle then follows after them. Coveners, led by HP and HPS, dance all around the outside area, arriving eventually at the maypole. There they each (including HP and HPS) take the end of a ribbon and dance around *deosil*, singing the "May Eve Chant" (see below) or another song or chant.

At a signal from HPS, every other person (possibly alternate males and females) turns about and the dancing continues, with the two teams going in opposite directions, ducking under one another as they go, to intertwine the ribbons. In this fashion, the ribbons will be plaited down the pole, symbolizing the joining together of male and female.

When the ribbons have gone all the way, each Witch takes the person next to him or her and they hug and kiss, then dance together around the maypole, in pairs. The "May Eve Chant" should be sung. This is a variation of a Rudyard Kipling poem that has become a Wiccan classic:

> *Oh, do not tell the priests of our rites,*
> *For they would call it sin.*
> *But we shall be in the woods all night*
> *A-conjurin' summer in!*
> *We bring you good news, by word of mouth,*
> *For women, cattle and corn;*
> *Now is the sun come up from the south,*
> *With oak and ash and thorn.*
> *Oh, do not tell the priests of our Art*
> *For they would call it sin.*
> *But we shall be in the woods all night*
> *A-conjurin' summer in!*

When HPS feels it is time, dancing ends and she leads the coven back to the east entrance. HP admits them and closes the Circle again, returning to his place beside HPS. The bell is rung seven times.

**HPS:** **So do we celebrate the time of the year, the safe arrival of our Lord and the return of our Lady. The wheel turns and turns and turns, without ceasing.**

HPS kneels and HP places the crown of flowers on her head. She rises and assumes the Goddess position. HP gives her the eightfold salute.

**HP:** God-Winter ends his reign and Goddess-Summer assumes the crown.

Each of the coveners moves around and gives HPS the eightfold salute. She remains in the Goddess position.

**HPS:** I return again to watch over my children, to germinate the fields and the flocks, to bring joy and love to all things. This is a time for sharing. This is a time for turning from the darkness to focus on the light. All acts of love and kindness are tributes to me. All celebrations of life are my desire. All plantings of the seeds are my delight.

She lowers her arms.

**HP:** Now let us enjoy a dramatic reminder of this season of the year.

One, two, or more of the coveners should have prepared a small play, mime, story, dance, or the like to enact the themes of Beltane: romance, love, and fertility; the turning of the wheel; communicating with nature spirits. These and many more themes can be used. Let the presentation be light yet earnest, so that everyone may enjoy it. At the end, the bell is rung seven times.

HPS assumes the Goddess position. HP gives HPS the threefold salute. One by one the coveners come forward and give her the threefold salute. The bell is rung nine times.

Then follows the Great Rite, after which Cakes and Ale are served and the Circle is opened. Games, dancing, and feasting end the celebration.

Although this is the light half of the year, ruled by the Goddess, the strength of the God is evident at midsummer, when the day is at its longest. At this Sabbat, the Holly King and Oak King we saw at Yule return to do battle again, but this time the Holly King is triumphant, taking the year into its waning cycle.

## MIDSUMMER (LESSER) SABBAT

The Circle should be decorated with appropriate flowers, heather, oak leaves, and the like. Some decoration should also be on the altar. It is appropriate to use white altar candles for this rite. A bale fire (contained within a cauldron, if working indoors) may be burning in the east, outside the Circle. Two male witches are chosen to be Holly King and Oak King. They may wear appropriate crowns.

The Circle is opened with the usual ritual. If it is or close to a full moon, this rite is performed next. Then the bell is rung three times. The High Priest moves to stand at the east entrance to the Circle.

**HPS:**     **Come! Let's away to the Sabbat!**
**ALL:**     **To the Sabbat!**

HPS leads the coveners around the altar and over to the east. HP opens the Circle and all, except HP, follow HPS out of the Circle. HP stays behind and closes the Circle after them. Coveners, led by HPS, dance all around the outside area, winding around, in and out, back and forth. Any small drums, tambourines, bells, or similar instruments may be piled outside the Circle to be picked up now and used during the dance. Any appropriate chant or song may be sung.

When HPS feels it is time, she leads the coven back to the east entrance, where they drop off their instruments. HP admits them and closes the Circle again, returning to his place beside HPS. The bell is rung seven times.

The Holly King sits beside the altar. The Oak King starts to dance *deosil* around the Circle, fairly fast to start but gradually slowing.

**HPS:**     **The Lord of life, of sunlight, and of all things has reached his zenith. Let his light shine throughout the world, awakening every corner and bringing love and joy to all.**

**HP:**     **Now have the days gained in light. The nights have shortened and the sun is at his highest. The year winds onward.**

**FIRST WITCH:**     **Turn, turn, turn the wheel. Round and round; around it goes.**

| | |
|---|---|
| SECOND WITCH: | The flame it dies, the flame it heals. |
| ALL: | Round and round; around it goes. |
| FIRST WITCH: | Return, return, no sign of strife. |
| ALL: | Round and round; around it goes. |
| SECOND WITCH: | Enjoy sunlight; celebrate life. |
| ALL: | Round and round; around it goes. |

The Holly King rises and moves to stand in the south. As the Oak King comes around, the Holly King stops him. They have a mock battle, first one, then the other almost falling. Eventually, the Oak King is thrown to the ground. The Holly King then starts to dance around the Circle in his place.

| | |
|---|---|
| HP: | The Sun Lord dies; the Sun Lord lives! |
| ALL: | Round and round; around it goes. |
| HPS: | Death opens hands and new life gives. |
| ALL: | Round and round; around it goes. |
| HP: | Turn, turn, turn the wheel. |
| ALL: | Round and round; around it goes. |
| HPS: | The flame that died, it now doth heal. |
| ALL: | Round and round; around it goes. |

All except the Oak King, who returns to sit by the altar, join the Holly King in dancing around the Circle three times.

| | |
|---|---|
| HP: | Wiccans all, let us give thanks to the Mighty Ones for the richness and goodness of life. |
| HPS: | As there must be rain with the sun to make all things good, so must we suffer pain with our joy, to know all things. |
| HP: | Mighty Ones, we thank you for all pain and suffering as we thank you for all love and joy. We know that there can be no light without darkness and no darkness without light. |
| HPS: | Bless us now, Lord and Lady. Keep us faithful in your service. Help us feel the joy that life and love can bring. And help us share what we have with those who have little. |

HPS takes the Holly King by the hand, and together they walk majestically around the Circle three times. The bell is rung seven times.

HPS assumes the Goddess position. HP gives HPS the threefold salute. One by one the coveners come forward and give her the threefold salute. The bell is rung nine times.

There follows the Great Rite, then the Cakes and Ale rite; the Circle is opened. Games, dancing, and feasting end the celebration.

Pronounced *LOO-nuss-uh*, Lughnasadh is a rite to celebrate the Celtic sun god Lugh. It is the first of the harvest thanksgiving rites. The altar and surrounding area are frequently covered with baked loaves of bread made from the first grain harvested, other food from the fields, and even fish from the stream.

This was the European harvest home ritual, the time to offer the gods the first fruits of the field, before they could be eaten by the people in the feast that followed the rites.

Observing Lughnasadh ensured a continuing harvest of wheat, corn, milk, fruit, and fish. After the religious rites and the feasting, the festival was often accompanied by athletic competitions and also a marriage fair, for finding suitable marriage partners.

> *Another vital feature of the [harvest celebration] proceedings was the copious beer and cider provided to wash down the goose, roast beef and plum pudding: some thoughtful farmers, therefore, "laid clean, loose straw outside the barn, for those requiring temporary rest and meditation."*
> —Charles Kightly, The Customs and Ceremonies of Britain

## LUGHNASADH (LESSER) SABBAT

The Circle should be decorated with appropriate flowers, poppies, grain, fruit, and the like. Some decoration, including fresh-baked bread, should also be on the altar. It is appropriate to use yellow or green altar candles for this rite. A bale fire (contained within a cauldron, if working indoors) may be burning in the east, outside the circle.

The Circle is opened with the usual ritual. If it is close to a full moon, this rite is performed next. Then the bell is rung three times. The High Priest moves to stand at the east entrance to the Circle.

> **HPS:**    Come! Let's away to the Sabbat!
> **ALL:**    To the Sabbat!

HPS leads the coveners around the altar and over to the east. HP opens the Circle and all, except HP, follow HPS out of the Circle. HP stays behind and closes the Circle after them. Coveners, led by HPS, dance all around the outside area, winding around, in and out, back and forth. Any small drums, tambourines, bells, or similar instruments may be piled outside the Circle to be picked up now and used during the dance. Any appropriate chant or song may be sung.

When HPS feels it is time, she leads the coven back to the east entrance, where they drop off their instruments. HP admits them and closes the Circle again, returning to his place beside HPS. The bell is rung seven times.

> **HPS:**    Through the sacred union of the Lady and her Lord is the harvest assured.
>
> **HP:**    May their power pass down to us, that we too may enjoy the gift of bounty. May the harvest grow and spread wide to all we love.
>
> **FIRST WITCH:**    May we draw the surplus from the land that our bodies be filled with strength.
>
> **SECOND WITCH:**    May the power of the Lord and the Lady reach down to us that young and old alike may wax anew.
>
> **ALL:**    Ever turn the wheel. Ever onward.

HPS picks up the loaf of bread from the altar and, holding it high, with HP she leads the coven in a dance *deosil* around the Circle. A harvest song may be sung. Returning to the altar, HPS replaces the loaf.

> **HP:**    Now let us enjoy a dramatic reminder of this season of the year.

All except HP and one male Witch sit in a circle. HP dances, *deosil*, around the outside of the seated circle of Wiccans (but still within the consecrated Circle). The Witch dances *widdershins* (counterclockwise) around the inside of them. As they pass one another, they strike hands over the heads of the seated coven members. Coveners clap at the same time and shout:

**ALL:**     **Lugh!**

HP and the Witch circle twelve times. On the last circling, HP drops to the ground after the hand slap, and the Witch jumps over the seated coveners. He runs, now *deosil*, once around the circle. Returning to HP, the Witch helps him to his feet and they embrace. All cheer and come to their feet.

The bell is rung seven times.

**HPS:**     **Lord and Lady, we thank thee for all that has grown from the soil. May it continue to grow in strength. So mote it be.**
**ALL:**     **So mote it be!**

HPS assumes the Goddess position. HP gives HPS the threefold salute. One by one the coveners come forward and give her the threefold salute. The bell is rung nine times. There follows the Great Rite and the Cakes and Ale rite. The Circle is opened, and games, dancing, and feasting end the celebration.

Also known as Mabon, from the Welsh fertility god, this is a time to rest from the labors of harvesting, for this is the final harvest. A symbol for this time of the year is the spiral, featured in a spiral dance at the Sabbat. One of the reasons, according to the Farrars, is that Mabon falls between Vine and Ivy, in Robert Graves' *Tree Calendar*. Both Vine and Ivy are the only ones of that listing that grow naturally in a spiral. The spiral, especially the double spiral—inward and outward—is a symbol of reincarnation.

The Sabbats always ended with games. An old Sabbat game, surviving today in parts of Britain as a children's game, was called Stacks. It was originally played in the farm rickyards and haystacks after the harvest had been gathered. According to an 1898 report, "Each lad tried to catch the lass he liked best so that he could kiss her. The lass then would 'gang wi' the lad that catched her first."

But the chief pleasure, if not the purpose, of such games was often more than kissing. In *Round About Our Coal Fire* (1731), it says that in one such game, "The parties have the liberty of hiding where they will, in any part of the house. If it should prove to be in bed, and if they then happen to be caught, the dispute ends in kissing, etc."!

## AUTUMN (LESSER) SABBAT

The Circle should be decorated with appropriate flowers, pine branches with pinecones, red poppies, oak branches and acorns, and the like. Some decoration, such as acorns and pinecones, should also be on the altar. It is appropriate to use brown or orange altar candles for this rite. A bale fire (contained within a cauldron, if working indoors) may be burning in the south, outside the Circle. A bowl of apples sits on the altar.

The Circle is opened with the usual ritual. If it is, or is close to a full moon, this rite is performed next. Then the bell is rung three times. The High Priest moves to stand at the east entrance to the Circle.

**HPS:**     **Come! Let's away to the Sabbat!**
**ALL:**     **To the Sabbat!**

HPS leads the coveners around the altar and over to the east. HP opens the Circle and all, except HP, follow HPS out of the Circle. HP stays behind and closes the Circle after them. Coveners, led by HPS, dance all around the outside area, in a great spiral winding out from the Circle area and then back in again. As the Witches pass one another, on the return spiral, they lean across and kiss. Any appropriate chant or song may be sung.

HPS leads the coven back to the east entrance, where HP admits them and closes the Circle again. He returns to his place beside HPS. The bell is rung seven times.

**HPS:**     **Here is the balance of day and night, yet at no point does time stand still. Throughout the year, the mighty wheel turns and turns again. Death comes but so does life, as children are born to grow and develop.**

HP:      As surely as the sun rises, so comes death to each and every one of us. Yet he comes as a friend, to take us to his bosom and to join us once again with the Goddess and with those who have gone before. For death is but the doorway to life, and life itself leads to death.

HPS chooses a Witch, who comes forward and takes the bowl of apples from the altar. The Witch moves around, *deosil*, giving each covener an apple. Returning to the altar, the Witch takes one and returns to sit with the others. HP and HPS each take an apple. HPS turns to the coven and, with her athame, cuts the apple crosswise then opens it to show the inside, revealing the pentagram of seeds within.

HPS:     Behold the symbol of life within the fruit.
HP:      Within all life lie the seeds of future lives.
HPS:     Let us give thanks to the gods for this bounty.

All spend some minutes reflecting on the joys of life and on the blessings they enjoy. As they finish contemplating, each may eat his or her apple.

The bell is rung seven times.

HP:      Now the season of plenty draws to a close as we view the beauties of autumn all around us.
HPS:     The Lord and the Lady are generous with their blessings, yet there are many who have lessons to learn and, therefore, do not have all that we have. Let us never forget them and let us send out our love to them, and to all living things, at this time and always. So mote it be.
ALL:     So mote it be!

HPS assumes the Goddess position. HP gives HPS the threefold salute. One by one the coveners come forward and give her the threefold salute. The bell is rung nine times.

There follows the Great Rite, then the Cakes and Ale rite; the Circle is opened. Games, dancing, and feasting end the celebration.

# ~ 20 ~

# The Tools of Witchcraft

The tools used in Witchcraft are relatively few and fairly easy to construct. These days there are a number of stores across the country, together with mail-order companies, that offer just about anything you might require. However, *the tool you make yourself is the best tool there is!* It's the same as doing magic and making talismans; you put power into the product by doing it and making it yourself.

There are certain items that it *is* acceptable to purchase, however, such as crystal balls, swords, bells, and incense burners, or thuribles. These can be made, but the process is complex and the imbuing of personal power is less critical.

There are two types of tools: personal tools and coven tools (for the solitary, of course, they are one and the same). The personal tool, as its name implies, is that owned and used by the individual Witch. The athame is a personal tool; every Witch has an athame. The incense burner, or thurible, is a coven tool; there is just one, which is kept on the altar and used by the whole coven. Various items used for working magic that can be done by the individual are often kept by individual Witches even when the Witch belongs to a coven.

A cord, or cords, is a good example. Cord magic (see chapter 7) can be done by a coven, but it can also be done by an individual Witch, so cords are both personal and coven tools. The High Priestess' or High Priest's cords are usually kept on the altar and used as coven cords when the need arises.

*It is an old belief that the best substances for making tools are those that have once had life in them, as opposed to artificial substances. Thus, wood or ivory is better for a wand than metal, which is more appropriate for swords or knives. Virgin parchment is better than manufactured paper for talismans, etc. And things which have been made by hand are good, because there is life in them.*
—Gardnerian Book of Shadows

# Athame

Let me start with the making of the most important tool of all. If you are going to have only one tool, this is it. It is the athame; the Witch's personal tool.

First, get used to referring to this as a tool, *not* a weapon. As you have seen from the foregoing rituals, its use is restricted to ritual applications and it is never used as a weapon, neither to harm nor even to protect. Some Witches will use it to cut herbs or to engrave candles with names or words, for example, but other than this it would not be used for any physical cutting.

Like the bell and the censer, the athame might be considered difficult to make. For this reason, it is acceptable to purchase a suitable knife, but *only if you do at least some work on it yourself.* As your own personal tool, it is very important to put your energies into it.

Starting with the store-bought knife, then, you should purchase one with a straight, double-edged blade. The reason for this is that when you describe a pentagram in the air to open or seal a Circle, you will be moving the blade through the air in both directions, so you will need an edge on both sides of the blade. Many traditions say that the handle should be black, as black is the most absorbent color and will best absorb your energies, constantly charging the athame whenever you hold it. If your store-bought knife does not have a black handle, it is fairly simple to make it black by either painting it or staining it. But not all traditions insist on black, so if you are not of a specific tradition, decide for yourself on the color.

Most of the work you will do is the engraving of the athame. This can be steel engraving on the blade or carving on the handle. The handle marking is the easier and more usual. Engraving can be done, though, with something like a Dremel electric engraving tool. Unless the handle is of some extremely difficult material, try to avoid simply painting on it. If it is wood, bone, or leather, for example, you can mark it by using either a hand engraving tool (a sharpened large nail will do for this) or a wood-burning tool.

Exactly what is marked on the athame will depend upon the Wiccan tradition to which you belong. Some traditions have very specific *sigils*, or signs, that are marked on the tool. If yours is a family tradition, a new tradition, or a single coven or solitary, you can decide what you would prefer on it. You can use symbols that have particular relevance to you or your group, construct an appropriate *sigil* (as in chapter 15), or simply put your Craft name on it in one of the magical alphabets.

If you want to do a little more than just put your name on the handle of a store-bought knife, yet don't feel up to making an entire athame from scratch, you could change the handle on a bought knife. Most knives come apart fairly easily. Usually the pommel, or boss, at the end of the handle simply unscrews, allowing the whole handle to slide off the shaft. By doing this, you can make your own handle—possibly carving one out of wood—and put it on in place of the one you took off. You can decorate your handle as you wish, perhaps even binding it around with leather, or beading it. In this way, you have done much more toward "making" the athame than just marking the handle.

The ultimate, of course, is to make one from scratch. This is not as hard as it might seem. There are a number of books on making knives (found in hunting equipment stores, or from your local library), and I go over the details in *Buckland's Complete Book of Witchcraft*.

Basically, you shape a piece of metal to be the blade and the shaft of the handle. You can cut out the metal from a blank sheet, or you can adapt something like an old file. The blade part is sharpened (though since it is a ritual tool, it does not have to be too sharp); it can also be heated and tempered, though this can be a tricky process.

Some traditions also have a coven tool termed a white-handled knife. This looks basically the same as an athame, though it does not have to have a double-edged blade and the handle is white, as its name implies. This is used for engraving candles and other instruments of magic. Making one of these follows the same lines I gave for making an athame.

A sword is used by some covens as the coven tool for consecrating the Circle, since it is possible to bring the tip of the blade close to the drawn line and thence direct the power into it. To make one is similar to making an athame but, with the long blade, can be tricky to do from scratch. If you opt for a sword, I suggest buying one and changing the handle to personalize it, in the same way as described previously for the athame.

Athames, white-handled knives, and swords should all be consecrated before use (see page 269).

# Bracelets

The High Priestess usually wears a wide silver bracelet as a badge of office. In recent years, many ordinary Witches (by which I mean regular coveners, not the official High Priestess or leader of the coven) have taken to also wearing the bracelet. Here again, what is correct depends upon what tradition you belong to.

The bracelet is wide, flat, and silver—the metal of the moon. Usually it has the HPS' or Witch's name engraved on it in Theban or one of the other magical alphabets. There might also be signs for the degrees if the HPS belongs to a degree-oriented tradition. If you are a solitary, or of your own tradition or family group, you can decide what should be on the bracelet. I have seen bracelets ranging from highly elaborate, with a multitude of magical *sigils* on them, to absolutely plain with nothing on them.

In the Gardnerian tradition, the High Priest whose High Priestess is also a Witch Queen, or Queen of the Sabbat, is known as a Magus and will wear a gold bracelet (brass is acceptable these days) with this tradition's specific signs worked into it. Some other traditions have adopted copper bracelets for the High Priest.

# Crowns

In Gardnerian, and other older traditions the crown is only worn by a Witch Queen; a High Priestess who has had other covens break off from her original one. The Gardnerian crown is a simple band of silver with a silver crescent moon on the front. Today, in other traditions, there are many variations on this, from silver to copper crowns with crescent moons, three phases of the moon, additional decorations all around the crown, and so on.

Many High Priestesses, and even ordinary Witches, wear a crown believing that it is the everyday dress of a Witch! It has almost become a case of "too many leaders and not enough followers." If everyone wears a crown, it loses its significance altogether.

I think it's fine for each female Witch to wear a crown, but only if there is some system of distinguishing one from another: Perhaps the High Priestess' or Witch Queen's crown is of silver, while the other ones are copper. But here again, the most treasured crown is one that is handmade. I have seen some beautiful crowns made for a Witch Queen by all the High Priests under her, each putting something into its construction. A crown such as this has a lot of meaning for its wearer.

An item needed by a Witch Queen is a garter. This carries buckles to show how many covens have hived off from her. There will, then, be at least two buckles on it (her own original coven and the first one to break away, making her a Witch Queen). Traditionally, the garter is of green leather with a blue silk lining; the buckles are silver. The main, first, buckle is often more elaborate than the others, which are uniform. The garter is worn just above the left knee.

At the Imbolc Sabbat (see chapter 19), a candle crown is worn by the High Priestess. This can be constructed of virtually anything. The main thing is that it should be able to carry thirteen small birthday-cake candles on it. I have seen such crowns ranging from as simple as made from cardboard to as elaborate as being of crafted silver. The design can vary.

The main thing is that there should be no fear of candle wax dripping on the High Priestess' head, or of the candles falling over. The Farrars suggest building one based on a skullcap of aluminum foil. If you make a permanent one, it is a good idea to make little cups and solder them, or attach them in some way, to the band of the crown.

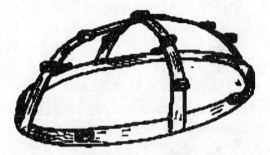

*SUGGESTED DESIGN OF SIMPLE BANDS OF COPPER WITH THIRTEEN*

*CANDLE-HOLDERS ATTACHED*

The High Priest has a crown, or helmet, that he wears in his role of representing the Horned God. This can be a horned or an antlered helmet. A basic head covering can be made or adapted (my original one, back in the early 1960s, was based on a metal mixing bowl!), and the horns or antlers attached to it. It may be easier to use horns, such as cow horns. Fill the inside of the base of the horn with a large wooden block shaped to fit, and then put a screw through the helmet base into that block to hold the horn in place. It is a little more difficult to attach an antler, since it has a much smaller-diameter base, but it can be done by attaching a metal base to the root of the antler and then to the helmet. The sort of base used as the tip of a chair leg, obtainable from a hardware store, can be used for this.

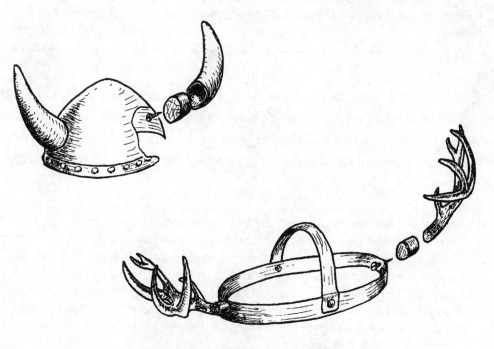

*HORNED HELMET AND ANTLERED HELMET*

# Besom

A Witch's broom, known as a besom, can be brought into play in various rituals as a coven tool (see "Spring Sabbat" in chapter 19). It once was used, along with pitchforks and long poles, when the fields were first planted. The villagers would ride astride the poles, like hobbyhorses, and dance around the fields. They would leap up in the air as they danced, to show the crops how high to grow—true sympathetic magic! Some covens ritually sweep the Circle as part of their rites. The broom is easily enough made by cutting a suitable handle and gathering twigs to be bound to it. Remember to cut your handle length from a fallen tree, not from a living one.

> *Sometimes we are lucky enough to find the gifts of the tree already lying on the ground. More often than not, though, we find ourselves harvesting their products for magical use. The collection process isn't as simple as just taking what we need. Trees are living creatures that eat, drink, breathe, and rest. Like members of humankind, they communicate and have individual personalities. For these reasons, we owe them the same respect and consideration we give our human siblings.*
> —Dorothy Morrison, *Everyday Magic*

In the past, the besom has been made of thorn branches, bulrushes, bean stalks, straw, and a variety of other things. The most traditional one, however, has a handle of ash with birch twigs bound to it by strips of willow. It does not have to be meticulously done; in fact, the cruder it appears, the more character it seems to have.

> *Shamanism teaches that a tree spirit, unlike a human spirit, remains in one place. However, if a partnership is formed with a human, the tree spirit can attain a certain mobility and extend the range of its awareness. It does this by giving up a part of itself—a branch perhaps—which retains the spirit of the tree within it. . . . A tree is like a pipeline from the sky to the earth. It is a living pipeline that carries energy. The same life force energy surges through all living things. When you embrace someone you feel good energy surging between the two of you. This is the same life force that is in trees.*
> —Eleanor and Philip Harris, *The Crafting and Use of Ritual Tools*

# Wand

Some traditions like to use a wand as a ritual coven implement. I feel that this is a carryover from ceremonial magic and does not truly belong in Witchcraft.

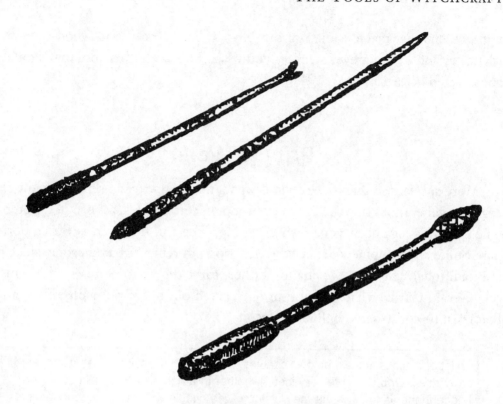

*WANDS AND PRIAPIC WAND*

Certainly anything that is done with a wand can be done equally well with the athame. Nonetheless, it has come to be regarded as a typical Witch's tool.

There are a number of formulas for its construction, depending upon which of the old *grimoires* (books of magic) you refer to. Some say that the length should equal the length of the magician's arm, from the elbow to the tip of the middle finger. Others state that it must be exactly twenty-one inches in length. Some *grimoires* specify willow as the wood of choice, others ash, oak, cherry, or a variety of other woods.

Since we are Wiccans and not ceremonial magicians, it doesn't matter what these books state! We can simply make it any length we want, out of any wood. In the same way, it can be of any form of construction you wish. I have a beautiful old one made of polished ebony decorated with engraved silver. But I have seen many a wonderful wand simply cut from a tree branch and decorated with love. Some are straight, some are bent, some are forked. The decorations are up to you, since it is not a ceremonial magic tool. You can bind it, bead it, carve it, wood-burn it, or whatever, and use whatever symbols you wish. This is another tool that should be consecrated before use.

# Priapic Wand

More specialized than the previous wand, the priapic wand represents the male organ of generation. It is used as a coven tool in certain rites, as seen in chapter 19. The length is, again, of your own choosing. The tip, however, is the important part. Some attach a pinecone, or carve the wood to represent a pinecone, since this is a traditional symbol of the phallus. Others carve the tip to represent the penis itself. Gerald Gardner had a beautiful one carved out of ivory. Again, this is a tool that must be consecrated before use.

> A lot of Witches make their own candles, which is not difficult and can add a lot to any ritual. One little trick, or nicety, whether in a homemade candle or a store-bought one, is to decorate the outside of the candle with things embedded into the wax. Large, fat, candles can look wonderful with pine needles embedded in the side, or even ringed with sticks of cinnamon or peppercorns. Just attaching such items as decorative buttons and the like can make a candle look special.

# Cords

All Witches may have a cord for doing cord magic (see chapter 7). It is usually red in color and nine feet long. This can vary from tradition to tradition, however. I believe Alexandrian Witches have three cords: one red, one white, and one blue. Gardnerians use three coven cords, all red. But you need only be concerned with one personal cord.

A Witch will generally keep the cord by doubling it over and then wrapping it and tying it around the waist. Sometimes referred to as a *cingulum*, it can serve as a belt for a robe or something from which to hang the athame's sheath. The main thing is, by being worn in Circle all the time, it absorbs much of your energy, making it most suitable for cord magic work.

Nine feet is a good length for a number of reasons, not the least because it is a magical number.[24] Also, at this length it can be very handy for marking a magical Circle of the traditional nine-foot diameter. If you stick something in the ground and then loop your cord around it at its halfway point, you can then hold a stick or knife at the extended two ends and walk around the center point, marking the Circle. It will be exactly nine feet in diameter.

The cord is usually made of some soft material. Many cords are silk. In the tradition of making all your tools yourself, you can take three long lengths of cord and braid them together to form your magical cord.

A word of caution: If you are going to dye the finished product (red or whatever color you prefer), do the dyeing before cutting it to length. I have known many Witches who made beautiful cords, exactly nine feet long, then dyed them—only to find that they shrink. When you are ready to cut to length, bind the ends with thread so they will not unravel. Your finished cord should be consecrated before use.

# Scourge

The scourge is used in Initiations, as has been shown. Some Witches also use it in working magic. One way of building power is to bind a person and scourge him or her, thus causing the blood to course through the body and increase the power. But this is a delicate balance and one best taught on a personal basis. The main thing to remember is that no scourging, in Witchcraft, is done to hurt.

The scourge is simply a handle to which is attached a number of thongs or "tails." There can be three, seven, or nine—all are considered magical numbers. The tails are anywhere from nine to twenty-one inches in length and are *not* knotted. They are simply attached to a short handle, which may be marked or inscribed in much the same way as the athame.

Many covens make the tails of silk cord. For the same reason that they are not knotted (to avoid hurting), we seldom use leather as the material. The scourge should be consecrated before use.

---

24. Three has always been regarded as magical, mainly because of the three aspects of the Goddess: Maiden, Mother, Crone. Nine, then, is especially magical, since it is three times three.

# Corn Dolly

Traditionally, the straws for making the corn dolly have been taken from the last sheaf of wheat or corn[25] from the final harvest. Straws are plucked and fashioned into the Imbolc corn dolly—the Maiden aspect of the Mother Goddess. This is called, in Gaelic, *Brídeóg*, the "biddy." Some corn dollies are in the crude form of a human, but many are elaborate knots, intricate designs of braided cornstalks, in spirals, woven into squares, formed into crosses, and other variations. In Germany, the dolly was made in animal form—pigs, goats, wolves, hares—and referred to as the corn cock. The Bride bed, in which the corn dolly is laid, is frequently a simple basket.

*CORN HUSK DOLLY*

25. In Britain, almost all grain is referred to as corn, though much of it is actually wheat. It is not to be confused with the American maize, or corn on the cob. British corn is the hollow-stemmed variety with a head of ears (of wheat or corn).

There are many ways of making a corn dolly, most of them traditional. In Britain, different parts of the country produced different styles, ranging from a simple bunch of wheat to elaborate braided-straw figures, often of abstract form. An easier way is to use American corn husks and fashion a corn (maize) dolly. These are actually more lifelike than the traditional corn dollies.

Using a total of about fifteen corn husks, soak them in hot water to make them pliable. Place two across each other to form a cross, and in the center place a ball made from scraps of husks. Pull the two strips down around the scraps and tie them around, making a crude head, with short lengths of the husks hanging below. Make the arms of two or three husks rolled together in a tube and tied at the ends. Push these through the base of the head husks and tie them in (see the illustration on page 268). You can tie more husks at their tops, over the base of the head-arms section, to hang down like a skirt. Often such a figure is finished off with a husk folded thinly and wrapped around like a shawl.

> But Shakespeare' magic could not copied be;
> Within that circle none durst walk but he.
> —John Dryden (1631–1701), *The Tempest* (Prologue)

# Consecration of Tools

The tools you are going to be using are essentially sacred tools. Because they will be used in the sacred space "between the worlds," they must be consecrated. This is done in a simple ritual, which may be performed as part of an Esbat or can be done as a rite in itself.

## CONSECRATION OF TOOLS RITUAL

The tool to be consecrated rests in the center of the altar. If the coven uses a sword, then the item should be on, or touching, the sword. (If the sword is the item being consecrated, then it should be touching HPS' or HP's athame.)

After the Circle has been cast and at some point before the Cakes and Ale, the consecration is performed. If the item is a personal tool, it will be consecrated by the Witch to whom it belongs. If it is a coven tool, it will be consecrated by HPS or HP, as appropriate.

The bell is rung three times.

The consecrator takes up the object and holds it over the altar, raised up to the gods:

*Lord and Lady, here I do bring a new tool of the Craft, to be dedicated in your names and in your honor. I have crafted this item in love of you and with the good of the Craft and my brothers and sisters in mind. Be with me now and bless this item.*

Lower the item and sprinkle it all over with the salted water that is on the altar. Then hold it in the smoke of the incense. Take up the item again and walk to the east corner. Hold it up and say:

*Here I do present my [name of item] to the gods and to all who worship and adore them. May this never be used in any way to bring harm to another. May it be used only in the service of the Lord and of the Lady. So mote it be!*

Proceed to the south and repeat the statement, then to the west, and to the north. The item is raised again in the east, to complete the Circle. Return to the altar, put down the item, and touch your athame to it:

*The blessings of the Lord and of the Lady be in this [name], from this day forward. Let all within this sacred Circle witness the dedication I have made. So mote it be.*

Everyone repeats:

*So mote it be!*

Now take up the item and use it in the way it is meant to be used,[26] so that its first use will be within the sacred Circle.

The bell is rung seven times.

---

The Tibetans have an interesting practice that might well be copied by Witches and Pagans. From homes and temples throughout Tibet, Nepal, and Bhutan, colorful prayer flags flutter in the wind. On these flags are written various mantras. The fluttering in the wind is believed to vibrate the mantras into the atmosphere. Along with the mantras are various sacred symbols. The five elements are represented by the flags being in the colors red, green, yellow, blue, and white.

---

# Ritual

Ritual is perhaps the most important tool of Witchcraft. In this book I have given sample rituals for all the main occasions, but I encourage Witches to write their own rituals. Only in this way will you get what is exactly right for *you;* what you will be most comfortable performing. You can use my rituals as a foundation, to see what should come where, and exactly what should be contained in a particular ritual, but write your own words and do your own actions.

All Wiccan rites start with the Casting of the Circle and end with its Closing. After the opening, if close to the full moon, there must be a Drawing Down the Moon. Then comes the particular Sabbat rite, if it is a Sabbat being celebrated. There is then a Cakes and Ale segment.

If it is an Esbat, rather than a Sabbat, then at the Cakes and Ale you can discuss what, if any, magic is to be done. (And don't feel you have to do magic. It should only be done if there is a very real need for it.) Or if there is healing to be done, that can be discussed during the Cakes and Ale.

Remember, the Esbat is the working meeting; the Sabbat is the celebration,

---

26. If it is an athame, describe a pentagram in the air with it, to the east, south, west, and north. If it is a wand, the same thing will be done. If it is cords, HP or HPS (the opposite sex to you) will bind you and lead you *deosil* around the Circle, before unbinding you. Whatever the item, it will be first used in the Circle at this time.

when no work should be done. At a Sabbat, the Closing of the Circle is followed by great celebration, with feasting and games.

A suggested basic composition of a ritual might follow the following lines: Casting the Circle; a processional; a hymn of praise or similar recognition of the gods; an enactment, if a Sabbat; a litany (call and response between the coven leader and the group); dance, song, or chant; offerings (Cakes and Ale); Closing.

# ~ 21 ~

# Personal Development of a Witch

A Witch never stops developing. She whets and sharpens her healing skills, her divination skills, her magic skills. Many Witches specialize in one area or another, much as people do in all walks of life. But the Witch's specialization is reflected in her Book of Shadows where, along with all the rites and rituals, she will find notes and experiments on the skills she is developing.

> The mind in its domination of the body exercises a causal influence which cannot be otherwise than kinetic. Thus, psychokinetic action . . . is the basis on which every man interprets his routine experience of daily life.
> —Dr. J. B. Rhine, *Journal of Parapsychology* 7, 1943

## Psychic Development

This is something worked on by all Witches. Everyone is psychic. This is obvious when you study young, unspoiled children—though in today's television age, the unspoiled child is becoming a rarity! Still, children do have a natural psychic ability. Apart from their acceptance of the world of fairy, their acknowledgement of spirits and entities in different dimensions from ours, they naturally tune in to others' thoughts and feelings.

I recall when I was still living in London and my elder son was about four years old. One day, I was sitting thinking about a television script I had to write. It dealt with the army, and in my mind I was playing around with various key words in an attempt to spark a story line. My son was playing with his toys at my feet. As I focused on the army clothing, my mind lingered for a moment on the word *khaki*. (In England, it is pronounced with a long *a*, as *KAR-ki*.) Just as I thought of it, my son looked up and said "What *about* the car key, Dad?" There had been a total and natural bonding of minds with no conscious effort on his part. This is not in the least unusual with children. Unfortunately, it gets driven out of us as we get older.

With some, psychic ability seems to come out more naturally than with others. There are those who know who is at the door or on the phone before ever answering it. They may even know that the doorbell or phone is going to ring before it actually does. These people have their psychic powers just below the surface. Others of us have to work at it, but we do all have them.

Here are some exercises that can be done to help bring out your powers. Try these and persevere with them. Practice them until they work every time.

The first exercise is a simple ESP (extra-sensory perception) test that can be done with a regular deck of playing cards. Take out the cards bearing the maximum number of "pips"—the eight, nine, and ten of each suit—giving you twelve cards in all. Shuffle them and lay them facedown on the table in front of you, in a line from left to right. You will need a notebook to keep score of all your practice runs.

Slide the first card a little apart from the rest and hold the palms of your hands over it. You can move your hands around if you like—back and forth, or up and down, or around and around, whatever seems right. See if you can sense whether the card is black or red. At this stage, don't worry about the suit, just the color. If you don't seem to get anything with the palms of your hands, then concentrate with your fingertips. When you feel you know (rather than just guessing), write it down and, without turning over the card, go on to the next.

Go through all twelve cards before turning them over and noting what the correct answer was. Write this down also. You will end up with a list something like this:

|  | SENSED | ACTUAL |
|---|---|---|
| 1: | BLACK | Red |
| 2: | BLACK | Black |
| 3: | RED | Black |

|  | SENSED | ACTUAL |
|---|---|---|
| 4: | BLACK | Black |
| 5: | RED | Red |
| 6: | RED | Black |
| 7: | RED | Red |
| 8: | BLACK | Red |
| 9: | RED | Black |
| 10: | BLACK | Red |
| 11: | RED | Red |
| 12: | RED | Black |

Since there are only two possible answers to each try, the average score would be six out of the twelve. In the above run, you got five correct—almost average. But one run tells us nothing. The more runs, the better. Going through ten times (for a total of 120 cards, in effect), the average score would be 60. If you scored, say, 73, that would be quite good; the odds are 20:1 against this just being chance. If you scored, say, 78 that would be excellent—odds of 100:1 against chance. As I've said, the more times you go through, the truer the picture presented of your psychic ability. Here are the odds on various run-throughs:

| No. of Runs | Chance Score | Good Score (20:1 against chance) | Excellent Score (100:1 against) |
|---|---|---|---|
| 10 | 60 | 73 | 78 |
| 20 | 120 | 144 | 152 |
| 30 | 180 | 215 | 222 |
| 40 | 240 | 286 | 295 |
| 50 | 300 | 356 | 365 |

Many Witches do this as a regular daily exercise, building up a very large number for a total of run-throughs and therefore presenting a much more accurate picture of the odds against chance. They find that the more they do it, the better their score becomes. There are many variations on this that can be done—using photographs in envelopes, zener cards, tarot cards, dominoes, and so on—to attune the psychic abilities.

Interestingly, if you consistently score way *below* the average, this too is significant. There is also a whole range of other possibilities, such as finding that you have gotten the card correct for the next one that you pull up rather than the one you're actually working on. That's referred to as "one ahead." There are also people who get the card two ahead! If your scores are always way off, then check out such possibilities, which show not only ESP but also precognition (knowing ahead of time).

To move an object just by thinking, without actually physically touching it, is known as psychokinesis (PK); it's also sometimes referred to as telekinesis (TK). This can be practiced by a number of Witches together, even in the Circle. It can even be treated like a game, perhaps with two teams going against each other. The teams sit one on each side of the Circle. Let's call them Team A and Team B.

A single individual first stands up in the north quarter of the Circle, with his back to the group. The two teams decide which will be the "attraction" team and which the "repellent." This can be decided by whispering, signs, or by writing, so that the individual does not know the decision. Then the individual comes to stand in the center of the Circle. He should be relaxed, standing at ease with his eyes closed.

Each team now concentrates, one team on attracting the individual to them and the other team on sending him away from them toward the other team. So if Team A is the "attraction" team, its members will try to *pull* the individual across the Circle space, while Team B tries to *push* him across.

What will happen is that the individual will get strong feelings to move in a particular direction (toward Team A) and should follow those feelings. In almost all cases, the person moves as he is being willed by the two groups. This can be repeated any number of times, changing the person in the middle and even changing who is in which team. It is good practice in moving something by willpower; this method is also especially useful in that you can get feedback from the person as to how he feels, and what sort of sense he gets of being moved.

Another exercise for anyone at any time is to suspend a pendulum from a holder of some sort and make it swing. For instance, place a ring on the end of a piece of ribbon, and hang it from a ruler sticking out from the top of a chest of drawers. Make sure the object (in this case, the ring) is hanging perfectly still and unmoving. Then simply concentrate on making it swing. It is surprising how quickly it will happen. The harder you concentrate and the more you practice, the easier it is to get it swinging, and the wider it will swing. If you have a lot of difficulty in getting it to move initially (and do be patient the first few times), then point your finger at it, from a very close distance, though be sure to not actually touch it. Direct the power down your arm and out of your finger to cause it to swing away from you.

You will find that the lighter the object is, the easier it is to move it. A good idea is to start with something very light, such as a cork ball. (These can be obtained from a fishing supply store.) Just push a pin attached to a thread into the cork ball and hang it from something.

There are many exercises you can do to develop your psychic abilities, and many books written on the subject. The main thing is to practice and keep practicing. Don't be disheartened if it takes a long time to get results. Just know that you *do* have the power. However deeply it may be buried initially, it can be brought out.

> I had traveled some distance down the Inner Path, and had developed my psychism to the point where it was as reliable as psychism is ever likely to be—that is to say, I could trust it in matters in which I had no personal concern. . . . But there is a big difference between the psychic and the adept . . . the adept, to be worthy of the name, must be not only a psychic but a magician—that is to say, he must be able to wield the powers of the spirit objectively as well as subjectively.
> —Dion Fortune, *Moon Magic*

# Affirmations

A very useful tool for psychic development, magic, healing, and most of the things we have talked about, is affirmations. Affirmations are simple, positive statements that, repeated over and over again like a mantra, get down to your unconscious mind and reinforce the powers you have, helping bring them out.

An example would be a phrase like "I have the power to heal and I can use it to help others." It's simple enough that you can remember it, especially once you've repeated it a few times. But more than this, write it down and display it where you will keep seeing it. Put it up by your bathroom mirror, so you will see it every time you go near the mirror. Put it on the refrigerator door and the doors to your office, workshop, garage. Write it on a small piece of paper and slip it into your checkbook, your diary, your purse. Put it on the sun visor of your car.

In other words, put it everywhere and anywhere that it will catch your eye and remind you to repeat it. To make it more interesting, and remarkable, use bright-colored paper that attracts you and makes you feel good. Write the words in colored ink(s).

Here are a few suggested affirmations, though those you think up yourself will be the most effective:

- All Witches have natural powers and I also have them.
- My natural psychic powers are constantly revealing themselves.
- My healing abilities grow from day to day.
- I am fully capable of building my personal power whenever I need to.
- Since becoming a Witch, my powers have emerged and are constantly developing.
- I have a natural ability to skry (read cards, heal, use herbs, and so on).

> *An Affirmation of word will serve for almost anything—health, wealth, happiness—whatever you are concentrating on at the time.*—Stuart Wilde, *Affirmations*

# Meditation

I have spoken about the benefits of meditation in chapter 16. It is a remarkable tool for calming, adjusting, developing, centering, attuning. It can be used to discipline your mind, heal your body, control your emotions, solve problems, and put you in touch with the gods.

There are many different ways of meditating, with various schools offering their particular variations. All, however, come down to the same foundation: Meditation is simply *listening* to the Higher Self, the Inner Self, the Universal Mind—whatever label you wish to use. It involves quieting your mind and body and relaxing to the point where your mind can accept what comes into it.

One school of thought holds that the lower, subconscious mind, which controls involuntary body functions, reflex actions, and the like, is attuned by turning the eyes downward. The Higher Mind, or superconscious, is attuned by turning the eyes upward. The normal conscious mind is attuned by looking straight ahead and seeing the regular, physical world.

So, to facilitate the connection with the superconscious, and thereby open to the Higher Self, you need to turn your eyes upward. In fact, some suggest that, when meditating, you try to focus your eyes on the position of the Third Eye, which lies between and a little above the eyebrows. This is the position of the pineal gland, one of the crown chakras. I have personally found this something of a strain (perhaps I didn't persevere) and thus a distraction, but you might want to give it a try.

But before we get to where to look, let's examine how to sit. First of all, you do not have to adopt some strange yoga posture with your legs wrapped around each other unless that is your preference. The secret is to sit *comfortably*, but with your back straight. If you are not comfortable, if you are in some strange position, your mind will be drawn to that and away from what you seek. So be comfortable. You can sit on the ground or in a chair. If in a chair, I recommend one with arms on which you can rest your own arms. But again, the main thing is that you have your back straight.

Try to reduce the presence of human-made material by finding a chair that is all wood, preferably pegged rather than nailed or screwed. Avoid plastics or synthetics. A sheepskin rug to sit on is preferred by many as comfortable and natural. In fact, you can lie flat on the floor if you wish. The only drawback to that is that you may fall asleep!

You should be in a place where you will not be disturbed and, so far as possible these days, where where you will not hear any extraneous noise. Make sure that you are secure; in other words, that no one will walk in on you unawares.

The time of day is not important, though early-morning or early-evening hours do seem to work better for many people. More important is that you try to meditate at about the same time of day each time. Clothing, if worn, should be loose and comfortable; unhook that bra, loosen that belt, slip off those shoes. In short, try to eliminate everything that would in any way be a distraction.

Many Witches meditate in the consecrated Circle, if available. If there is no easy access to it, then cast your own small Circle about the place where you are going to sit. At the very least, cast such a Circle around you in your mind. Then go through the deep breathing and white light building that I described earlier in this book. Build up the white light, get rid of all negativity, and let the light fill the Circle in which you sit, whether it is marked or imaginary.

Now the meditation begins. Clear your mind of all mundane material. Don't worry about next week's dental appointment, or where your next car payment will come from. If you have great difficulty, focus your mind on something pleasant and positive. See an open field, perhaps with sheep or cattle at a distance. Or see a clearing in a wood, or a small stream babbling over stones as it hurries along. Relax your body and enjoy the moment.

Eventually something *will* come into your mind unbidden. It will slip in almost unnoticed. It may be something you see, in your mind, or something you hear. Whatever it is, try to remember it. In fact, when you have finished your meditation, write down everything you remember. Some disciplines tell you to meditate for at least twenty minutes twice a day. I don't think you have to do this much, though of course you may if you wish. But I do think you should meditate for at least ten minutes every day, to benefit from it.

> Meditation is emptying self of all that hinders from the creative forces rising along the natural channels of the physical man to be disseminated through those centers and sources that create the activities of the physical, mental and spiritual man.
> —Edgar Cayce, *Reading 281-13*

# Divination

There are a tremendous number of forms of divination, some of the most popular being cards, I Ching coins, astrology, runes, palmistry, skrying, tea-leaf reading, dice, and dominoes. Try as many as you can to find the one or ones that work best for you. And give each a really good try, over a period of time. Don't just try it once and give up. Not all of them will work for you; most of us have forms of divination that become favorites, and others at which we have no success whatsoever.

Cards—tarot cards especially—are probably the most popular. And within the category of tarot cards, there are still choices to be made. Today, there are something like two thousand different decks on the market! Experiment and try different ones over a long period. There are also plenty of books on tarot card reading as well as the cards themselves.[27] Read as much as you can. And also try regular playing cards, as well as the tarot variety. They can be equally as effective.

---

27. I have recently put out my own deck and book (*The Buckland Romani Deck*), which I hope you will enjoy.

> *Divination is a great and powerful art, there are numerous ways of recognising signs of divinity radiating through nature. Some techniques of divination are highly sophisticated and almost scientific, and others are so amazingly simple that even an intuitive child could understand.*
> —Cavendish House, *The Complete Book of Fate and Fortune*

Astrology is a lifelong study, and again, there are a number of excellent books on the subject. There are also classes and home study courses available. It is an exacting science and one well worth the study.

This book would be ten times its size if I tried to teach all these forms of divination in it! I will just stress that we all have the power to do these things, though some of us are better at some than others. Investigate, experiment, practice, and find the forms that are right for you. Rather than making the future look grim from the amount of work that lies ahead, I think it makes the future look bright with all the many possibilities and opportunities that are there. Witches, more than anyone, are attuned to these practices, so immerse yourself in them and enjoy!

# Healing

Healing is one of the oldest traditions of Witchcraft. The very earliest Witches were healers before all else. They developed their knowledge of herbs to heal but also performed healing by such practices as the laying on of hands. This, together with healing by directing power (working magic), is still used today.

In chapter 7, I gave details on working magic as a coven: dancing and chanting, visualizing, building up the power, and finally projecting it to the target. The same process takes place with healing at a distance. In doing this, you would visualize the person *as healed*; as already better, fit, and well. If he has a broken leg (for example), you would see him running and jumping. If she has a sore throat, see her singing and shouting. Always picture the end result of the magic. As an individual Witch, you can do the same projected-power healing magic as done by the coven. And don't forget to get the person's permission to do a healing.

You can also do healing by simply sending out your thoughts of the healed person, without the whole magical ritual buildup of power. If you do this, do it consistently every day, at the same time every day. If possible, have a photograph of the

> *A practical art and science of color holds great potential benefit. From a study of the therapeutic and psychological aspects of the hues of the spectrum, it becomes possible to exert greater control over color mediums and to attain many vital ends.* —Faber Birren, *Color Psychology and Color Therapy*

person to help you concentrate on her. Again, think of her as already healed. You can add color magic to this by visualizing the appropriate color surrounding her. Green is the all-purpose color of healing, but you can find the applicable color for a specific problem and use that color (see my *Practical Color Magick*). Basically, the red end of the spectrum invigorates as a stimulant, while the blue end cools and soothes.

If the patient is physically available, the color can be projected directly onto her by using sheets of colored gel, either over a window or in a projector. This form of therapy has been practiced for millennia, and was used by the ancient Egyptians. In addition to projecting, color can be introduced through color-charged water and by placing appropriate-colored stones over the chakras, and even over the relevant parts of the body.

Auric healing is another form. The body has an etheric double (it is seen in the form of a ghost when the physical body has gone but the spirit delays leaving this earthly plane). It can be seen by sensitives as a dark outline around the physical body. But stretching out from the body for two or three inches more is an "inner aura" (the mental body) and, for three to six inches, the "outer aura" (the spiritual body). These have been captured on film through Kirlian photography. In early art, these auras were depicted as *halos* or *glorias*.

Auras are colored, and sensitives can tell your health, mood, emotion, and more from your colors. For example, a person deeply in love has a strong pink tinge to his aura. A very spiritual person has a lavender and blue hue. Anger shows as red. Sickness and injury can show up in a number of ways; as yellow, brown, or black spots, for example. By projecting, with your mind, the appropriate color onto a person's aura, you can help heal him. For blood problems and trouble with various organs, projection of clear dark blues is soothing. Grass greens are invigorating, and reds stimulating. For the nervous system, violet and lavender have a soothing effect, yellow and orange are inspiring, and grass green is invigorating. For fevers and high blood pressure, blue is soothing and relaxing. For chills and lack of bodily warmth, project red.

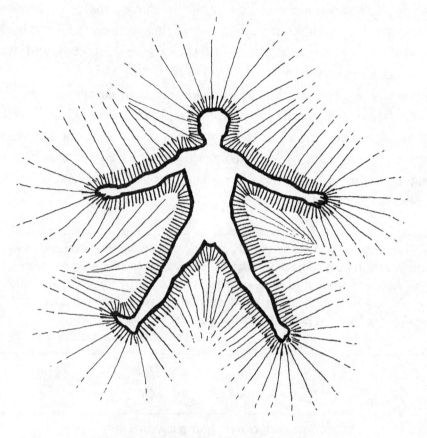

*ASTRAL BODY, INNER AURA AND OUTER AURA*

When doing hands-on healing, first draw off all negative energy from the person's body. This is done by running your hands down the body, on each side from head to toe, and then shaking your hands vigorously as though trying to shake water off them. If the person is standing, then do it front and back as well as the sides. As you draw your hands down, visualize the negativity being pulled from her and get her to work with you. Both of you can do deep breathing, drawing in the good and pushing out the negative. When you have done the drawing off a number of times—I recommend at least seven or even nine—then relax and take some deep breaths before continuing. Go to the problem area and lay your hands gently on the skin. Draw white light down from the gods, or up from the earth (however you feel most comfortable working), and see it traveling through your body, down your arms and hands, and into her body.

Keep this up for some time, then gradually change the color from white to green. Send in the green light of healing, visualizing the body well and healthy. Do this for as long as you can before changing back to the white light and, finally, relaxing and removing your hands.

There is an old Gypsy method of hands-on healing that I came across in recent years; I have found it to be extremely effective. I detail it in my *Gypsy Witchcraft and Magic*. Basically it goes into more detail than the previous method by concentrating on specific areas, many of which coincide with the chakras. But for the majority of healing, the previous method works wonders and has been used in Wicca for generations.

---

*The most potent charms were secret, known only to the wiseman who used them and inherited them from some other white witch who passed on his knowledge in old age. . . . A wise woman of Brackley who cured ague by means of blessing cords and who was already ninety years old had not yet named her successor, and great anxiety was felt lest the charm should die with her.*
—Christina Hole, *Witchcraft in England*

---

*Life has the power of manifesting itself to life.*
—F. W. H. Myers, *Human Personality and Its Survival of Bodily Death*, 1903

# Appendix

## *Full Coven Initiation*

This is a larger version of the Initiation given in chapter 3. There we were dealing with the coven leader and the neophyte—only these two people were involved. But when there is a full coven, be it a family group or any other coven, then it is good to involve as many people as possible. So here is the Initiation ritual with full participation. Again, I will assume it is a male who is being initiated. Feel free to adapt this ritual for the number of people you have in your coven.

I will name the participants: High Priestess, High Priest, Initiate, Maiden, Squire, Gatekeeper, and Witches 1, 2, 3, and 4.

All are properly prepared. The High Priestess and the High Priest stand in front of the altar, which has all of the tools on it. Along with the regular tools are a container of anointing oil, a blindfold, a nine-foot length of red silken cord, and a scourge. The initiate's own athame also lies on the altar, to one side. The candles are alight beyond the Circle, but not the four quarter candles around the Circle nor the altar candles, which should be white. The wine goblet is full.

The other Witches, with the exception of the Gatekeeper, stand in a Circle around the altar. The Gatekeeper stands just inside the Circle, to the east, with the Initiate opposite him, on the outside of the Circle. (See the note below, regarding the Initiate's appearance.)

The High Priestess (HPS) rings the bell three times then takes up her athame, kisses the blade, and holds it high in salute.

**HPS:** Hail, Lord and Lady. Here I do build a temple of life in which to honor you. Assist us as we lay down the foundation stones on which to build our cone of power.

HPS lowers the blade and walks over to the east point in the Circle. She points the tip of the blade at the line drawn on the ground and slowly walks around the Circle, directing energy as she goes. She continues until she returns to the point where she started. There she raises the athame in salute and describes a pentagram in the air. She kisses the blade and returns to the altar.

Witch 1 now walks over to the east point in the Circle, taking with him a lighted taper. He lights the east candle.

**WITCH 1:** Here is light at the east, where the life-giving sun rises each day. Here is erected the Watchtower of Air, standing guard over this temple of the gods.

He returns to the Circle and passes the taper to Witch 2. She takes it and moves around to the south, where she lights that candle from the taper.

**WITCH 2:** Here is light at the south, where fires rise up to warm and illuminate the earth. Here is erected the Watchtower of Fire, standing guard over this temple of the gods.

She returns to the Circle and passes the taper to Witch 3, who moves around to the west and lights that candle from the taper.

**WITCH 3:** Here is light at the west, where waters move gently to give the moisture of life to the earth. Here is erected the Watchtower of Water, standing guard over this temple of the gods.

He returns to the circle and passes the taper to Witch 4. She moves around to the north and lights that candle from the taper.

**WITCH 4:** Here is light at the north, where the earth forms a solid

**foundation for all life. Here is erected the Watchtower of Earth, standing guard over this temple of the gods.**

Witch 4 goes to the altar and puts down the taper, then returns to her place in the Circle. Standing before the altar, HP lights the altar candle(s).

**HP:**  **Here is light that I bring into the temple. Let it light the way through the darkness of ignorance to the world of knowledge. Light to life, in all things.**

HPS dips the tip of her athame blade into the bowl of salt.

**HPS:**  **Salt is life. Let this salt be pure and let it purify our lives, as we use it in this rite dedicated to the God and Goddess in whom we believe.**

She takes three pinches of the salt and drops them into the water. Moving her athame blade across to the water dish, she dips it in there.

**HPS:**  **Let the sacred salt drive out any impurities in this water, that together they may be used in the service of these deities, throughout these rites and at any time and in any way we may use them.**

She mixes the water and salt with the athame blade, stirring in a clockwise direction three times around, then lays down the athame and picks up the dish of salted water. She hands it to the Maiden, who goes to the east point of the Circle and raises the dish.

**MAIDEN:**  **I use this sacred liquid now in the building of this, our sacred temple. I dedicate it to the gods, in love and light.**

Lowering the dish, she starts to walk slowly *deosil* around the Circle, dipping her fingers into the water and sprinkling it along the line of the Circle. She returns to the east point and raises the dish briefly in salute, then returns to the altar. She puts down the salt dish.

HP takes up the censer and passes it to the Squire, who goes to the east point, where he raises the censer.

**SQUIRE:** **The fire of this censer, with the fragrance of its smoke, serves to cement the foundation of this our temple, dedicated to the Lord and the Lady.**

He lowers the censer and again passes along the line of the Circle, swinging the censer so that the fumes and smoke pass along it. When he returns to the starting point, he again raises the censer in salute and then returns to the altar.

HP replaces the censer and takes up his athame. All raise their athames in salute and describe a pentagram in the air.

**HPS:** **Lord and Lady, God and Goddess, I invite you to enter into this temple we have constructed to venerate you.**

**HP:** **Be with us here and witness these rites we hold in your honor.**

**ALL:** **So mote it be!**

All kiss their blades.

HPS dips her forefinger into the water and marks a cross within a circle on the forehead of the High Priest, followed by a pentagram over his heart, saying:

**HPS:** **Here I do consecrate you in the names of the Lord and the Lady. Let us be here in peace and love, with honor to all life.**

She gives the dish of holy water to the High Priest, who then does the same to her. He dips his forefinger into the water and marks a cross within a circle on the forehead of the High Priestess, followed by a pentagram over her heart, saying:

**HP:** **Here I do consecrate you in the names of the Lord and the Lady. Let us be here in peace and love, with honor to all life.**

All of the Witches, including the Gatekeeper, in turn move around and stand before the High Priestess or High Priest. HPS consecrates the male Witches, and

HP consecrates the female Witches. Each returns to his or her place after being consecrated.

The Maiden rings the bell three times three, or nine times in all.[28]

HPS, taking up her athame, faces the east where the Initiate waits outside the Circle. She points the tip of the athame at the Initiate.

| | |
|---|---|
| **HPS:** | **Who stands outside this temple of the ancient gods?** |
| **GATEKEEPER:** | **It is a seeker who has traveled far, looking for peace, joy, and the light of knowledge.** |
| **HP:** | **Is he here of his own free will?** |
| **INITIATE:** | **I am.** |
| **HPS:** | **What steps brought you here?** |
| **INITIATE:** | **First curiosity, then learning, and finally love. Curiosity about the Old Religion; learning about the ancient ways; love for the gods, for life, and for my brothers and sisters of the Craft.** |
| **HP:** | **What two words will bring you into this Circle, this temple of the gods?** |
| **INITIATE:** | **Love and trust.** |
| **HPS:** | **All who bring such words are welcome.** |

HPS lowers her athame. She takes up the blindfold and cord, and goes to the east. The Gatekeeper cuts a door for her to leave the Circle. She goes out, kisses the Initiate, then blindfolds him and binds him.

HPS guides the Initiate over the lines of the Circle into the temple. When they have passed through, the Gatekeeper closes and seals the Circle. HPS guides the initiate to stand before the altar.

The Maiden rings the bell three times.

HPS takes up the water and marks a cross within a circle on the Initiate's forehead, a pentagram over his heart, and then touches it to his genitals, right breast, left breast, and genitals.

28. Some covens prefer to have had the initiate waiting outside the temple while the Circle was being cast. If this is the case, he would be brought in by the gatekeeper at this point, to stand outside the Circle facing in.

HPS:    With this holy water I anoint and cleanse you, that you may be clean and pure within this Circle, the temple of the gods.

The Initiate now kneels in front of the altar.

HP:         I ask, why are you here in this temple of the gods?
INITIATE:   I am here to be made one with those gods. I wish to become one of the children of the Lord and the Lady. I wish to be part of the family of Wicca.
HPS:        To do what you wish you must end life as you have known it. Are you ready to do that?
INITIATE:   I am.
HP:         You will be setting your feet on the path that leads to purity, truth, and love.
HPS:        The first step is to leave your life of old, to face death and joyously pass beyond it. Are you ready to do so?
INITIATE:   I am.
HP and HPS: So mote it be.

HPS takes up the scourge and (lightly, so as *not* to hurt) strikes the Initiate across the buttocks nine times.[29] She then lays down the scourge. The maiden rings the bell seven times.

HP helps the Initiate to his feet and removes the cord and blindfold. HPS embraces him and they kiss.

HPS:        Now you enter into the world newborn. To start life anew, you will need a new name. What is that name by which you wish to be known, within this sacred Circle?
INITIATE:   I take the name . . . [Witch name].

HPS again consecrates him: forehead, heart, and sacred triangle, this time with the anointing oil.

29. This is the symbolic death found in mystery religions universally. An example may be seen in the seventh scene of the frescoes at the Villa of Mysteries in Pompeii.

HPS:    **I consecrate you now in the names of the Lord and the Lady. Henceforth you will be known, in this sacred Circle and to all your brothers and sisters of the Craft, by your new name . . . [Witch name] . . . With this sacred oil I anoint and cleanse you, giving new life to one of the children of the Gods. So mote it be!**

HPS replaces the oil on the altar and salutes the Initiate.
The Maiden rings the bell nine times.

HPS:    **Now I present to you the working tool of a Witch.**

She takes the Initiate's athame from the altar and presents it to him. They both hold it as she speaks:

HPS:    **This is the true tool of a Witch. It has all the powers of a magic wand and may be used in forming other instruments of the Craft. It must be properly used within the sacred Circle.**

HPS lets go of the athame and the Initiate holds it over the altar.

HPS:    **Now you must consecrate it, so that it may be properly used within this Circle and in the service of the gods.**

The Initiate sprinkles some of the water on the athame, then holds it in the smoke of the incense.

INITIATE:    **I cleanse and consecrate this, my magical athame, that it may serve me as I serve the Lord and the Lady. May it be my strength and my love and may it never be used in anger nor to harm anyone or anything. So mote it be!**

He then draws a pentagram in the air with it, kisses the blade, and lowers it.

| | |
|---|---|
| HP: | Now you are truly one of us. As such you will share our knowledge of the gods, of the arts of healing, divination, and magic. |
| HPS: | You will learn all the mystic arts. All these things you will learn as you progress down the path of the Old Religion. |
| HP: | But first, I must caution you to always remember the Wiccan Rede: An it harm none, do what thou wilt. |
| INITIATE: | An it harm none, do what thou wilt. |
| HPS: | So mote it be. |
| INITIATE: | So mote it be. |
| ALL: | So mote it be! |

HPS and the Initiate embrace and kiss. HPS then takes his hand and leads him around the Circle, starting at the east point, where she raises her athame in salute.

| | |
|---|---|
| HPS: | Hail, Lord and Lady. Here do I present, for the first time, the Witch . . . [Witch name] . . . , a brother of the Craft. A true member of the Old Religion. |

She leads him on to the south point, where she repeats the announcement, then to the west and to the north, repeating at each. Back at the east, HPS raises her athame again in salute and kisses the blade. She then leads the Initiate back to the altar.

HP raises the goblet, pours a libation, then hands it to HPS, who drinks from it. She passes it to the Initiate, who also drinks.

| | |
|---|---|
| HPS: | To the gods! |
| INITIATE: | To the gods! |

Now should follow the ritual of Cakes and Ale (see chapter 4), followed by singing or dancing or celebrating in any other appropriate way. The final step is always the Closing of the Circle (see chapter 4).

# Magical Properties of Herbs

- Adam-and-Eve roots (*Aplectrum hyemale*)—For love and happiness. Ruled by Venus.

- Adder's-tongue (*Erythronium americanum*)—Also known as adder's mouth, serpent's tongue. Great healing properties. Ruled by the moon.

- African violet (*Saintpaulia ionantha*)—For protection and spirituality. Ruled by Venus.

- Agrimony (*Agrimonia eupatoria*)—Also known as cocklebur, sticklewort, and church steeples. For sleep and protection. Ruled by Jupiter.

- Alfalfa (*Medicago sativa*)—Also known as buffalo herb and purple medic. For prosperity and money. Ruled by Venus.

- Allspice (*Pimenta officinalis*)—For healing, luck, and money. Ruled by Mars.

- Aloe (Aloe vera)—Also known as burn plant. For luck and protection. Ruled by the moon.

- Anemone (*Anemone pulsatilla*)—Also known as windflower. For heatlh, healing, and protection. Ruled by Mars.

- Angelica (*Angelica atropurpurea*)—Also known as masterwort and archangel. For healing, protection, and exorcism, and to bring visions. Ruled by the Sun.

- Anise (*Pimpinella anisum*)—Also known as aniseed. For protection and purification and to bring or maintain youth. Ruled by Jupiter.

- Apple (*Pyrus malus*)—Also known as fruit of the gods, the silver bough, and tree of love. For healing and for love. Supposed to bring immortality. Ruled by Venus.

- Asafetida (*Ferula foetida*)—Also known as devil's dung. For protection, exorcism, and purification. Ruled by Mars.

- Aster (*Callistephus chinensis*)—Also known as Michaelmas daisy and starwort. For love. Ruled by Venus.

- Bachelor's-button (*Centaurea cyanus*)—Also known as devil's flower. For love. Ruled by Venus.

- Barley (*Hordeum* spp.)—For love, money, protection, and healing. Ruled by Venus.

- Basil (*Ocimum basilicum*)—Also known as American dittany, St. Joseph's wort, witches' herb. Good for love, protection, exorcism, and wealth. Supposed to give the power to fly. Ruled by Mars.

- Bay (*Laurus nobilis*)—Also known as laurel, lorbeer, sweet bay, bay laurel, daphne, and Grecian laurel. Good for healing, psychic powers, strength, and protection. Ruled by the sun.
- Bedstraw (*Galium triflorum*)—Also known as cleavers and madder's cousin. Good for love. Ruled by Venus.
- Beet (*Beta vulgaris*)—Good for love and for making wishes come true. Ruled by Saturn.
- Belladonna (*Atropa belladonna*)—Also known as banewort, deadly nightshade, death's herb, great morel, devil's cherries, witch's berry. Good for producing visions. Ruled by Saturn.
- Be-still (*Thevetia nereifolia*)—Also known as trumpet flower and yellow oleander. Good for luck. Ruled by Venus.
- Bistort (*Polygonum bistorta*)—Also known as dragon weed, Easter giant, red legs, snakeweed, and patience dock. Good for fertility and for developing psychic powers. Ruled by Saturn.
- Bittersweet (*Celastrus scandens*)—Also known as climbing staff tree, fever twig, waxwork, yellow root. Good for healing and protection. Ruled by Mercury.
- Blackberry (*Rubus villosus*)—Also known as cloudberry root, dewberry, bramble-kite, goutberry, and thimbleberry. Good for healing, money, and protection. Ruled by Venus.
- Black cohosh (*Cimicifuga racemosa*)—Also known as black snakeroot, squawroot, rattle root, and bugbane. Good for courage, protection, love, and potency. Ruled by Jupiter.
- Bladderwrack (*Fucus viesiculosis*)—Also known as cutweed, sea spirit, and seawrack. Good for money, protection, psychic powers, and weather working (sea and wind spells especially). Ruled by the moon.
- Bleeding-heart (*Dicentra spectabilis*)—Good for love. Ruled by Venus.
- Bloodroot (*Sanguinaria canadensis*)—Also known as Indian plant, king root, and red puccoon. Good for purification, love, and protection. Ruled by Mars.
- Bluebell (*Campanula rotundifolia*)—Also known as harebell. Good for luck and to find the truth. Ruled by Mercury.
- Blue flag (*Iris versicolor*)—Also known as fleur-de-lis, iris, poison lily, poison flag, snake lily, water flag. Good for money. Ruled by Venus.
- Boneset (*Eupatorium perfoliatum*)—Also known as ague weed, crosswort,

feverwort, sweating plant, thoroughstem, Indian sage, vegetable antimony. Good for protection and exorcism. Ruled by Saturn.

- Borage (*Borago officinalis*)—Also known as bugloss, herb of gladness, burage. Good for courage and to develop psychic powers. Ruled by Jupiter.

- Briony (*Bryonia alba*)—Also known as gout root, mad root, ladies' seal, snake grape, tetter berry, wild hops, wood vine. Good for money, protection, and image magic. Ruled by Mars.

- Broom (*Cytisus scoparius*)—Also known as Irish broom, basam, besom, bizzon, genista green broom, Scotch broom. Good for purification, protection, divination, and wind spells. Ruled by Mars.

- Buckthorn (*Rhamnus cathartica*)—Also known as purging berry, waythorn, purging buckthorn. Good for exorcisms and protection. Ruled by Saturn.

- Burdock (*Arctium lappa*)—Also known as burr seed, bardana, bardane, clotbur, hardock, hareburr, hurr-burr, happy major, personata. Good for healing and protection. Ruled by Venus.

- Calamus (*Acorus calamus*)—Also known as myrtle flag, myrtle sedge, sweet cane, sweet root, sweet grass. Good for healing, luck, money, and protection. Ruled by the moon.

- Camellia (*Camellia japonica*)—Good for amassing riches. Ruled by the moon.

- Caper (*Capparis spinosa*)—Good for love, lust, and potency. Ruled by Venus.

- Caraway (*Carum carvi*)—Good for health, protection, and developing mental faculties. Ruled by Mercury.

- Cardamom (*Elettaria cardamomum*)—Good for love and lust. Ruled by Venus.

- Catnip (*Nepeta cataria*)—Also known as catmint, cat's wort, field balm, nip. Good for beauty, love, and happiness. Ruled by Venus.

- Celandine (*Chelidonium majus*)—Also known as chelidonium, tetterwort, kenning wort, devil's milk, swallow herb. Good for protection and legal matters, and to bring happiness. Ruled by the sun.

- Celery (*Apium graveolens*)—Good for developing psychic powers and for lust. Ruled by Mercury.

- Chamomile (*Anthemis nobile*)—Also known as Roman chamomile, ground apple, maythen, whig plant. Good for purification, love, and money. Ruled by the sun.

- Cherry (*Prunus virginiana*)—Also known as black cherry, sweet cherry. Good for divination and love. Ruled by Venus.

- Chickweed (*Stellaria media*)—Also known as adder's mouth, stitchwort, satin flower, tongue grass, passerina, star chickweed, winterweed. Good for love and fidelity. Ruled by the moon.

- Chicory (*Cichorium intybus*)—Also known as succory, wild cherry. Good for removing obstacles, invisibility, obtaining favors, and frugality. Ruled by the sun.

- Cinnamon (*Cinnamomum zeylanicum*)—Also known as sweet wood. Good for healing, protection, love and lust, spirituality, and protection. Ruled by the sun.

- Cinquefoil (*Potentilla canadensis*)—Also known as crampweed, five finger grass, goosegrass, goose tansy, Moor grass, silverweed, sunkfield. Good for sleep, prophetic dreams, protection, and money. Ruled by Jupiter.

- Cloth-of-gold (*Crocus angustifolius*)—Good for understanding the speech of animals. Ruled by the sun.

- Clover (*Trifolium pratense; T. repens*)—Also known as cleaver grass, three-leaf grass, trefoil, honeystalks. Good for love, fidelity, protection, money, success, and exorcism. Ruled by Mercury.

- Coltsfoot (*Tussilago farfara*)—Also known as bullsfoot, British tobacco, butter burr, foles foot, horse hoof, ass's foot, coughwort. Good for love and visions. Ruled by Venus.

- Columbine (*Aquilegia canadensis*)—Also known as lion's herb. Good for love and courage. Ruled by Venus.

- Comfrey (*Symphytum officinale*)—Also known as gum plant, healing herb, knitback, boneset, bruisewort, knit bone, miracle herb, slippery root, wallwort, yalluc. Good for money and travel safety. Ruled by Saturn.

- Coriander (*Coriandrum sativum*)—Also known as cilantro, Chinese parsley. Good for love and healing. Ruled by Mars.

- Cowslip (*Primula veris*)—Also known as arthritica, buckles, drelip, fairy cup, key of heaven, lady's key, password, plumrocks. Good for healing, retaining youth, and success in treasure seeking. Ruled by Venus.

- Cumin (*Cuminum cyminum*)—Also known as cumino, black and sweet cummin seed. Good for protection, exorcism, and fidelity. Ruled by Mars.

- Cyclamen (*Cyclamen* spp.)—Also known as groundbread, slow bread, swine bread. Good for protection, happiness, lust, and fertility. Ruled by Venus.

- Daisy (*Chrysanthemum leucanthemum*)—Also known as bruise daisy, oxeyes, moon daisy. Good for love and lust. Ruled by Venus.
- Damiana (*Turnera aphrodisiaca*)—Also known as Mexican damiana. Good for love and lust. Ruled by Mars.
- Dandelion (*Taraxacum officinale*)—Also known as lion's tooth, priest's crown, cankerwort, puffball, swine snout, wild endive. Good for divination and for contacting spirits. Ruled by Jupiter.
- Datura (*Datura* spp.)—Also known as ghost flower, devil's apple, jimsonweed, mad apple, thorn apple, madherb, love-will, stinkweed, sorcerer's herb, witch's thimble. Good for protection and curse breaking. Ruled by Saturn.
- Deer tongue (*Liatris odoratissima*)—Also known as vanilla leaf. Good for developing psychic powers, and also for lust. Ruled by Mars.
- Devil's-shoestring (*Viburnum alnifolium*)—Good for gambling luck, power, protection, and employment. Ruled by Mars.
- Dill (*Anethum graveolens*)—Also known as filly, dill weed, aneton. Good for protection, money, love, lust. Ruled by Mercury.
- Dittany (*Cunila mariana*)—Also known as mountain dittany, stone mint, sweet horse mint, wild basil. Good for astral projection. Ruled by Venus.
- Dock (*Rumex crispus*)—Also known as curled dock, narrow dock, yellow dock. Good for healing, money, and fertility. Ruled by Jupiter.
- Dogbane (*Apocynum androsaemifolium*)—Also known as bitter root, catch fly, flytrap, honey bloom, wandering milkweed, western wallflower. Good for love. Ruled by Venus.
- Dogwood (*Cornus florida*)—Also known as boxwood, budwood, green osier, Virginia dogwood. Good for protection and granting wishes. Ruled by Mercury.
- Dragon's blood (*Daemonorops draco*)—Also known as blume, calamus draconis. Good for protection, exorcism, love, and potency. Ruled by Mars.
- Elder (*Sambucus canadensis*)—Also known as alhuren, battree, eldrum, lady ellhorn, old lady, pipe tree, tree of doom. The Romani call it *Yakori bengeskro*—"devil's eye." Good for exorcism and protection, for healing and for prosperity. Ruled by Venus.
- Endive (*Cichorium endivia*)—Good for love and lust. Ruled by Jupiter.
- Eyebright (*Euphrasia officinalis*)—Also known as euphrosyne. Good for psychic development. Ruled by the sun.

- Fennel (*Foeniculum vulgare*)—Good for healing, protection, and purification. Ruled by Mercury.
- Fenugreek (*Trigonella foenum-graecum*)—Also known as bird's foot, Greek hayseed. Good for bringing money. Ruled by Mercury.
- Fern (*Dryopteris filix-mas*)—Also known as male fern, bear's paw root, knotty brake, male shield fern, sweet brake, shield root. Good for protection, exorcism, luck, riches, health, and eternal youth. Ruled by Mercury.
- Feverfew (*Chrysanthemum parthenium*)—Also known as featherfew, febrifuge plant. Good for protection. Ruled by Venus.
- Figwort (*Scrophularia nodosa*)—Also known as knotty-rooted figwort. Good for health and protection. Ruled by Venus.
- Flaxseed (*Linum usitatissimum*)—Also known as linseed. Good for healing, beauty, psychic powers, protection, and money. Ruled by Mercury.
- Fleabane (*Erigeron canadense*)—Also known as butter weed, blood staunch, colt's tail, horse weed, pride weed, scabious. Good for exorcism, protection, and chastity. Ruled by Venus.
- Foxglove (*Digitalis purpurea*)—Also known as dead men's bells, cowflop, floptop, fox bells, witches' bells, dog's finger, fairy petticoats, fairy thimbles, digitalis, fairy gloves, folks' glove, ladies' glove, purple foxglove. Good for protection. Ruled by Venus.
- Garlic (*Allium sativum*)—Also known as clove garlic, poor man's treacle, stinkweed. Good for healing, protection, and exorcism. Ruled by Mars.
- Gentian (*Gentiana lutea*)—Also known as bitter root, yellow gentian, felwort. Good for love and power. Ruled by Mars.
- Geranium (*Pelargonium* spp.)—Good for love, fertility, health, and protection. Ruled by Venus.
- Ginseng (*Panax quinquefolius*)—Also known as wonder of the world root, sang, dwarf ground nut, fivefingers root, garantogen, ninsin, red berry. Good for beauty, love, lust, healing, protection, and wishes. Ruled by the sun.
- Goat's rue (*Galega officinalis*)—Good for health and healing. Ruled by Mercury.
- Goldenrod (*Solidago odora*)—Also known as sweet-scented goldenrod, Aaron's rod, blue mountain tea, solidago, goldruthe, wound weed, woundwort. Good for divination and for bringing money. Ruled by Venus.

- Goldenseal (*Hydrastis canadensis*)—Also known as eye root, eye balm, ground raspberry, Indian plant, jaundice root, orangeroot, Ohio curcuma, yellow puccoon, yellow paint root, yellow eye, tumeric root. Good for healing and for bringing money. Ruled by the sun.

- Ground Ivy (*Nepeta glechoma*)—Also known as cat's foot, alehoof, haymaids, hedgemaids, gill-go-over-the-ground, Lizzy-run-up-the-hedge. Good for divination. Ruled by Mercury.

- Groundsel (*Senecio* spp.)—Also known as groundswallower, ground glutton, grundy swallow, simson. Good for health and healing. Ruled by Venus.

- Gum arabic (*Acacia vera*)—For purification. Ruled by the sun.

- Hawthorn (*Crataegus oxyacantha*)—Also known as bread-and-cheese tree, hagthorn, ladies' meat, mayblossom, may bush, quick thorn, tree of chastity, gaxels, haw. Good for fertility, chastity, happiness, and successful fishing. Ruled by Mars.

- Heather (*Calluna* spp.)—Also known as heath, ling, Scottish or common heather. Good for luck, protection, and rain making. Ruled by Venus.

- Hellebore (*Helleborus niger*)—Also known as Christmas rose. Good for exorcism, astral projection, and invisibility. Ruled by Saturn.

- Hemlock (*Conium maculatum*)—Also known as herb Bennet, keckies, kex, musquah root, poison parsley, spotted corobane, water parsley. Good for astral projection and purification. Ruled by Saturn.

- Hemp (*Cannabis sativa*)—Also known as gallowgrass, marijuana, neckweede. Good for love, healing, meditation, and visions. Ruled by Saturn.

- Henbane (*Hyoscyamus niger*)—Also known as fetid nightshade, black nightshade, hog bean, symphonica, poison tobacco, stinking nightshade, Jupiter's bean, cassilago. Good for love. Ruled by Saturn.

- Henna (*Lawsonia inermis*)—Good for headaches and for love. Ruled by Mercury.

- Hickory (*Carya* spp.)—Good for protection from the law. Ruled by Saturn.

- High John the Conqueror (*Ipomoea purga*)—Good for love, happiness, success, and money. Ruled by Mars.

- Holly (*Ilex aquifolium*)—Also known as bat's wings, holy tree, holm chaste, hulver bush, tinne. Good for protection, especially from lightning and for luck and dream magic. Ruled by Mars.

- Honesty (*Lunaria* spp.)—Also known as money plant, silver dollar, lunary. Good for bringing money and repelling monsters. Ruled by the moon.

- Honeysuckle (*Diervilla canandensis*)—Also known as goat's leaf, woodbine. Good for development of psychic powers, protection, and money. Ruled by Jupiter.
- Hops (*Humulus lupulus*)—Also known as beer flower. Good for inducing sleep and for healing. Ruled by Mars.
- Horsetail (*Equisetum arvense*)—Also known as bottle brush, dutch rushes, horsetail rush, paddock pipes, shavegrass, pewterwort. Good for fertility. Ruled by Saturn.
- Hound's-tongue (*Cynoglossum officinale*)—Also known as tory weed, Canadian bur, dog bur, dog's tongue, gypsy flower, sheep lice, woolmat. Good for protection from dogs. Ruled by Mars.
- Hyacinth (*Hyacinthus orientalis*)—Good for protection, love, and happiness. Ruled by Venus.
- Hyssop (*Hyssopus officinalis*)—Also known as isopo, ysopo. Good for protection and purification. Ruled by Jupiter.
- Irish moss (*Chondrus cripus*)—Also known as pearl moss, salt rock moss, carrageen. Good for luck, protection, and money. Ruled by the moon.
- Ivy (*Nepeta glechoma*)—Also known as alehoof, cat's paw, cat's foot, carrion flower, gillrun. Good for healing and protection. Ruled by Saturn.
- Jasmine (*Jasminum officinale*)—Also known as jessamine, woodbine, moonlight on the grove. Good for love, money, and prophetic dreams. Ruled by the moon.
- Job's-tears (*Coix lacryma-jobi*)—Also known as tear grass. Good for healing, luck, and wishes. Ruled by the moon.
- Juniper (*Juniperus communis*)—Also known as gin berry, gin plant, geneva. Good for preventing theft and for protection, exorcism, love, and health. Ruled by the sun.
- Knotweed (*Polygonum aviculare*)—Also known as cowgrass, hogweed, knotgrass, nine joints, pigrush, pigweed, armstrong, red robin, ninety knot, sparrow's tongue. Good for health and all binding. Ruled by Saturn.
- Lady's-mantle (*Alchemilla vulgaris*)—Also known as bear's foot, lion's foot, nine hooks, stellaria. Good for love. Ruled by Venus.
- Lady's-slipper (*Cypripedium calceolus* var. *pubescens*)—Also known as nerve root, American valerian, Noah's ark. Good for protection. Ruled by Saturn.
- Lavender (*Lavandula angustifolia*)—Also known as garden lavender, elf leaf,

spike, nardus. Good for protection, purification, love, chastity, sleep, and peace. Ruled by Mercury.

- Lemon balm (*Melissa officinalis*)—Also known as bee balm, Melissa, and sweet balm. Good for love, healing, and success. Ruled by the moon.

- Lemongrass (*Cymbopogon citratus*)—Good for lust, psychic powers, and to repel reptiles. Ruled by Mercury.

- Lemon verbena (*Aloysia triphylla*)—Also known as cedron, yerba louisa. Good for love and purification. Ruled by Mercury.

- Lettuce (*Lactuca sativa*)—Also known as sleepwort, lattouce. Good for chastity, protection, sleep, and love divination. Ruled by the moon.

- Life-everlasting (*Gnaphalium polycephalum*)—Also known as balsam weed, chafe weed, cudweed, field balsam, golden motherwort, Indian posey, poverty weed, everlasting. Good for health, healing, and longevity. Ruled by Saturn.

- Lilac (*Syringa vulgaris*)—Good for protection and exorcism. Ruled by Venus.

- Lily (*Nymphaea odorata*)—Also known as cow cabbage, pond lily, toad lily, water cabbage. Good for protection and breaking love spells. Ruled by the moon.

- Liverwort (*Hepatica triloba*)—Also known as crystalwort, kidney liver leaf, liver moss, liver weed, trefoil, herb trinity. Good for love. Ruled by Jupiter.

- Lobelia (*Lobelia inflata*)—Also known as asthma weed, bladder podded lobelia, emetic weed, eyebright, gag root, puke weed, vomitwort, Indian tobacco. Good for love and stopping storms. Ruled by Saturn.

- Loosestrife (*Lythrum salicaria*)—Also known as blooming sally, lythrum, purple willow herb, rainbow weed, sage willow. Good for peace and protection. Ruled by the moon.

- Lovage (*Levisticum officinale*)—Also known as lavose, love rod, lubestico, smellage, sea parsley. Good for love. Ruled by the sun.

- Mace (*Myristica fragans*)—Good for psychic and spiritual powers. Ruled by Mercury.

- Maidenhair (*Adiantum pedatum*)—Also known as rock fern. Good for love and beauty. Ruled by Venus.

- Mallow (*Malva rotundifolia*)—Also known as blue mallow, cheeses, dwarf mallow. Good for protection, exorcism, and love. Ruled by the moon.

- Mandrake (*Mandragora officinarum*)—Also known as anthropomorphon, brain thief, gallows, herb of Circe, ladykins, mandagor, mannikin, raccoon berry, wild lemon, semihomo. Good for protection, fertility, health, love, and money. Ruled by Mercury.

- Marjoram (*Origanum majorana*)—Also known as joy of the mountain, sweet marjoram, pot marjoram, mountain mint, knotted marjoram, wintersweet. Good for health, protection, love, happiness, and money. Ruled by Mercury.

- Mayapple (*Podophyllum peltaltum*)—Also known as American mandrake, duck's foot, hog apple, raccoon berry, wild lemon. Good for bringing money. Ruled by Mercury.

- Meadow rue (*Thalictrum* spp.)—Also known as flute plant. Good for protection. Ruled by the moon.

- Meadowsweet (*Filipendula ulmaria*)—Also known as bride of the meadow, dollor, bridewort, gravel root, little queen, meadowwort, steeplebush, trumpet weed. Good for divination, love, peace, and happiness. Ruled by Jupiter.

- Mint (*Mentha* spp.)—Also known as garden mint. Good for travel, money, lust, healing, protection, and exorcism. Ruled by Mercury.

- Mistletoe (*Viscum verticillatum*)—Also known as golden bough, all heal, birdlime, devil's fuge, holy wood, witches' broom, wood of the cross. Good for protection, exorcism, love, health, and hunting. Ruled by the sun.

- Moonwort (*Botrychium* spp.)—Also known as unshoe horse. Good for love and money. Ruled by the moon.

- Morning glory (*Ipomoea* spp.)—Also known as bindweed. Good for peace and happiness. Ruled by Saturn.

- Moss (*Byrum argenteum*)—Also known as silver moss. Good for luck and money. Ruled by Mercury.

- Mugwort (*Artemisia vulgaris*)—Also known as Artemis herb, felon herb, muggons, naughty man, old man, sailor's tobacco, St. John's plant. Good for strength and protection, healing, astral projection, psychic powers, and prophetic dreams. Ruled by Venus.

- Mullein (*Verbascum thapsus*)—Also known as bullock's lungwort, candlewick plant, flannel flower, graveyard dust, hare's beard, hig taper, Jupiter's staff, shepherd's club, velvet plant. Good for protection, exorcism, courage, health, and love divination. Ruled by Saturn.

- Mustard (*Brassica nigra*)—Good for fertility, protection, and psychic powers. Ruled by Mars.

- Myrtle (*Myrtus communis*)—Good for love, fertility, peace, youth, and money. Ruled by Venus.

- Nettle (*Urtica dioica*)—Also known as stinging nettle. Good for healing, protection, and exorcism. Ruled by Mars.

- Nutmeg (*Myristica fragrans*)—Also known as mace. Good for health, fidelity, money, and luck. Ruled by Jupiter.

- Oleander (*Nerium oleander*)—Good for love. Ruled by Saturn.

- Onion (*Allium cepa*)—Also known as onyoun, oingnum. Good for protection, exorcism, healing, prophetic dreams, and lust. Ruled by Mars.

- Orange bergamot (*Mentha citrata*)—Also known as orange mint. Good for bringing money. Ruled by Mercury.

- Orchid (*Orchis* spp.)—Also known as Satyrion. Good for love. Ruled by Venus.

- Orris (*Iris florentina*)—Also known as Queen Elizabeth root, florentine iris. Good for divination, love, and protection. Ruled by Venus.

- Pansy (*Viola tricolor*)—Also known as banewort, bird's-eye, heart's ease, Johnny-jump-up, kiss-me-at-the-garden-gate, love-in-idleness, love lies bleeding, meet-me-in-the-entry. Good for love, love divination, and rain magic. Ruled by Saturn.

- Parsley (*Petroselinum crispum*)—Also known as persil, devil's oatmeal, rock parsley. Good for protection, purification, and lust. Ruled by Mercury.

- Passionflower (*Passiflora incarnata*)—Also known as maypops, passion vine, grandilla. Good for sleep, peace, and friendships. Ruled by Venus.

- Patchouli (*Pogostemon cablin*)—Also known as pucha-pot. Good for money, fertility, and lust. Ruled by Saturn.

- Pennyroyal (*Hedeoma pulegioides*)—Also known as squaw mint, stinking balm, thick weed, tick weed, pudding grass, lurk-in-the-ditch. Good for peace, protection, and strength. Ruled by Mars.

- Peppermint (*Mentha piperita*)—Also known as brandy mint, lammint. Good for development of psychic powers, healing, sleep, purification, and love. Ruled by Mercury.

- Periwinkle (*Vinca minor*)—Also known as blue buttons, devil's eye, sorcerer's violet, joy on the ground. Good for love and lust, mental and spiritual powers, money, and protection. Ruled by Venus.

- Pimpernel (*Pimpinella* spp.)—Also known as blessed herb, herb of Mary, poorman's weatherglass, shepherd's weatherglass. Good for health and protection. Ruled by Mercury.

- Poke (*Phytolacca americana*)—Also known as crowberry, garget, inkberry, pigeon berry, pokeberry root, poke root, Virginia poke. Good for courage and hex breaking. Ruled by Mars.

- Poppy (*Papaver somniferum*)—Also known as blindeyes, blind buff, headaches. Good for love, fertility, money, sleep, invisibility, and luck. Ruled by the moon.

- Prickly ash (*Zanthoxylum americanum*)—Good for love. Ruled by Mars.

- Purslane (*Portulaca sativa*)—Also known as garden purslane, pigweed. Good for protection, love, happiness, sleep, and luck. Ruled by the moon.

- Ragweed (*Ambrosia* spp.)—Good for courage. Ruled by Mars.

- Ragwort (*Senecio* spp.)—Also known as cankerwort, fairies' horses, staggerwort, dog standard, stammerwort. Good for protection. Ruled by Venus.

- Rattlesnake root (*Polygala senega*)—Good for money and protection. Ruled by Saturn.

- Rhubarb (*Rheum rhaponticum*)—Good for protection and fidelity. Ruled by Venus.

- Rose (*Rosa gallica*)—Good for love, love divination, healing, psychic abilities, luck, and protection. Ruled by Venus.

- Rosemary (*Rosmarinus officinalis*)—Also known as compass weed, dew of the sea, elf leaf, polar plant, sea dew. Good for protection, love, lust, purification, healing, and psychic powers. Ruled by the sun.

- Rowan (*Sorbus acuparia*)—Also known as delight of the eye, mountain ash, ran tree, sorb apple, wicken tree, wild ash, witchbane, witchwood. Good for healing, protection, success, and psychic powers. Ruled by the sun.

- Rue (*Ruta graveolens*)—Also known as countryman's treacle, mother of the herbs, ruta, German rue, garden rue. Good for health and healing, exorcism, love, and psychic powers. Ruled by Mars.

- Sage (*Salvia officinalis*)—Also known as sawge. Good for protection, wisdom, long life, and immortality. Ruled by Jupiter.

- St.-John's-wort (*Hypericum perforatum*)—Also known as amber, goat weed, tipton weed, sol terrestis. Good for health, protection, strength, love divination, and happiness. Ruled by the sun.

- Sassafras (*Sassafras albidum*)—Good for money and health. Ruled by Jupiter.

- Skullcap (*Scutellaria lateriflora*)—Also known as blue skullcap, helmet flower, hoodwort, mad-dogweed, blue pimpernel, madweed. Good for love, peace, and fidelity. Ruled by Saturn.
- Skunk Cabbage (*Symplocarpus foetidus*)—Also known as meadow cabbage, polecat weed, suntull. Good for legal matters. Ruled by Saturn.
- Slippery Elm (*Ulmus fulva*)—Also known as Indian elm, moose elm, red elm. Good for stopping gossip. Ruled by Saturn.
- Snakeroot (*Aristolochia serpentaria*)—Also known as serpentary rhizome, snagree, pelican flower, snakeweed. Good for money and luck. Ruled by Mars.
- Solomon's-seal (*Convallaria multiflora*)—Also known as dropberry, sealwort, seal root, lady's seal. Good for protection and exorcism. Ruled by Saturn.
- Spearmint (*Mentha spicata*)—Also known as brown mint, green mint, garden mint, lamb mint, mackerel mint, Our Lady's mint, spire mint, yerba buena. Good for love, healing, and psychic powers. Ruled by Venus.
- Spikenard (*Aralia racemosa*)—Also known as nard. Good for health and fidelity. Ruled by Venus.
- Star anise (*Illicum verum*)—Also known as Chinese anise. Good for luck and psychic development. Ruled by Jupiter.
- Sunflower (*Helianthus annuus*)—Also known as marigold of Peru, comb flower, garden sunflower, corona solis. Good for health, fertility, wishes, and wisdom. Ruled by the sun.
- Sweetgrass (*Hierochloe odorata*)—Good for calling spirits. Ruled by Jupiter.
- Sweet pea (*Lathyrus odoratus*)—Good for courage, strength, friendship, and chastity. Ruled by Venus.
- Tansy (*Tanacetum vulgare*)—Also known as buttons, hindheel, double-flowered tansy. Good for health and longevity. Ruled by Venus.
- Thistle (*Cirsium arvense*)—Also known as blessed thistle, cursed thistle, holy thistle, lady's thistle. Good for strength, protection, exorcism, healing, and curse breaking. Ruled by Mars.
- Thyme (*Thymus vulgaris*)—Also known as garden thyme. Good for health and healing, psychic powers, purification, love, and courage. Ruled by Venus.
- Tonka (*Dipteryx odorata*)—Also known as tonqua bean. Good for money, wishes, love, and courage. Ruled by Venus.
- Turmeric (*Curcuma domestica*)—Good for purification. Ruled by Mars.
- Valerian (*Valeriana officinalis*)—Also known as all-heal, setwell, vandal root,

capon's trailer, cat's valerian, bloody butcher, St. George's herb, garden heliotrope. Good for protection, purification, love, and sleep. Ruled by Venus.

• Vervain (*Verbena officinalis*)—Also known as Brittanica, enchanter's plant, herb of enchantment, simpler's joy, traveler's joy, wild hyssop, Juno's tears, pigeon's grass, verbena, van-van. Good for protection, purification, love, chastity, peace, money, sleep, and healing. Ruled by Venus.

• Witchgrass (*Agropyron repens*)—Also known as couch grass, dog grass, quick grass, witches' grass. Good for love, lust, happiness, and exorcism. Ruled by Jupiter.

• Witch hazel (*Hamamelis virginiana*)—Also known as winterbloom, pistachio, snapping hazel, spotted alder, wood tobacco. Good for chastity and protection. Ruled by the sun.

• Wolfsbane (*Aconitum napellus*)—Also known as aconite, leopard's bane, monkshood, Thor's hat, storm hat, wolf's hat, Cupid's car. Good for protection and invisibility. Ruled by Saturn.

• Wood betony (*Stachys officinalis*)—Also known as bishopwort, lousewort, purple betony. Good for protection, purification, and love. Ruled by Jupiter.

• Woodruff (*Asperula odoratum*)—Also known as master of the woods, sweet wodruff, herb Walter, wood rove. Good for money, protection, and victory. Ruled by Mars.

• Wood sorrel (*Oxalis acetosella*)—Also known as fairy bells, cuckowe's meat, sourgrass, stickwort, leaved grass, wood sour. Good for health and healing. Ruled by Venus.

• Wormwood (*Artemisia absinthium*)—Also known as absinthium, old woman, crown for a king. Good for love, protection, psychic powers, and communicating with spirits. Ruled by Mars.

• Yarrow (*Achillea millefoilum*)—Also known as milfoil, nose-bleed, arrowroot, carpenter's weed, military herb, old man's pepper, seven years' love, tansy, thousand-seal, wound wort. Good for courage, exorcism, love, and psychic powers. Ruled by Venus.

# Color Symbolism

| | |
|---|---|
| RED | Courage, health, sexual love, strength, vigor. |
| PINK | Honor, love, morality. |
| ORANGE | Adaptability, attraction, encouragement, stimulation. |
| YELLOW (GOLD) | Attraction, charm, confidence, persuasion, protection. |
| WHITE | Purity, sincerity, truth. |
| GREEN-YELLOW | Anger, cowardice, discord, jealousy, sickness. |
| GREEN | Fertility, finance, healing, luck. |
| BROWN | Hesitation, neutrality, uncertainty. |
| LIGHT BLUE | Health, patience, tranquillity, understanding. |
| DARK BLUE | Changeability, depression, impulsiveness, sincerity. |
| VIOLET | Healing, peace, spirituality. |
| PURPLE | Ambition, business progress, power, tension. |
| SILVER (GRAY) | Cancellation, neutrality, stalemate, brilliance, reflection. |
| BLACK | Confusion, discord, negativity, loss, neutrality, indecision. |

# Astral Colors

| Astrological Sign | Birth Date | Primary Color | Secondary Color |
|---|---|---|---|
| Aquarius | Jan. 20–Feb. 18 | BLUE | Green |
| Pisces | Feb. 19–Mar. 20 | WHITE | Green |
| Aries | Mar. 21–Apr. 19 | WHITE | Pink |
| Taurus | Apr. 20–May 20 | RED | Yellow |
| Gemini | May 21–Jun. 21 | RED | Blue |
| Cancer | Jun. 22–Jul. 22 | GREEN | Brown |
| Leo | Jul. 23–Aug. 22 | RED | Green |
| Virgo | Aug. 23–Sep. 22 | GOLD | Black |
| Libra | Sept. 23–Oct. 22 | BLACK | Blue |
| Scorpio | Oct. 23–Nov. 21 | BROWN | Black |
| Sagittarius | Nov. 22–Dec. 21 | GOLD | Red |
| Capricorn | Dec. 22–Jan. 19 | RED | Brown |

# Days of the Week

MONDAY          White
TUESDAY         Red
WEDNESDAY       Purple
THURSDAY        Blue
FRIDAY          Green
SATURDAY        Black
SUNDAY          Yellow

# Planetary Rulers and Attributes

| Day | Planet | Activity |
|-----|--------|----------|
| SUNDAY | Sun | Agriculture, beauty, creativity, fortune, guardianship, hope, money, self-expression, victory |
| MONDAY | Moon | Ancestors, childbearing, dreams, healing, instinct, memory, merchandise, purity, theft, virginity |
| TUESDAY | Mars | Enemies, initiation, loyalty, matrimony, prison, protection, war, wealth |
| WEDNESDAY | Mercury | Business, communication, debt, fear, loss, travel |
| THURSDAY | Jupiter | Clothing, desires, harvests, honor, marriage, oaths, riches, treaties |
| FRIDAY | Venus | Beauty, family life, friendship, fruitfulness, growth, harmony, love, nature, pleasures, sexuality, strangers, waters |
| SATURDAY | Saturn | Building, doctrine, freedom, gifts, life, protection, real estate, sowing, tenacity |

# Planetary Hours

In addition to working magic on the appropriate day (see "Planetary Rulers," above), some Witches like to start the ritual on the actual planetary hour also. In other words, if they are working for love (for example), they not only start the ritual on a Friday but also start it in the hour of Venus. How do you determine which is the hour of Venus (or any other particular planet)? First of all, you need to know your local times of sunrise and sunset. They vary across the country, and at different times of the year, of course.

Let's say that in your locality, at the time of year you want to do this magical ritual, sunrise comes at 6:25 A.M. and sunset at 8:20 P.M. That means there are more hours of daylight than of darkness (obviously, it must be summer!). You need to divide the daily hours into twelve *parts*, and do the same with the nighttime hours. With a total of 835 minutes of daylight (6:25 A.M. to 8:20 P.M.) and 605 minutes of darkness (8:20 P.M. to 6:25 A.M.), dividing each into twelve parts (not hours) gives you twelve 69.58-minute daylight sections (835 divided by 12), and twelve 50.42-minute nighttime sections (605 divided by 12). For the purposes of working with planetary hours, these 69.58-minute sections and 50.42-minute sections will be called "hours" even though we know they are not regular 60-minute hours.

Now the first "hour" of daylight on a Friday is the planetary hour of Venus. (If we had been doing this for a Wednesday, for example, the first "hour" would be the planetary hour of Mercury.) They then follow through the twelve rulers in order, each daylight "hour" taking, in this case, 69.58 minutes and each nighttime "hour" taking 50.42 minutes. Different days of the year will vary in the lengths of their hours according to the local times for sunrise and sunset. Here, then, is a table.

## SUNRISE
### Daytime Hours

| Hour | Sun | Mon | Tue | Wed | Thu | Fri | Sat |
|---|---|---|---|---|---|---|---|
| 1 | Sun | Moon | Mars | Mercury | Jupiter | Venus | Saturn |
| 2 | Venus | Saturn | Sun | Moon | Mars | Mercury | Jupiter |
| 3 | Mercury | Jupiter | Venus | Saturn | Sun | Moon | Mars |
| 4 | Moon | Mars | Mercury | Jupiter | Venus | Saturn | Sun |
| 5 | Saturn | Sun | Moon | Mars | Mercury | Jupiter | Venus |
| 6 | Jupiter | Venus | Saturn | Sun | Moon | Mars | Mercury |
| 7 | Mars | Mercury | Jupiter | Venus | Saturn | Sun | Moon |
| 8 | Sun | Moon | Mars | Mercury | Jupiter | Venus | Saturn |
| 9 | Venus | Saturn | Sun | Moon | Mars | Mercury | Jupiter |
| 10 | Mercury | Jupiter | Venus | Saturn | Sun | Moon | Mars |
| 11 | Moon | Mars | Mercury | Jupiter | Venus | Saturn | Sun |
| 12 | Saturn | Sun | Moon | Mars | Mercury | Jupiter | Venus |

## SUNSET

### Nighttime Hours

| Hour | Sun | Mon | Tue | Wed | Thu | Fri | Sat |
|------|---------|---------|---------|---------|---------|---------|---------|
| 1 | Jupiter | Venus | Saturn | Sun | Moon | Mars | Mercury |
| 2 | Mars | Mercury | Jupiter | Venus | Saturn | Sun | Moon |
| 3 | Sun | Moon | Mars | Mercury | Jupiter | Venus | Saturn |
| 4 | Venus | Saturn | Sun | Moon | Mars | Mercury | Jupiter |
| 5 | Mercury | Jupiter | Venus | Saturn | Sun | Moon | Mars |
| 6 | Moon | Mars | Mercury | Jupiter | Venus | Saturn | Sun |
| 7 | Saturn | Sun | Moon | Mars | Mercury | Jupiter | Venus |
| 8 | Jupiter | Venus | Saturn | Sun | Moon | Mars | Mercury |
| 9 | Mars | Mercury | Jupiter | Venus | Saturn | Sun | Moon |
| 10 | Sun | Moon | Mars | Mercury | Jupiter | Venus | Saturn |
| 11 | Venus | Saturn | Sun | Moon | Mars | Mercury | Jupiter |
| 12 | Mercury | Jupiter | Venus | Saturn | Sun | Moon | Mars |

# Magical Alphabets

| | Theban | Passing the River | Malachim | Angelic | Runic |
|---|---|---|---|---|---|
| A | | | | | |
| B | | | | | |
| C | | | | | |
| D | | | | | |
| E | | | | | |
| F | | | | | |
| G | | | | | |
| H | | | | | |
| I | | | | | |
| J | | | | | |
| K | | | | | |
| L | | | | | |
| M | | | | | |
| N | | | | | |
| O | | | | | |
| P | | | | | |
| Q | | | | | |
| R | | | | | |
| S | | | | | |
| T | | | | | |
| U | | | | | |
| V | | | | | |
| W | | | | | |
| X | | | | th | |
| Y | | | | ng | |
| Z | | | | | |

# Chants and Songs for Sabbats and Esbats

*The Veil Between the Worlds* (Samhain)
Tune: traditional—"Amarillis" (1670)
Words: Raymond Buckland

### THE VEIL BETWEEN THE WORLDS

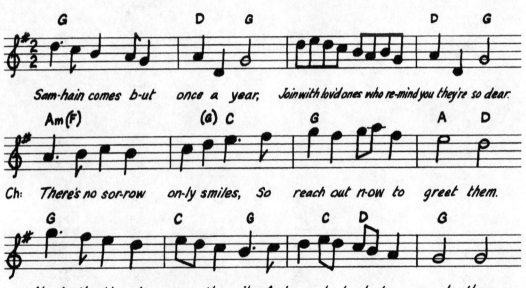

Samhain comes but once a year,
Join with lov'd ones who remind you they're so dear.

Chorus  There's no sorrow only smiles
     So reach out now to greet them.
     Now's the time to cross the miles
     And so at last to meet them.

The veil between the worlds is thin,
Now's the time to open up and let them in. *Chorus*

Happy now to see this day,
When we've waited many months to feel so gay. *Chorus*

Now the day that's between the years;
Summer-winter turning point, so lose your fears. *Chorus*

*Note:* The chorus may be used alone as a chant.

*Summer's Leaving* (Samhain)
Tune: traditional—"The Waters of Holland"
Words: Raymond Buckland

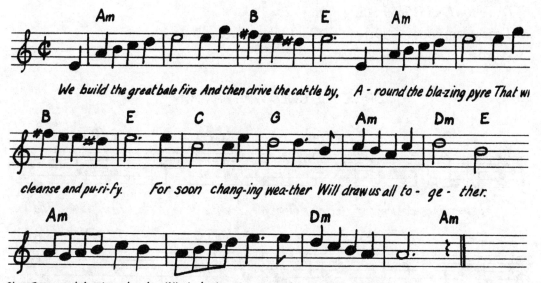

SUMMER'S LEAVING

We build the great bale fire
And then drive the cattle by,
Around the blazing pyre
That will cleanse and purify.
For soon changing weather
Will draw us all together.

*Chorus*     Summer's leaving slowly,
                Winter's drawing near.
                Yet we have naught to fear.

Across the many hills
We can see the bale fires bright.
A-lifting to the stars,
How they make the dark sky light.
The flocks and the herds now
Will huddle under tree bough. *Chorus*

*Drive the Cold Winter Away* (Yule)
Tune: traditional—"Drive the Cold Winter Away" (1650)
Words: Raymond Buckland

## DRIVE THE COLD WINTER AWAY

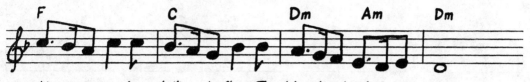

cold o-ver-came As we built up the flame To drive the cold win-ter a - way.

As winter winds blow,
And icicles form,
We huddle close to the fire.
The shadows grow long,
The birds are all gone,
All animals seem to tire.
We're safe in our home
With no need to roam,
Nor leave it from night to day.
We cold overcame
As we built up the flame
To drive the cold winter away.
We cold overcame
As we built up the flame
To drive the cold winter away.

*Ice Queen* (Yule)
Tune: traditional—"In the Fields of Frost and Snow"
Words: Tara Buckland

### ICE QUEEN

Ice Queen comes when the north winds blow, To touch our fields with frost and snow.

Ice Queen comes when the north winds blow,
To touch our fields with frost and snow.
Ice Queen comes in a gown of sleet,
To lay a white blanket at our feet.
When the frost comes,
When the snow falls,
Tend the hearth,
Feed the hearth,
Tend and feed the soul.
Ice Queen sits enthroned in the north wind,
Crowned with diamonds, ice, and snow.
Ice Queen sits enthroned in the north wind,
Crowned with diamonds, ice, and snow.

*Note:* This may be done as a song or a chant.

*Harvest Bride* Chant (Imbolc)
(*Note*: "Bride" is pronounced *breed*)
Tune: traditional—"Nonesuch" (1650)
Words: Raymond Buckland

## HARVEST BRIDE

Here comes the Corn Sheaf Mo-ther now, Here comes the Queen of Har-vest: Here comes the Mo-ther of the grain, So

sing and praise the har-vest. In Bride we see the grain re-born. For Bride we light the ta-per. The

crown of lights is on her head. In joy we dance and ca-per.

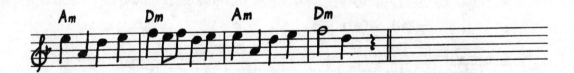

Here comes the Corn Sheaf Mother now,
Here comes the Queen of Harvest.
Here comes the Mother of the Grain,
So sing and praise the harvest.

In Bride we see the grain reborn.
For Bride we light the taper.
The crown of lights is on her head.
In joy we dance and caper.

*Note:* Both the major key and the minor key are given here. It may be done in either or—as is often done—you can do both verses twice (or three times) in the major, then both two or three times in the minor key.

The last time through, repeat the last two lines.

*The Turning Wheel* (Imbolc)
Tune: traditional—"The Free Mason"
Words: Raymond Buckland

THE TURNING WHEEL

The nights go by as do the days
Yet ev'ry hour is full of praise.
For the lives we live are filled with light
And lead us on our ways.

*Chorus*  The turning wheel goes round and round,
    The seasons all go hurrying by.
    The turning wheel from ancient times
    Has brought us here to live and die.

A new life come, an old life go,
And so the wheel turns fast and slow,
But the lives we live are filled with joy
And praises high and low. *Chorus*

The boy today is soon a man
The girl grows fast, as fast as she can,
Yet the fields stay green and trees grow tall,
As part of Nature's plan. *Chorus*

*Note:* The chorus may be used alone as a chant.

*Now Is the Time* (Spring)
Tune: traditional—"Gathering Peascods" (1650)
Words: Raymond Buckland

### NOW IS THE TIME

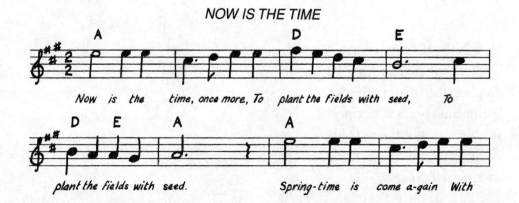

Now is the time, once more,
To plant the fields with seed,
To plant the fields with seed.
Springtime is come again,
With many mouths to feed,
With many mouths to feed.
So let us all go now,

Off to planting in the soil.

To sow the seeds of joy.

For blessings they will flow,

As we labor and we toil.

It is the time to toil.

The gods will bless as before,

For they know what we do.

The mighty Lord and his Lady fair

Will bless our labors true.

*SPRINGTIME* (Spring)

Tune: traditional—"Argeers" (1650)

Words: Raymond Buckland

SPRINGTIME

Let us all go dancing in the woods;
Leaping high and low we'll swing.
Let us all make merry in the fields
As ev'ryone welcomes in the spring.

Chorus    Leaping high; swinging low.
                Eko! Eko!
                Up and down; round we go.
                Eko! Eko!
                Voices are loud as we sing and we shout,
                And all the people's faces are aglow.

Boy and girl are laughing as they dance.
Raising voices as they sing.
Echo 'cross the pastures and the woodlands,
As with joy; welcome in the spring. *Chorus*

*The Queen of May* Chant (Beltane)
Tune: traditional—"The Maid Peeped Out the Window" (1670)
Words: Tara Buckland

THE QUEEN OF MAY

sing and dance ce-le-brat-ing May, With buds and pe-tals in their hair.

Ev'-ry-one with-out a care For sum-mer's born at the dawn-ing.

The silver moon casts its magic sheen,
The Queen of May she is dressed in green.
Heartsease is woven into her hair.
Fairies are dancing without a care.
They sing and dance celebrating May
With buds and petals in their hair.
Ev'ryone without a care,
For summer's born at the dawning.

*Cornish May Song* (Beltane)
Tune and words: traditional

CORNISH MAY SONG

We have been rambling half the night
And almost all the day-a,
And now returned back again,
We've brought you a branch of May-a.

*Chorus*    With Holanto* sing merry-o,
        With Holanto sing merry!

O, we were up as soon as day,
To fetch the summer home-a,
The summer is a-coming on
And winter is a gone-a. *Chorus*

*Holanto is a May garland.

Then let us all most merry be
And sing with cheerful voice-a,
For we have good occasion now,
This time for to rejoice-a. *Chorus*

*The Maypole Dance* (Beltane)
Tune: traditional—"Childgrove" (1701)
Words: Raymond Buckland

THE MAYPOLE DANCE

we wind rib-bons round the May-pole. For we know in our hearts that joy ov-er-flows True to the promise of the Gods

Dance around the maypole,
We laugh and shout and sing together now.
Dance around the maypole
To welcome in the spring.
Turn around the maypole,
We dance and turn and twist the ribbons round.
Dance around the maypole
To welcome in the spring.

As it stands so tall, like a growing tree,
We decorate the rising maypole.
For we know in our hearts that joy overflows
True to the promise of the gods.
Yes, it stands so tall, like a growing tree,
And we wind ribbons round the maypole.
For we know in our hearts that joy overflows
True to the promise of the gods.

*Note:* The first verse may be used alone as a chant.

*Oak King and Holly King* (Summer)
Tune: traditional—"Prince William" (1731)
Words: Raymond Buckland

## OAK KING AND HOLLY KING

Two kings, Oak and Hol-ly, Now fight for who will be the ru-ler Un-til Sam-hain comes When again they fight a-lone. The Oak King has been rul-ing For six months, now it's time to find out If he still has power Or must give up his throne. Ch: And the year will be cut in twain Each takes his turn till it comes a-gain Oak King first and then Hol-ly King too, As the vic-tor has his reign.

Two kings—Oak and Holly—
Now fight for who will be the ruler
Until Samhain comes
When again they fight alone.
The Oak King has been ruling

For six months, now it's time to find out
If he still has power
Or must give up his throne.

*Chorus*     And the year will be cut in twain—
            Each takes his turn till it comes again—
            Oak King first and then Holly King, too,
            As the victor has his reign.

Midsummer is here now,
The longest day of the year.
The sun is shining down
And springtime has now flown.
But soon winter will come
And the battle will be fought again
To place another king
Upon his six-month throne. *Chorus*

*Note:* The chorus may be used alone as a chant.

*Our Sun* (Summer)
Tune: traditional—"Hardiman the Fiddler"
Words: Tara Buckland

OUR SUN

Oh, our sun, our sun, our sun,

Bright yellow orb in the sky.

Our sun, our sun, our bright yellow orb in the sky,

Our son.

Oh, our sun, our sun, our sun,

Bright yellow orb in the sky.

Our sun, our sun, our bright yellow orb in the sky,

Our son.

Kiss the earth with gold,

Kiss her and tell her you love only her,

And your heart is gay

To touch her and squeeze her and kiss her and

Kiss the earth with gold,

Kiss her and tell her you love only her,

And your heart is gay

To touch her and squeeze her and kiss her and

Oh, our sun, our sun, our sun,

Bright yellow orb in the sky.


*First Harvest* Chant (Lughnasadh)

Tune: traditional—"Lady in the Dark" (1665)

Words: Raymond Buckland


### FIRST HARVEST

The start of harvest is here.
The way to year's end is clear.
Corn grain, good cheer,
That is so dear,
Our harvest truly is here!


*Evening Shadows* (Lughnasadh)
Tune: traditional—"The Mulberry Garden" (1670)
Words: Raymond Buckland


EVENING SHADOWS

The lady goes to the stream to bathe
With flowers in her hair.
The doe and fawn are passing by

Raise heads and sniff the air.
The bright-color'd birds among the trees
All happily sing their song,
As gentle breezes rustle leaves
With evening shadows long.

The farmers shoulder their forks and scythes
And cross the fields of grain.
The sheep and cows are grazing near
Begin to move again.
The lengthening shadows reach across
From harvest sheaves stacked high,
As comes day's end, it's time to send
The moon up into the sky.

*Spiral Dance* (Autumn)
Tune: traditional—"Epping Forest" (1670)
Words: Raymond Buckland

SPIRAL DANCE

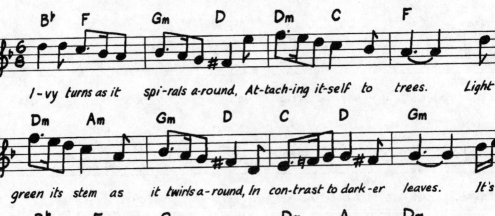

I-vy turns as it spi-rals a-round, At-tach-ing it-self to trees. Light

green its stem as it twirls a-round, In con-trast to dark-er leaves. It's

"turn and cling," Cling to a - ny - thing. It's

hold - ing        tight        As it        fights        for        light.        The

I - vy    turns as it    spi-rals a-bove,    A - reach-ing up high to    see.        It

rea-ches the top, in its    spi-ra-ling dance, To    get    to the sun and be    free.

Ivy turns as it spirals around,
Attaching itself to trees.
Light green its stem as it twists around,
In contrast to darker leaves.
It's "turn and cling,"
Cling to anything.
It's holding tight
As it fights for light.
The ivy turns as it spirals above,
A-reaching up high to see.
It reaches the top, in its spiraling dance,
To get to the sun and be free.

*Autumn* (Autumn)
Tune: traditional—"The Merry Andrew"
Words: Raymond Buckland

## AUTUMN

Au-tumn wea-ther soon will fill with rain That quick-ly turns to snow.

In the autumn ev'ning
Shadows lengthen while animals all start to
Nest and build their houses
For the coming snow.
Winter's in the offing;
Winds blow coldly; falling leaves descend,
Start to quickly cover
All that lies below.
Barns are full of harvest nuts and grain,
There's no time to grow the food again.
Autumn's weather soon will fill with rain
That quickly turns to snow.
Barns are full of harvest nuts and grain,
There's no time to grow the food again.
Autumn's weather soon will fill with rain
That quickly turns to snow.

# Bibliography

## A Suggested Reading List on Witchcraft and Magic

Anderson, Mary. *Color Healing*. New York: Samuel Weiser, 1975.

Anderton, Bill. *Fortune Telling*. North Dighton, MA: JG Press, 1996.

Bardon, Franz. *Initiation Into Hermetics*. West Germany: Osiris-Verlag, 1962.

———. *The Practice of Magical Evocation*. Austria: Pravica, 1967.

Birren, Faber. *Color Psychology and Color Therapy*. Secaucus, N.J.: University Books, 1961.

Blofeld, John. *I Ching: the Book of Change*. New York: Dutton, 1968.

Bolton, Brett L. *The Secret Powers of Plants*. New York: Berkley, 1974.

Branston, Brian. *The Lost Gods of England*. London: Thames & Hudson, 1957.

Buckland, Raymond. *The Tree: Complete Book of Saxon Witchcraft*. York Beach, ME: Samuel Weiser, 1974.

———. *Practical Candleburning Rituals*. St. Paul: Llewellyn, 1982.

———. *Practical Color Magick*. St. Paul: Llewellyn, 1983.

———. *Buckland's Complete Book of Witchcraft*. St. Paul: Llewellyn, 1986.

———. *Scottish Witchcraft*. St. Paul: Llewellyn, 1991.

———. *Witchcraft From the Inside*. St. Paul: Llewellyn, 1995.

———. *Ray Buckland's Magic Cauldron*. St. Paul: Galde Press, 1995.

———. *Advanced Candle Magick*. St. Paul: Llewellyn, 1996.

———. *The Witch Book*. New York: Visible Ink Press, 2001.

———. *Secrets of Gypsy Fortunetelling*. St. Paul: Llewellyn, 1992.

———. *Doors to Other Worlds*. St. Paul: Llewellyn, 1996.

———. *The Buckland Romani Deck*. St. Paul: Llewellyn, 2001.

———. *Gypsy Witchcraft and Magic*. St. Paul: Llewellyn, 1998.

Buckland, Tara. *How to Make an Easy Charm to Attract Love Into Your Life*. St. Paul: Llewellyn, 1990.

Butler, E. M. *Ritual Magic*. New York: Noonday Press, 1967.

Campanelli, Pauline. *Pagan Rites of Passage*. St. Paul: Llewellyn, 1998.

Cheasley, Clifford W. *Numerology*. Boston: Triangle, 1916.

Cheiro (Louis Hamon). *Cheiro's Book of Numbers*. New York: Arc, 1964.

———. *Cheiro's Language of the Hand*. New York: Rand McNally, 1900.

Collins, Terah Kathryn. *The Western Guide to Feng Shui*. Carlsbad, CA: Hay House, 1996.

Cooper, J. C. *The Aquarian Dictionary of Festivals*. Wellingborough, UK: Aquarian Press, 1990.

Crowther, Patricia. *The Witches Speak*. Isle of Man: Athol, 1965.

———. *Witch Blood!* New York: House of Collectibles, 1974.

———. *Lid Off the Cauldron*. London: Frederick Muller, 1981.

Cunningham, Scott. *Wicca*. St. Paul: Llewellyn, 1988.

———. *Living Wicca*. St. Paul: Llewellyn, 1993.

———. *Cunningham's Encyclopedia of Magical Herbs*. St. Paul: Llewellyn, 1985.

Da Liu. *I Ching Coin Prediction*. New York: Harper & Row, 1975.

Dunwich, Gerina. *Wicca A to Z*. New York: Carol, 1997.

———. *The Wicca Source Book*. New York: Citadel, 1998.

Farrar, Janet, and Stewart Farrar. *The Witches' Goddess*. Custer, WA: Phoenix Publishing, 1987.

———. *The Witches' God*. Custer, WA: Phoenix Publishing, 1989.

———. *Eight Sabbats for Witches*. London: Robert Hale, 1981.

Frater, U. D. *Secrets of Sex Magic*. St. Paul: Llewellyn, 1995.

Frazer, James G. *The Golden Bough*. London: Macmillan, 1890.

———. *The Worship of Nature*. London: Macmillan, 1926.

Gardner, Gerald. *High Magic's Aid*. London: Houghton, 1949.

———. *Witchcraft Today*. London: Rider, 1954.

———. *The Meaning of Witchcraft*. London: Aquarian Press, 1959.

Garrison, Omar. *Tantra: The Yoga of Sex*. New York: Avon, 1973.

Goldberg, B. Z. *The Sacred Fire: The Story of Sex in Religion*. New York: University Books, 1958.

González-Wippler, Migene. *The Complete Book of Amulets and Talismans*. St. Paul: Llewellyn, 1991.

Gray, Magda, ed. *Fortune Telling*. London: Marshall Cavendish, 1974.

Gunther, Max. *Wall Street and Witchcraft*. New York: Bernard Geis Associates, 1971.

Harris, Eleanor, and Philip Harris. *The Crafting and Use of Ritual Tools*. St. Paul: Llewellyn, 1998.

Hawken, Paul. *The Magic of Findhorn*. London: Souvenir Press, 1975.

Hoebel, E. Adamson. *Anthropology: The Study of Man*. New York: McGraw-Hill, 1966.

Hole, Christina. *Witchcraft in England*. New York: Scribners, 1947.

———. *A Mirror of Witchcraft*. London: Chatto & Windus, 1957.

Horne, Fiona. *Witch: A Magical Journey*. New York: Thorsons, 2000.

Hughes, Pennethorne. *Witchcraft*. London: Longmans Green, 1952.

Kennedy, David Daniel. *Feng Shui Tips for a Better Life*. Pownal, Vt.: Storey Books, 1998.

Kightly, Charles. *The Customs and Ceremonies of Britain*. London: Thames & Hudson, 1986.

Kraig, Donald Michael. *Modern Sex Magick*. St. Paul: Llewellyn, 1998.

Leland, Charles G. *Aradia, Gospel of the Witches*. London: Nutt, 1899.

Lethbridge, T. C. *Witches*. London: Routledge & Kegan Paul, 1962.

Loehr, Rev. Franklin. *The Power of Prayer on Plants*. New York: New American Library, 1969.

Madden, Kristin. *Pagan Parenting*. St. Paul: Llewellyn, 2000.

Malbrough, Ray T. *Charms, Spells and Formulas*. St. Paul: Llewellyn, 1986.

Martello, Leo. *Witchcraft: The Old Religion*. Secaucus, N.J.: University Books, 1974.

Mayer, Gladys. *Colour and Healing*. Sussex: New Knowledge Books, 1974.

Mermet, Abbé. *Principles and Practice of Radiesthesia*. London: Watkins, 1975.

Morrison, Dorothy. *Everyday Magic*. St. Paul: Llewellyn, 2000.

Mumford, Jonn. *Sexual Occultism*. St. Paul: Llewellyn, 1975.

Murray, Margaret A. *The Witch Cult in Western Europe*. London: Oxford University Press, 1921.

———. *The God of the Witches*. London: Sampson Low Marston, 1931.

O'Gaea, Ashleen. *The Family Wicca Book*. St. Paul: Llewellyn, 1998.

RavenWolf, Silver. *To Ride a Silver Broomstick*. St. Paul: Llewellyn, 1993.

———. *Teen Witch*. St. Paul: Llewellyn, 2000.

Starhawk. *Spiral Dance*. New York: Harper & Row, 1979.

Time-Life Books. *The Celts* (The Emergence of Man series). New York, 1974.

Valiente, Doreen. *Where Witchcraft Lives*. London: Aquarian Press, 1962.

———. *An ABC of Witchcraft Past and Present*. New York: St. Martin's, 1973.

———. *Witchcraft for Tomorrow*. New York: St. Martin's, 1978.

———. *The Rebirth of Witchcraft*. London: Hale, 1989.

———. *Natural Magic*. Custer, WA: Phoenix Publishing, 1975.

Ventimiglia, Mark. *The Wiccan Prayer Book*. New York: Citadel, 2000.

Wilde, Stuart. *Affirmations*. Taos, N.M.: White Dove, International, Inc., 1987.

Williams, David. *Astro-Economics*. St. Paul: Llewellyn, nd.

Wing, R. L. *The I-Ching Workbook*. New York: Doubleday, 1979.

# Index